Jno. H. Pitezel

LIGHTS AND SHADES

OF

MISSIONARY LIFE:

CONTAINING

TRAVELS, SKETCHES, INCIDENTS,

AND

MISSIONARY EFFORTS,

DURING

NINE YEARS SPENT IN THE REGION OF LAKE SUPERIOR.

BY

REV. JOHN H. PITEZEL,

ALIAS, WA-ZAH-WAH-WA-DOONG, OR "THE YELLOW BEARD."

"Every matter in the universe is linked in such wise unto others,
That a deep, full treatise upon one thing might reach to the history of all things."
TUPPER.

CINCINNATI:

PRINTED AT THE WESTERN BOOK CONCERN,

FOR THE AUTHOR.

R. P. THOMPSON, PRINTER.

1861.

PREFACE.

VARIETY is said to be the "spice of life." In general this sufficiently marks the devious walks of human life to break the spell of monotony. But of some stations this is more especially true. In such, if not more frequent, it is at least more marked. The "ups and downs" differ like hillocks when compared with cragged and steep mountains. To some the transition is greater from toil to rest, from imminent danger to safety; consequently, the thermometer, indicating the degrees of pleasure or distress felt, is subject to rise higher or fall lower, proportionately.

The life of a missionary, in a wild and uncultivated field, is far from being monotonous. He is constantly brought into contact with extremes. His life is often a checkered scene not all made up of thorns, not all of clouds and storms. The cheerful sunlight often breaks in upon his path. Hardship itself imparts a power of endurance not a gift of nature, enabling its possessor to frown down formidable obstacles. It is often the lot of missionaries to wade through the deepest trials and experience the greatest consolations.

The sketches given in the following narrative, it is hoped, may not prove entirely uninteresting to the indulgent reader. Often it is the case that, in new and unsettled portions of the country, the travels and labors of missionaries form an important link in its after history. And without these, the history of the Church can not be fairly written; and unless the missionary make the record, it is not likely to be made by others. Indeed, in many instances, none but he can make it.

Much of the early history of the vast territory stretching along Lakes Huron and Superior, and extending far into the western wilds, has been gleaned from the accounts of Jesuit missionaries.

We can not but admire the pains taken by Macaulay, in his History of England, to describe what England was a hundred and fifty years ago, compared with what England is now. So when we read over the privations and conflicts of the early settlers of our own country, we are inspired with gratitude at the onward march of improvement and our own superior advantages. The means of conveyance; the different methods of travel; the difference between the exposures of the wilderness and the comforts of a country where the forests have been cleared and towns and cities have sprung up, with all the new inventions for annihilating distance and labor, weigh not a little in the scale. It is certainly not unworthy of note whether, in crossing the great deep, we are to be conveyed in a bark canoe, an open boat, in filthy and uncomfortable schooners, the proud brig, or the stately steamer, where ease itself becomes painful and luxury begets loathing. Nor is it of less interest whether journeys made by land be performed on foot, with the aid of snow-shoes, through a wintery wilderness where the habitation of man is seldom seen, where the pedestrian is compelled to shoulder his own bed and *ne-wah-poo*, or provisions, and erect his rude shelter of boughs for temporary sojourn, or whether the route is the beautiful turnpike over which the traveler rolls on elliptic springs, finding, at frequent intervals, commodious inns, or flies, in the rail-car, over mountain and valley.

In a letter from Rev. D. P. Kidder, D. D., in reference to the unpretending work now offered to the public, he says: "Indeed, I think it the duty of those who can, to furnish the Church with suitable records of their missionary labors, and to perpetuate some knowledge of the aboriginal races of our continent, now so fast fading away." Such has been the aim of the writer, so far as his material and the time he could devote to this work would admit. How far he has succeeded is left to the good sense and judgment of the reader.

Tremblingly hoping that this little volume may be acceptable to ministers and members of the Methodist Episcopal Church and the reading public generally, and that its influence, as far as it extends, may tend to promote the great *missionary cause*, and thus advance the Redeemer's kingdom in the salvation of man, it is now sent forth without apology.

J. H. Pitezel.

Paw Paw, Mich., June 5, 1857.

CONTENTS.

CHAPTER I.

Author appointed missionary—A new era—Missionary spirit—Arrive at Detroit—John Owen—J. S. Harrison—Geo. W. Brown—Sabbath—Steamer Constitution—Accommodations—Lake St. Clair—Scenery—Indians—Wesleyan missionaries—Lake Huron—Reunion—Saginaw Bay—Island of Mackinaw—Indian lodges—Indian annuity—"Big Turtle"—Mr. Balotes—Traders—Whisky—Drunkenness—Results—Mr. Stuart—Transparent waters—A Christian Indian family—Rev. Mr. Daugherty—Catholicism—Its time-serving policy—Fort Mackinaw—Rev. Mr. O'Bryan—Fort Holmes—Sugar Loaf—Arch Rock—The Scenery—Poetical impromptu—Preaching—"General Scott"—Garden River—Saut Ste. Marie—James Ord, Esq.—Fort Brady—Rev. W. H. Brockway .... PAGE 21

CHAPTER II.

Saut Ste. Marie mission—John Kah-beege—Introduction to the mission—Mission-house—Gloomy aspect—Improvement—Site of the mission—Scenery—Religious aspect—Indian devotion—First Sabbath—Preaching—Indian meetings—S. Spates—Family worship—S. Hall—Schools—Domestic cares—Roman Catholic Indians—Wedding—Christmas and New Year—Baptism—Sunrise scenery—Travels—Nimrod—Scene of wigwams—Domestic scene—Indian heathenism—Fishes and Fishing—Close of winter—Summer—Visitors—Temptation—Sabbath desecration—Notes of Study—Close of the year—Appointment to the Kewawenon mission 35

CHAPTER III.

Voyage to Kewawenon—Outfit—Embarkation—Rough waters—Grand Sable—Pictured Rocks—Grand Island—Dead River—Arrival 61

CHAPTER IV.

Kewawenon mission—Kewenaw Bay—"*L'Anse*"—Indian cabins—Preparations for winter—Mr. and Mrs. Marksman—Produce from the mission garden—Furniture—Schools—Sabbath school—Scarlet fever—Manual labor—Religious aspect—Indian membership—Meetings—Encouraging tokens—Severity of winter—Providential deliverance........PAGE 72

CHAPTER V.

Trip to La Pointe—The canoe—The company—Wind-bound—Coasting—James Schoolcraft—Heavy sea—Missionaries of American Board—Their mission—Religious exercises—S. Hall—New Testament in Ojibwa—Rev. Mr. Wheeler—Schools—Hospitality—Indians from the woods—Their condition—Their wretchedness—War-dance and heathen burial—Indian burial—The feast—Return—Becalmed—Rock Harbor—Copper Harbor—A *fix*—Dr. Houghton—Bay Degree—Hazardous landing—Dreary night—Unsuccessful attempt to re-embark—Sabbath—Arrive at the mission.. 86

CHAPTER VI.

Second year—Potato crop—Eagle river—Author dubbed *Captain*—G. Bedell—Backslidings and revivals—"Man's extremity, God's opportunity"—Christmas eve—Pastoral visiting—David King—Indian notion of weeping—Rowdies—Accession to the Church—Fiery trials—Better days—Travels—Chief Monomonee—Efforts of a Catholic priest—Outfit for traveling—Character of the country—Lodging at night—Carp river—Hospitable reception—Snow-shoe lameness—Contrivance for the emergency—Indian treatment for the case—W. B.—His misrepresentation—Reach home—Handicraft—Making shoes—Fortune seekers—Town election—Author attends conference at Marshall...............104

CHAPTER VII.

Interesting conference—Author reappointed to Kewawenon mission—J. W. Holt, assistant—Arrive at the Saut—Schooner *Fur Trader*—Fair winds and deceitful prospects—Head winds and heavy seas—Imminent danger—Panic among the passengers—Uncomfortable condition—Captain R. and his crew—Driven back to Fort Brady—Captain B.—Grand Island—Mr. W.—His family—Arrival home—Mr. B.—His sudden death—Silver mountain—A mine *in prospect*—Location a bone of contention—Disappointment and loss—The uncertainty of worldly riches..121

CHAPTER VIII.

First visit among the miners—Reception—Preaching and traveling—Returning—Bewildered—Wanderings by day—Lodging by night—Fare in the wilderness—Impassable swamps—Situation perplexing—Comes to Portage river—Is relieved by a boat—Author reaches home after much fatigue and suffering—Statistical table—Subsequent visits among the miners—State of things at Kewawenon—Conversion of J. T. and wife from Popery—Erection of a church—The young Indian, *Joshua Soule*—His sad end—Visits of the Superintendent .... PAGE 131

CHAPTER IX.

Michigan annual conference—A change—Difficulties—P. O. Johnson and wife—The new field—The cabin—Wants supplied—Mining—The perpetual din—Speculation—"Humbug"—Visitations—The English miners—German and Irish—Backsliding—Meeting-place—Dancing—Author invited to a Christmas ball—Declines the invitation—Four reasons for declining—Some favorable characteristics among the miners—Congregational singing 150

CHAPTER X.

Eagle river—Origin of the name—The town—The cliff—View from the top—Trouble—Soil—Farming—Picturesque scenery—Number of workmen at the Cliff Mine—Captain Jennings—L. Hanna—Character of the miners—A look into the mine—The stamps—Monthly amount of copper mined—The *whim*—The *sheer*—Preparations to enter the mine—The descent by ladders—The *stull*, or *pent-house*—Exceeding richness of the mine—Best time for visiting the mine—The various operations of the workmen 165

CHAPTER XI.

Close of the conference year—Conference at Kalamazoo—Delightful Sabbath at sea—Public worship—Author tarries at the Saut during conference—New acquaintances—Little Rapids—Favorable religious aspect—Mr. Richmond—Ramsey Crooks—Mrs. Hanna—Rough sea—Arrival at Copper Harbor—Author appointed Superintendent of the missions in the District—Birth of a son—Arrival of missionaries—Case of *delirium tremens*—Arrival at the Saut—A new home—Reflections—Sad end of a drunken Indian—Dreadful influence of rum upon the Indians 175

CHAPTER XII.

Visit to Garden river—Trips to Naomikong—Cold journey—Reach Carp river—Te-quah-me-non—The old squaw—King-hawk—Kah-ba-noden—Interview with him—Return to Naomikong—Waishkees Bay—Reach home—Trip during the "crust-moon"—Derivation of the name—Nodaway—The Ojibwas—Slaughter of the Nodaway—Indian *medicine men*—Ceremonies of initiation—Precepts binding upon medicine men—Caraboo meat—She-gud—Interesting love-feast—An aged widow—Return home .... PAGE 187

CHAPTER XIII.

Summer tour among the missions—Arrive at La Pointe—Preaching aboard ship—Schooner exchanged for a canoe—Appropriate Scripture reading—Sabbath on shore—A heavy storm—Reach St. Louis river—Fond du Lac mission—Fall of the native missionary—Slight progress at the mission—Indian council—The chief, *Shingobe*—Author addresses the Indians—Nah-gah-nup replies—Author rejoins—Nah-gah-nup replies again—The head chief speaks—Discouraging prospect for Sandy Lake—Interview with Dr. Norwood—The route—Reach Knife Portage—Grand Rapids—Difficult ascent—Tempest—Musketoes—Arrive at Sandy Lake—A conjurer—His maneuvers—Modern spiritualism—Council—Sandy Lake mission—Contest between paganism and Christianity—Leave Sandy Lake—Sabbath at La Pointe—Arrive at Kewawenon—Mrs. Barnum—Kewawenon mission—Baptism—Arrive at Eagle river—Eagle River mission—Arrival home 200

CHAPTER XIV.

Saut de Ste. Marie mission—Little Rapids—J. D. Bingham—P. O. Johnson—National fast—Appearance of cholera—Death of Mr. Stevens and Captain Hicks—Other deaths—Embark for Detroit—Arrive at Adrian, the seat of the conference—Dr. Hinman—An interesting conference—Return to Saut Ste. Marie—Missionaries in company 221

CHAPTER XV.

Naomikong—A new mission-house—Collecting the materials—Return home—A second trip to Naomikong—A third trip—Memorable love-feast—Additions to the Church—Mother Waishkee—Remarkable Instance of filial affection—Fourth trip—Return—Sermon on the occasion of the death of Zachary Taylor, President of the United States 227

CHAPTER XVI.

Trip to Sandy Lake—Mr. Sawyer—Rough sea—Precarious situation—Storm ceases—Safe arrival—Fort Wilkins—Grand Portage—Mrs. Hughs—East Savan river—No-ko-mis—War-dance—Appearance of the savages—Speech of an old chief—Martin Luther's speech—Another speech of the chief—His marriage—Baptism of his children—Astonishment of the wild Indians—Famine—Dreadful suffering—Cannibalism .... PAGE 234

CHAPTER XVII.

Return from Sandy Lake—A storm—Reach Grand Portage—Windbound—Reflections—Reading—Trial of faith necessary—Voyage continued—Great boat—Reach La Pointe—Mr. Oaks—Black river—Drunken squaw—Land at Iron river—A trying day—Reach Ontonagon—Mrs. Douglas—The fatal cup—Fatal results—John Southwind—David King—Mr. Sheldon—D. D. Brockway—Arrive at the Saut 249

CHAPTER XVIII.

Condition of the missions—The extreme posts—Kewawenon—Labors of Mr. Crane—His success and sorrows—Eagle river—The Saut—Missionary news—Condition of Sunday schools—"Angels unawares"—John Peterson—Rev. A. Atwood—Liberality of Mr. Peterson—*En route* for conference—Arrive at Detroit—Tiffin City—Great changes—Adrian—Albion—Interesting session—Winter supplies—Arrival at the Saut—Death of little Henry—Sorrow—Dr. Durbin 264

CHAPTER XIX.

Quarterly meeting at Naomikong—Snow—Illness—Improvements—Religious prospects—Interesting meeting—Sacrifices—Author takes charge of a school—Temperance—Meetings and lectures—Result—Mysterious disease—Deaths—Collision on the Lake—Foundering of the Manhattan—Lives saved 274

CHAPTER XX.

Visits among the missions—Entering the St. Louis river—Arrive at Fond du Lac—Sandy Lake—Mrs. Spates—Public worship—Sermon to the Indians—Behavior of a heathen Indian—Lawlessness—Route homeward—Bad River station—Musketoes and gnats—Rough sea—Ontonagon river—Minnesota Mine—The Monticello—Independence—Manner of the Author's spending the day—Kog-wa-on—What he said to the missionary--The missionary's reply—Phœnix Mine—Arrival at the Saut.......PAGE 283

CHAPTER XXI.

Impediments to the evangelization of the Indians—Removal of the place of payment—Destitute situation of the Indians at Sandy Lake—Sickness and death—Numerous graves—Destruction of canoes—Distress of the Indians—Report of the missions as published—Saut Ste. Marie—Naomikong—Waishkees Bay—Kewawenon—Carp river—Sandy Lake and Mill Lac—Fond du Lac—Eagle river—Ontonagon.......298

CHAPTER XXII.

Author commences the labors of another year—Improvements at Naomikong—Rev. Mr. M'Dougall—S. P. Church—Trip to the Bruce Mine—Cordial welcome—Temperance speeches—Preaching—Baptism and the Lord's supper—Return home—Trip to Naomikong—Difficult traveling—Preaching and awakening.......312

CHAPTER XXIII.

Religious prospect at Saut Ste. Marie—Increased attention and interest—Rev. Mr. Porter and Rev. Mr. Bingham—Rev. John Clark—Conversion of a lady—Her great joy in God—Author visits her husband and other soldiers in the Fort—Some interest—Conversions—A class organized—An incident—Interesting meetings—The inebriate—Melancholy casualty—Death of a wicked man—His funeral.......321

CHAPTER XXIV.

Author commences a tour of visitation—Steamer Baltimore—Accommodations—Reading—Contrast—Marquette—Mr. and Mrs. Benson—Mrs. Barnum—Kewawenon—Appearance of the mission—Mr. Barnum's missionary report—Quarterly meeting—Council—Rev. S. Steele—E. H. Day—Visit to various mines—Man killed by falling—Illness—Dr. Senter—Reach home—Trip to Carp river—Great change wrought around Lake Superior—Return—Providence—Summerfield—National discourse.......332

CHAPTER XXV.

Camp meeting at White Fish Point—Published account—Rev. L. Warner—His preaching—Peter Jones—Description of him—Sallows,

M'Dougall, and Blaker—Indians at the meeting—Their conduct—Marriage—Missionary meeting—Love-feast and sacrament—Remarks at the love-feast—Close of the meeting—Indian christening—Temperance meeting—Peter Jones's account of the temperance meeting··PAGE 345

CHAPTER XXVI.

Revival at the Saut—Declension—Troops at the Fort ordered to California—Sergeant M. and family—Remove to Wisconsin—Members left—The congregation—Sunday School—Naomikong—Prosperity—Extract from the annual report—Deaths—Dying sister—Account of a pagan woman—Revival meetings—Statistics—Day school—Sabbath school—The children—Value of the mission property—Houses built by the Indians—Industrial pursuits among them—Camp meeting—Small-pox at the Saut—Kewawenon—Report—Usual prosperity—Indians converted—Number of members—The schools—Eagle River mission—A laborious field—S. Steele—Well sustained—A prosperous year—Missionary money raised—German mission—Statistics of Church and Sabbath school—Letter from S. Steele to the author—Ontonagon—E. H. Day—His labors encouraged by the people—Sunday school statistics—Carp river—Great iron mines—Rev. William Benson—Failure of supplies—Result—Supplies forwarded—"Old stamp" Methodists—Another call for missionary help—Isle Royal—Lumbermen visited—General tables of statistics··363

CHAPTER XXVII.

Communication from Dr. Durbin—Transfer of missions to Wisconsin conference—Author and family embark for Detroit—Rev. Mr. M'Dougall—Touch at Mackinaw—Steamer Atlantic—Reflections on the close of the conference year—Arrive at Detroit—Toledo—Cholera—Confined mostly to emigrants and the intemperate—Reach Adrian—Pleasant greetings—Great changes—Reach Chicago—Arrive at Sheboygan—Fond du Lac—The conference—Its appearance—Rev. E. Yocum—W. H. Sampson—Dr. Adams—Rev. C. Hobart—Sabbath meetings—Conference love-feast—Sermon of Bishop Ames—Its character—Catholic priest—His meetings—Michigan conference—Pleasant home—Preaching—Bishop Scott—Agreeable session—Author appointed to Kalamazoo station—Reflections on leaving the mission district—Reach Adrian and Albion—Arrive at Kalamazoo—The new charge—Journey to the Saut—Packing for removal—Missionaries—Sabbath—Farewell sermon—Rev. James Shaw—Last moments in the empty house—Humiliation, joy, and consecration—Last visit to little Henry's grave—Resignation and hope—Homeward bound—Arrive at Kalamazoo······························375

CHAPTER XXVIII.

Woman—Her part in the missionary work—The Christian lady at an Indian mission—New sights, sounds, and influences—Her associates—The charm and romance at first—The spell broken—Sympathy with the Psalmist—Domestic cares—Burdensome visitations—Training of children—Partnership of the wife in the labors and sufferings of her husband—Contrast of housewifery at the Protestant and Catholic stations—Long absences of the husband—Letter from a missionary's wife to her husband—Travels of the female missionary—Hardships incident—Revolting scenes—Letter from Mrs. Spates to Mrs. Pitezel—Desolation and famine—Potatoes the principal food—Great moral darkness··PAGE 385

CHAPTER XXIX.

Indian characteristics—His affection for his traditional history—The sad coming of the "pale faces"—A superficial glance not sufficient to estimate properly the Indian—The shades of the wilderness his home—The blessings of civilized life absent—The seeming natural inference—The Indian's want of opportunity—Fate of such as have resided among Indians—Names of renown—Intellectual capacity of such unquestionable—Fine specimens of impassioned eloquence—Speech of Sastarexy pending the giving up of *Le Pesant*—Speech of Logan after all his relatives had been murdered—Speech of Black-Hawk after failing to effect the deliverance of his people—Indians imitative beings—Skill of Indian women—Progress in the various arts of civilization—Indian love of liberty and independence—Indian history a history of wars—Savage ferocity and cruelty in war—Mr. Frost's testimony on this subject—Treachery—Indians seldom aggressors—Degradation of Indian women—The term *woman* a reproach—Gov. Cass and the disgraced Indian—Drudgery devolves upon the women—This not compulsory but voluntary—Simplicity of their language—Expressive terms—Coat of arms—Indian mythology and religion—Extract from Hall's Life of Clark—The Great Spirit—Polytheism—Divers divinities—Sacrificial offerings—Superstition—The priesthood—Universal deluge—Incarnation—Idolatrous and polytheistic worship—Signification of *Mackinaw*—Sacred rock in St. Louis river—*Ma-ne-bu-zho*, of the Ojibwas—Image representing this god—Greatest blessings attributed to him—Longfellow's song of Hiawatha······398

CHAPTER XXX.

Plea for Indian missions—Skepticism on this subject—Opinion of a gentleman of learning and talent—Reports of Messrs. Foster and Whitney—

Their disparaging statement of the result of Christian missions—The assumption denied as unfounded—Heaven's mandate to be obeyed—Result of the Indian wars—Statements of Government officers corroborate the favorable reports of missionaries—Mr. Tyler's message, 1842—Extract—Argument from the few as yet Christianized—Ratio of converted Indians to the whole favorable—Results of the Christianizing process—Wesleyan missionaries in Canada—Speech of *Yellow Head*, head chief of the Chippewas—Speech of *Penashe*, chief at Kewawenon, in reply to *Yellow Head*—Clear testimony of these speeches touching the power of the Gospel upon the Indian—Indians a part of the "purchased possession"—Christianity a debtor to the Indian—The Indian's choice is between two alternatives: Christian civilization or extinction—Encouragement from prophecy……………PAGE 410

CHAPTER XXXI.

Lake Superior region—Its exhaustless wealth—Hitherto mostly unknown—Great change—Commerce, mining, and agriculture—Reports of Messrs. Foster and Whitney—Dr. Houghton—His important services—The Jesuit missionaries—Native copper—How regarded by the Indians—Alexander Henry—Mining since 1844—Mining four hundred years ago—Samuel O. Knapp—Extract from Foster and Whitney's reports—Proof of high antiquity from the forest trees over the works—No traditions of the ancient mines—Lake Superior region not adapted to farming purposes—Soil of the south shore—Surprising rapidity of vegetation—Products—Fisheries and pineries the principal matters of commerce—Saut Ste. Marie canal—Advantages and attractions of the Lake Superior region—Romantic scenery—Setting sun—Aurora borealis—Mirage—Late twilight and early dawn—State of society not favorable—Laxity of morals—A proud destiny in the future—Conclusion……………422

LIGHTS AND SHADES

OF

MISSIONARY LIFE.

LIGHTS AND SHADES

OF

MISSIONARY LIFE.

CHAPTER I.

APPOINTMENT AS MISSIONARY—VOYAGE TO THE SAUT.

AT the Michigan annual conference, held at Ann Arbor, August 16, 1843, Rev. W. H. Brockway, then superintendent of the Indian missions of Lake Superior, applied to me to go as a missionary into his district. After prayerfully considering the matter, I gave my consent, in case the Bishop should assign me such a field. In a free conference with Mr. Brockway and Bishop Soule, it was arranged that we should take charge of the mission at Saut de Ste. Marie. To make the needful preparation, with the least possible delay, I left the conference in session, and repaired to Adrian, near which was Mrs. P. and our only child, then in her third year, at a sister's.

I had before formed some idea of the ruggedness of that northern clime, and of the obstacles in the way of missionary effort; and future experiment proved that they were not overrated. No one, who values the priceless blessings of civilized society, can consent to part with them without a struggle, and delve into such scenes as fill every land of paganism. To embark in this enterprise put the faith and resolution of Mrs. P. to a severe test. Her friends also felt as if we were about to be exiled. But sober second thought chased away gloomy apprehensions, and led to hopeful trust in God. I felt to look upon this date as a new era in my life. The missionary fire had before been enkindled in my heart, and an inward desire to cultivate mission ground; but up to this time no door seemed to open to me. I had made the language of the poet my own:

"Should Providence command me to the farthest verge of the green earth,
To distant barb'rous climes,
'Tis naught to me, since he is ever present, ever felt,
In the void waste as in the city full,
And where he vital breathes there must be joy."

The language of my heart, as recorded at the time, was, "Hitherto the Lord hath helped us, and here by his grace will we raise our EBENEZER."

August 25th we left Adrian, taking with us Mrs. P.'s sister, then a girl twelve years of age, for Detroit, *via* Monroe, where we arrived in the evening. The next day we were disappointed in the boat which was to take us to Detroit. Mr. Goodenough, the landlord, kindly furnished us with a good two-horse buggy, and sent his son to drive. After a ride of forty miles, through heat and dust, we arrived safely in Detroit. After the first night, during which we lodged at a tavern, we were kindly cared for under the roof of Mr. John Owen, long and widely known as a leading citizen of Detroit, and an influential member of the Methodist Episcopal Church.

Sunday morning we heard Rev. J. S. Harrison preach his introductory sermon, from Galatians vi, 14. In the afternoon Rev. Geo. W. Brown, a missionary bound for Kewawenon, Lake Superior, preached. At night it was my privilege to speak to a very large and attentive audience, on the amazing love of God to a lost world, from John iii, 16. To me it was a profitable season, and I trust it was not a lost opportunity to others. It seemed to me a matter of doubt whether I should ever again stand before such an intelligent congregation of white people. But this was resigned to Him whose I was and whom I served. The day throughout was hallowed by the presence and blessing of God.

Tuesday, 29th, after a pleasant stay of three days in the city, we were glad to take the steamer Constitution, bound for Mackinaw. We lay at the dock till two o'clock the next morning. Accommodations on board were very poor. Wife, daughter, and sister found lodgings in the ladies' cabin. I received a miserable berth in another part of the boat, and, being slightly unwell, much fatigued, and lodged in a sultry berth, I rested but little and slept less. In the morning we were in the beautiful little Lake St. Clair. Our way thence into the St. Clair river and up its rapid and pure current into Lake Huron, is too near home, and has been too often described, to need minute attention here. It is enough to say that we were charmed all the way with the picturesque scenery, both on the British and the American shore. Spacious farms, neat dwellings, smiling villas, and charming landscapes stretch along the banks of that majestic river. Near Port Sarnia we felt an interest in observing a number of Indians sporting on the shore. On the rising ground, for a long distance, appeared their neat and comfortable-looking cabins, connected with well-cultivated fields, affording proof of a near approach to civilization. They are under the care of British Wesleyan missionaries, who have done a great work for the Canada Indians. The mission buildings are on a slightly-elevated spot, and look tasteful and inviting. We had soon passed Port Huron and Fort Gratiot, and were, anon, laying our course across the majestic Lake Huron. It was delightful weather, with scarcely a ruffle on the water.

We were happy to have, as associates, Rev. George W. Brown and his estimable wife, who had but recently given him her hand and heart, as the companion of his joys and sorrows in his self-denying itinerancy. Brother B. and myself had spent several years together, in the same village, when boys. We had, for a time, attended a literary institution together. When but a youthful exhorter I had been permitted to point him to the Lamb of God, and invite him to the altar, where our prayers and tears were mingled and our hearts made to rejoice at his happy deliverance. Once more we found ourselves united in the noblest work to which man was ever called—a mission of love and salvation to perishing heathen. During this delightful trip the Lake was often made to echo the hymns and spiritual songs of the little band. What mystery is there in the ways of Providence!

That night we crossed Saginaw Bay. It was succeeded by another beautiful day. The sun seemed to burst upon the world, from the bosom of the deep, like a globe of fire, sending out his golden beams, as if to enliven the scenes around us, already wearing an aspect of loveliness. We had soon neared the land, and swept gracefully by points, islands, and landscapes on the American shore, which I shall not detain the reader to describe. A little before noon we came in full view of the lofty island of Mackinaw, about three hundred feet high above the level of the Lake. From its summit frowned upon us the imposing battery of the Fort. Situated at its base is the village, comprising several hundred inhabitants, mostly French, Indian, and half-breeds. As we drew near we could see the shore dotted with Indian lodges, in the shape of pyramids, looking, in the distance, like so many ant heaps. The Indians, three or four thousand in number, and about twenty-five chiefs, were here to receive their annuity—some of them from a distance of two or three hundred miles. They were to receive $27,000 that year. Before landing the captain kindly coasted along the eastern shore of the island, and pointed out some of its prominent objects, among which was the great natural curiosity, called Arch Rock. Turning about we glided leisurely into the straits, where we landed on the spot famed in the history of our country for daring exploits, scenes of slaughter and blood.

Michilimackinac signifies, according to some, "Big Turtle," owing to the peculiar shape of the island. Mr. Schoolcraft says, "that the present Indian signification of the name of this island is, 'place of the dancing spirits,' and that the popular etymology, which derives this word from 'Big Turtle,' dates still farther back, and is founded on the fact that the *michi* were turtle spirits." (Sheldon's Early Hist. of Mich., p. 41.)

We dined at a tavern, and as we wére to be detained for several days before we could go to the Saut, after some pains, we found quarters under the roof of a Mr. Balotes, a member of the Baptist Church. The place was so thronged with strangers that comfortable lodging, at a public house, was out of the question. We could not have desired kinder attention than we found with this pleasant family.

The afternoon was spent in strolling among the Indian wigwams, and seeing them receive their pay and spend it among the traders, who thronged the place, and were ready to grab the Indian's money as soon as it came into his hands, by fair or foul means. It was a little surprising to us to find cherries and currants, in their prime, the last of August.

Among our excursions brother B. and myself visited the mission establishment, once under the care of the Presbyterian Church, but now abandoned. It is a spacious building, and was once thronged with native and half-breed children and youth, there educated at vast expense. Little of the fruit of this self-sacrificing labor is thought now to be apparent. But it may be seen, in the revelations of eternity, that here was a necessary and very important link in the chain of events, connected with the Christianization of benighted pagans.

September 1. This morning I took a walk along the shore of the straits about a mile, where I saw scenes of woe and wretchedness. Some of the worse than heathen *whites, French, and half-breeds*, had been furnishing the Indians with whisky, and cheating them out of their money. The direst effects of drunkenness were witnessed among them. Some were raving and fighting, some singing, some dancing, or running and whooping, while in some of the lodges were men, women, and children, rolling and tossing, and making hideous noises or doleful moanings. What a very *pandemonium* was here seen—all the work of whisky! My soul sickened at this sight of woe. I was grieved to see such a mass, susceptible of high intelligence, debased below the level of the brute. Fearful, thought I, will be the final reckoning of the instigators of all this crime and misery, when the Judge of all the earth shall make inquisition for blood. The agent, Mr. Stuart of Detroit, took a noble stand in favor of temperance, and exerted a great influence among the Indians. But his utmost vigilance was insufficient to prevent the ravages of this destroyer. Bad as was the case here described, I was told that there was then much less drunkenness than was common at such times. Here is revealed to us an almost omnipresent obstacle to missionary success. It is but justice to say, that among the traders were several honorable exceptions to such as have been just mentioned.

The missionaries and their families, accompanied by brother Patterson and wife, from Detroit, took a ride on the straits, in a sail-boat. We sailed up and down the channel and into the verge of Lake Michigan. We had never before seen any thing to equal the transparency of those waters. The bottom, at a depth of twenty or thirty feet, was perfectly visible. The stones and pebbles are white lime, which makes them perceptible at greater depth than otherwise. We passed over to the opposite island, and then returned, singing as we crossed the channel,

"From Greenland's icy mountains," etc.

We felt our spirits refreshed and the missionary fire re-enkindled.

September 2. This morning brother Brown and myself visited a family of Christian Indians, from *Saut Ste. Marie.* A fire was burning in the center of the lodge and something cooking in a kettle. The ground around was covered with green branches of white cedar. On these were spread some neat mats of their own make. Opposite the door were two painted wooden trunks, which served as seats for visitors. Their blankets and bedding were carefully stowed away in the sides of the wigwam. They appeared glad to see us.

We sung one of their favorite hymns—

"Jesus my all to heaven is gone,"

such as could singing in the Ojibwa, and then prayed. Here were the visible fruits of our mission at the *Saut.* Contrast the scene presented here with that above. Let an infidel world judge between the philanthropic efforts of the Church to elevate the red man, and the avaricious and misanthropic endeavors of wicked men to build up their own fortunes by exterminating the tribes of the wilderness.

We here formed the acquaintance of Rev. Mr. Daugherty, a Presbyterian missionary, a pious and worthy man from Grand Traverse, who accompanied his Indians and had his tent among them. He was here to preserve his sheep from the destroyer.

We here found an influence which is deadly against the spread of a pure Christianity—it is Catholicism. The settlers are mostly Catholic. There was here a Catholic mission and a priest on the spot, with his followers. They wear the cross and count their beads, but are kept in ignorance of the Bible. This system of worship is fascinating to the Indians, for the very reason that its rites and ceremonies are mostly external, and require little exercise of the mind and heart.

The ever-changing nature of the pretended infallible Church, Jesuit-like, becomes a perfect time-server, and has a dexterity to show the side or put on the face which suits best, and so wins the favor of the Indians. That afternoon we visited Fort Mackinaw, and without enumerating the objects of interest which we here saw, we thought it difficult to imagine how any thing could be kept in a more neat and orderly manner. Rev. Mr. O'Brian, of the Episcopal Church, was chaplain. After conducting our wives back to their lodgings, brother Brown and myself reascended the hights of the island, and took a fatiguing though romantic stroll to see some of its wonders. We went first to Old Fort Holmes, which at different times had been in possession of the British and Americans. This is situated on the highest part of the island. There are still large excavations remaining. Two posts and a beam of the gateway were standing, on which many have aspired to immortality by carving their names. Except in one or two narrow places, we could see water all around the island, nine miles in circumference. We next went to see what is called Sugar Loaf, a huge rock, which, in shape, resembles a sugar loaf. Thence we followed a circuitous trail to the eastern extremity of the island, to take a more accurate view of Arch Rock. Advancing toward the arch we came first to a fearful precipice, suddenly breaking off, perhaps, a hundred and fifty or more feet to the bottom. Before us was the magnificent arch, extending across this chasm, which opened to the east on Lake Huron. A path to the right led us along the brink to the arch itself. We removed our boots from our feet—went on the arch to the center, the loftiest spot. In reaching this we must cross one place where the rock was not much over a foot wide—its summit is about three feet in width. The other side of the arch is in no part much over a foot wide. There were growing on the narrow part some small twigs of cedar. On this lofty spot we stood for some time, filled with wonder at the august exhibition around us. In the rear, and on each hand, the lofty eminence was clothed with trees and shrubbery—maple, birch, poplar, cedar, and balsam, giving to the landscape richness and variety. Before us were the majestic waters of Lake Huron, dotted with three little islands, in full view, called St. Martin's Islands. Is it wonderful that we should have felt like invoking the spirit of the muses, or that, if possessed of a whit of the *ideal* faculty, it should have sought embodiment in poetic measure? Here is given the substance of an *impromptu* sketched on the occasion; but please do not be hypercritical, kind reader, as you trace these lines:

Lo! on a rock I stand,
  Arch'd by the hand of God;
Beneath, the surges lash the strand,
  Terrific, at His nod!

Above, the tempest low'rs,
  Around, the waters sweep,
And distant islands tell the pow'r
  That placed them in the deep.

How mighty is the hand
  Which, from old chaos wild,
Heav'd up the rocks and fram'd the land,
  And form'd both seas and isles!

If great the hand which made,
  How wise the mind which plann'd
Creation, in her various grades,
  From matter up to man!

This God is our Great Rock,
  Our Hight, when torrents sweep,
Our Covert from the tempest's shock,
  Our Firm Foundation deep.

We returned from this excursion feasted in mind, if hungry and fatigued in body.

Sabbath, at half-past ten o'clock, A. M., we had the pleasure of hearing Rev. Mr. Daugherty preach, through his interpreter, to the Indians, who collected in the old Presbyterian church. His text was, "I counsel thee to buy of me gold tried in the fire," etc. Both the text and sermon were well adapted to the occasion. It fell to my lot to address the white congregation in the afternoon. At night brother Brown preached a very good, practical sermon to the Indians. It was refreshing to us in this land of comparative heathendom, for ministers and members of different persuasions, but all belonging, as we trust, to the true Church, to blend our hearts and our devotions together.

September 4. We left Mackinaw at eight o'clock, A. M., in the steamer General Scott, thence to the *Detour*, a distance of forty-five miles. The lake was quite rough. We now entered the mouth of the Ste.

Mary's river, and were ascending her majestic waters, in the midst of her thousand islands, sprinkled around us like dew-drops glittering in the sunlight. We swept by the dilapidated fortification on St. Joseph's Island, and several beautiful landscape scenes among the mountains to the north. Now we had reached the Indian settlement on the Canada shore, at a place called by the Indians *Ke-te-gon See-beh;* that is, *Garden River.* Soon before us rose up, in grandeur, the Falls of the St. Mary's. On our left was the Methodist mission. The shore on each side was lined with dwellings of the French and half-breeds up to the Falls. Here was seen, on the Canada side, the Hudson Bay Company's Fort. On the American shore, directly opposite, was the village of *Saut Ste. Marie* and Fort Brady.* But the most attractive spot, on the river, was that of the Indian Agency, occupied by James Ord, Esq., about half a mile east of the Fort. This was once an elegant building, but had become worse for the wear. It stands a little back from the river, on high ground, surrounded by a spacious inclosure, shaded by several balsam and spruce, and some large, venerable-looking elms, which have resisted the storms of many generations. As we gradually ascended into this high latitude we sen-

* In the rear of this, on a sightly spot, was the Baptist mission, under the superintendence of Rev. A. Bingham, who, for about twenty years, had been laboring to bring the Indians under Christian influence. Several children boarded at the mission, and a school was kept up which would have done credit to any land.

sibly felt that we were getting into a colder region. There appeared to be something in the very atmosphere so pure and bracing as to give buoyancy and elasticity to the physical and mental powers. One of our recent missionaries happily expressed his own sensation, when in that region, by saying, that he "felt all the time like making a speech." At seven o'clock in the evening we landed safely at Fort Brady, and were kindly entertained, for the night, in the quarters of Rev. W. H. Brockway, who, in addition to his charge of the missions, was chaplain in the Fort.

CHAPTER II.

YEAR SPENT AT THE SAUT STE. MARIE MISSION.

We had been realizing something of the romance of missionary life. The trip to the Saut had been delightful. From the time that we left Detroit every thing bore the charm of novelty. We were now about to assume the sober verities of mission life. Our first lessons were clear evidence to us that we had entered upon no sinecure. Every itinerant knows something about how matters in a station will often become deranged, even in the interval of conference. And preachers' wives know what it is to follow others into houses of all kinds, turned over to them, often not fit for occupancy. We were to take possession of premises from which the missionary had been absent about three months, and which had been consigned to the care of Indians, including the family of twelve children, boarded, clothed, etc., by the mission.

September 5. John Kah-beege, a native preacher, who was to be our interpreter, came from the mission in a boat, to take us to our new home. We went down immediately after breakfast, accompanied by Rev. G. W. Brown, who introduced us to the mission children, telling them that their father and mother had come to take care of them. At first they were very shy of us, and manifested a profound ignorance about every thing relating to the concern. They were shrewd enough to watch the movement of things before they threw off their reserve.

Our next business was to look about us and see where we were and what was to be done. There was ample room in the mission house, such as it was. One end was frame and partly finished, the other was built of hewed logs, much dilapidated, and has since been displaced by a substantial frame building. This dwelling, though looking very well from a distance, was, within, any thing but inviting, as a home. It had become the tenement of vermin, which gave us no little labor and care to expurgate. The children had worn their clothes to tatters, and had not a decent change. And, worse than this, several of them were infected with an odious cutaneous disease. But to enter into the details of these matters we should be compelled to write what would grate harshly upon refined sensibilities, and impose no pleasant task upon the writer. And yet it should be remembered that such domestic evils, disagreeable as they are to name, or read, must be met and disposed of by the missionaries, as existing realities; and should they make no pretenses to extraordinary refinement, they may at least claim to have *sensibilities* highly susceptible of such impressions.

We may ask the neat Massachusetts housewife to picture to herself, if she can, what would be her feelings to be ushered into such a home, laden with the care of such a family? Do you wonder that gloomy thoughts filled the mind of Mrs. P.? But no time was to be lost; something was to be done, and all hands went at it with the utmost determination and with such skill as we could command. In short, resolution and persistent effort overcame all such obstacles, and we were soon permitted to see the children well, comfortably and decently clad, the building cleansed from every thing offensive, and our forbidding home to wear an agreeable and comfortable aspect. If, as Mr. Wesley says, "cleanliness is next to godliness," those acts of physical renovation were intimately connected with the spiritual interests of the mission.

SITE OF THE MISSION.

Than this scarcely any thing could be more lovely. It is two miles down the river from Fort Brady. At the station a large branch of the river breaks off abruptly, from the main channel, flowing southwardly, studded with numerous beautiful islets. The current here is very rapid; hence the name of Little Rapids. The mission stands on a gentle slope, a few rods back from this channel, in full view of the beautiful river scenery to the east and north, and of the mountainous ranges on the Canada shore. The shore is very abrupt in front of the mission, the water being, a few feet from land, eight or ten feet deep, and perfectly clear and transparent. In the rear were the barn and out-houses. Lining the shore were about a dozen

Indian houses, several wigwams, and the school-house, an old log building, which served for chapel and schools. The land under cultivation was principally along this channel. Forty or fifty acres were then cultivated by the Indians, under the direction of the superintendent, aided by the other missionaries. A fine crop of vegetables were in the ground when we landed, to take care of which were among our first duties.

RELIGIOUS ASPECT.

Aside from its religious aspect a Christian mission possesses no intrinsic importance. The aim of this cause is a direct one; it contemplates the salvation of deathless immortals. When this end is not accomplished missionary efforts prove a failure. The Christianization of the heathen is fundamental—civilization is the legitimate fruit.

We found here a small society of fifty-five Indians. When in their meetings, even a stranger to their language could readily perceive that religion is the same among the untutored Indians as among the whites. Their fervent prayers—their devout hymns of praise—their subdued and often tearful attention to the preached word—their consistent religious experience, as they relate in the class or love-feast, and the correctness of their general deportment, may be favorably compared with that of their more knowing white brothers.

September 10th, we spent our first Sabbath among

them. Brother Brown had not yet left for Lake Superior, and preached to the Indians in the morning. At the same time I preached to the whites in Fort Brady. After noon, for the first time, it fell to my lot to preach, through an interpreter. I was much less embarrassed than I had anticipated, but it seemed like a tedious way of preaching. The Indians heard the word attentively, and all, we trust, were measurably blessed. Brother Brockway was with us, with whom we were permitted to join in receiving and administering the holy eucharist. Several Indians, from abroad, partook with us; some from Grand Island, 130 miles distant. It was a solemn and impressive season. The prayer meeting, at night, gave evidence of the presence of God.

Our Sabbath meetings consisted of the Sunday school, preaching twice, class and prayer meeting; sometimes only one sermon and prayer meeting. Besides, we had one or more meetings during the week. Some of these were seasons of special interest, as some facts, noted at the time, will show.

September 24. Preached in the morning, with good liberty, on the subject of prayer. At the evening meeting the Indians sung with much readiness and prayed with fervency. And although I could understand but little they said, I was much blessed in waiting upon God with them, and began to feel much at home in those meetings—felt, at the time, an inward consciousness that I was slowly advancing in the divine life, and panted for all the fullness of God.

October 2. We had Rev. S. Spates with us, on his way to Fond du Lac mission, Lake Superior. He had been several years in the work, and had acquired an experience to which we were strangers. We enjoyed a gracious season together—had a good congregation. There were several Indians from Garden River, Canada. I conducted the morning services. At two o'clock, P. M., brother Spates preached from, "Ye are the salt of the earth," etc. His remarks were brief, pointed, and appropriate, and had a good effect on the hearers. The prayer meeting, at night, was a spiritual and profitable season. The Indians prayed with great readiness, simplicity, and fervency. The Lord was with us of a truth. One said, in his prayer, "*Me very poor Indian.*" Becoming very happy, he exclaimed, "*Ah-pe-che-me-quaich, Ke-sha-mon-e-doo*"—very thank you, Good Spirit! They prayed fervently for their missionaries, as well as for themselves and their children. The next evening we had a missionary prayer meeting—a season of considerable interest. This may suffice as a specimen of our religious exercises; other incidents of the kind will be found as we pursue the thread of our narrative, and may be passed over here.

Our seasons of family worship were among the most deeply-interesting and profitable interviews. The family, including the Indian children, were called together, morning and evening, and a lesson read out of the holy Scriptures, and a hymn sung, generally in Ojibwa, and prayer, by some member of the family.

October 4. Rev. S. Spates was still with us, waiting for a vessel to sail to La Pointe. We were visited, the same day, by Rev. S. Hall, a missionary of the A. B. C. F. M., from La Pointe, who was on his way to Boston, accompanied by his family. He had spent twelve years there—wrote and preached in the Indian tongue. More will be said about this truly Christian gentleman, and devoted missionary, in another place.

Our religious prospects were, at times, very flattering, during the early part of the year. But we had two serious drawbacks. Several of the Indians went to the woods to hunt, and were some time absent. John Kah-beege, our interpreter, started early in the winter to visit the Indians at *Te-quah-me-non*, and the little band at Grand Island. Instead of returning immediately from Grand Island, as was expected, he went on to Kewawenon, and did not get back till the opening of spring. We were, therefore, left to do the best we could for interpreters, and had often to speak through persons poorly qualified for such a work; and our hands were tied, and our best efforts trammeled.

The members connected with the station were considerably scattered along the shore of Lake Superior, as far as Grand Island. Some lived twelve miles below the mission, on the American shore, and some at Garden River, Canada. As I had the care of the school, it was intended that brother Kah-beege would do most of the traveling and preaching at these outposts. During his long absence, in addition to the duties of the school, I made several visits to their encampments, for particulars of which see below:

OUR SCHOOLS.

The day school was made up of about thirty-five scholars. The average attendance, through the winter, was about eighteen. During sugar-making we had few, except the mission children, and the school was, for a time, discontinued, except as it related to the mission children. They were instructed at home. During the summer there was again better attendance, and the school was more prosperous. Several of the children spoke English quite well, and could read readily. The studies pursued were, of course, mostly elementary, and in English—spelling, reading, writing, arithmetic, geography, and grammar. The scholars gave evidence that, with proper help, they could readily acquire knowledge.

The Sunday school was made up of the scholars of the day school, and exerted a healthful moral and religious influence over the Indians. But the superintending and teaching devolved on the missionaries, and made their duties confining, if not arduous.

DOMESTIC CARES.

The care of the mission family imposed no small burden, especially on Mrs. P. Our family numbered sixteen. Besides, persons employed to work for the mission were fed under our roof. More than this, we were often visited by hungry Indians, who must be fed. One evening more than twenty crowded in upon us just after we had finished our supper. An additional meal was provided for them, and part lodged at the mission, and the rest distributed among our neighbors. This is one out of numerous instances of the kind. In those onerous duties Mrs. P. had little reliable help. Her sister did what she could. Two of the native girls were women grown. One was good help when so disposed; but the other had been recently taken from the wigwam. Some of the smaller children could render some assistance, but to see that they did it was, to Mrs. P., about equivalent to doing it herself. It was requisite also that the boys should be trained to habits of industry. They must work part of each day on the farm, and the missionary must generally be with them, or little would be done. So that, in doors and out, he was constantly taxed with the oversight of the children. Of this we were not disposed to complain. We had gone there to do what we could to better the condition of the Indians, and had anticipated all the work that we could perform. Our chief source of regret was that we could see so little fruit of our efforts.

ROMAN CATHOLIC INDIANS.

The following note was penned October 22d: "Yesterday we were visited by some Catholic Indians from Lake Michigan. They were intoxicated. Poor souls! How sunken in degradation and misery with all their religion! And how much more deserving of censure they who served as agents in their intoxication!"

WEDDING.

About this time *Betsy Ge-zhe-go-qua*, one of our mission girls, was married to John Tanner. By this means our number was diminished, but our best native help was taken away.

CHRISTMAS AND NEW-YEAR.

Christmas we met at half-past ten o'clock, A. M., for religious worship. There was a good turn-out on the occasion. Brother Brockway preached from, "He that believeth not is condemned already." His sermon was characteristic. He generally scores deep, and handles matters without much ceremony, especially when he comes in contact with the vices and abominations of the heathen.

On the approach of New-Year we had great preparations to make for the large number of Indians expected from abroad. A barrel of flour was baked into bread for the occasion, and a barrel of bean soup made, and sundry minor things placed in readiness. The Indians began to gather in before we were prepared for them. Several were pagan Indians recently from Lake Michigan, ignorant of God, but professed to be seeking religion. They were deplorably degraded.

On Friday night we had a refreshing meeting. Saturday the number of Indians from abroad was considerably augmented; on which day we had preaching both afternoon and night. Sunday morning we had a very spiritual love-feast. At the public meeting the house was filled to its utmost capacity. The sacraments were administered after preaching. I had here the privilege of baptizing Wyatt, a sprightly infant son of Rev. W. H. Brockway, who shortly after was taken to the better land.

Sabbath evening, at eight o'clock, being New-Year's eve, we assembled to hold a watch-night. It was introduced by a prayer meeting, in which the Indians participated with their usual fervency and devotion. I followed with a sermon from Psalm lxxiii, 24. We then closed the old year with a prayer meeting, in which God was evidently in the midst to bless. Brother Brockway and family participated with us in the watch meeting and the scenes that surrounded us at the dawn of the new year. One person professed religion and united with the Church.

New-Year's day burst upon us as one of the most delightful we had ever beheld. The weather was mild for the climate and season. The thermometer stood at 22° above zero in the morning, and 32° above at three o'clock, P. M. As the day dawned, the atmosphere was clear and transparent. A rich golden belt stretched along the eastern horizon, tinged with red, purple, and other hues. The still night had clad the shrubs and evergreens on the island opposite the mission with a rich, frosty drapery. The sun looked out from his nightly covering, and seemed to smile on the scene of loveliness. The beautiful river Ste. Marie's perfected the gorgeous picture, dashed upon nature's canvas by Him who painted the lily and colored the rainbow. As soon as it began to be light the Indians commenced to make their visits. Their custom at such times is to go, from the eldest to the youngest, and give every body a friendly shake of the hand, and say, "*Bush-oo*"—wish all a happy New-Year! Some will give you a kiss, if you will suffer it; and they will take all the cakes and provisions you see fit to give them, eating what they can, and carrying the rest away in their *mush-ke-mot*, or sack, which they carry for this purpose.

At ten o'clock we again had public worship with the Indians, when it fell to my lot to preach. After meeting we distributed some corn, pork, and other eatables among our visitors, including the barrel of bean soup, which was not the least among the luxuries of the day.

Thus ended our first New-Year's day among the Indians. We could but record with gratitude that we had, up to that time, from our arrival, been blessed with almost uninterrupted health. Our fare had been coarse and our labor arduous, but, with health and a peaceful conscience, we felt that it was to us really a happy New-Year.

TRAVELS.

It has before been intimated that we were occasionally called to visit the Indians at their encampments. This was done in a boat, or canoe, when the river was not frozen. During the winter we traveled on snow-shoes. I made five visits during the fall and winter to *Mah-shkoo-ta-sa-ga*, twelve miles from the mission, down the river, on the same shore. The place derives its name from the quantity of hay that grows in the vicinity. The channel there widens into a small lake, which in English is called Hay Lake. I went four or five times to preach to the Indians living at Garden River, eight miles off, on the Canada side; and once visited a place called *Shmo-na-ya-sing*, sixteen miles distant on the same shore, where some of our mission Indians were making sugar. These journeys were none of them performed without severe physical labor and exposure. Particularly the jaunts made on snow-shoes were sometimes accomplished with blistered feet and weary limbs. In one instance several of my toes became so badly bruised that the blood settled under the nails, which in a few days came off and gave place to others. We were, however, amply rewarded for these slight inconveniences to find our visits highly prized by the Indians. The influence of God's Spirit was often manifested in the quickening of believers, and in some instances we found those who were inquiring what they must do to be saved. It would be unnecessarily tedious to enter into the minutiæ of these trips—a description of one of them, made in mid-winter, must suffice.

February 3d, in company with a young man for interpreter, I left the mission for *Mah-shkoo-ta-sa-ga.* For an outfit we had snow-shoes, a dog-train, and two dogs, to draw our bed and provisions. The train was constructed of two narrow boards, about nine feet in length, made thin and light, and fastened with screws to small cleats, which were on the upper side. The fore end was bent over like a skate. A hole was made through the cleats at each end, and a rope drawn through from one end of the train to the other. Then the provision basket, made narrow and long for the purpose, and one buffalo robe and blanket, were lashed fast to the bottom ropes with a strong cord. One of our dogs was nine or ten years old, and had performed important services of this kind for years. His name was Nimrod. He was a noble specimen of the canine race, and a universal favorite. He, however, came to a bad end. Like poor Tray of old, the next summer he fell into the bad company of some Indian dogs, and commenced killing the mission calves. Our superintendent found it necessary to make an example of the Indian dogs; and, though no doubt one of his most painful acts, as a matter of impartiality, he was compelled to shoot Nimrod with the rest. But the mission family were filled with sorrow, as at the loss of a friend.

But to return from this digression. Thus equipped

we took up our line of march on the ice, which in some places was bare, but was mostly covered with snow. Here and there water was standing on the ice, thinly crusted with snow, through which we would sometimes break with our snow-shoes. This made them clog, and rendered the walking heavy. We overtook an Indian train drawn by a pony, on a fishing tour. By the kind invitation of the owner, I rode a short distance. About two o'clock, P. M., we arrived at the encampment, which was about half a mile from shore, in the dense woods. As we approached the scene presented was novel and interesting to one who had never seen the Indians in their winter retreat. The smoke from the wigwams was seen curling up among the hemlocks. The lodges looked like huge brush heaps covered with snow, with long smoky poles pointing up in the center. The lodges were first constructed as usual, generally conical in shape; then thickly covered with boughs, and these deeply imbedded in snow, which served to break the severity of the cold. A large shed was sometimes made over the door, covered on all sides in the same way, which served for a wood-shed and store-room.

The numerous, lofty, and wide-spreading evergreens were clad in the verdure of spring, in the dead of winter. Where is the spot on earth, however wild and desolate, in which the beneficent Author of our being has not placed something worthy of admiration?

We stopped with *I-ah-be-dah-sing*, a subordinate chief. His was the interesting family we visited at Mackinaw. We gave provision to the chief's wife, who did our cooking to admiration. They had just caught several rabbits, and the boys, that day, caught a fine lot of fish, which, with the stock of eatables we had with us, made us fine living. The chief was employed in making a gill-net, which labor he performed with great ease and dexterity. He was industrious, and seemed to thrive.

At night we had preaching, and several prayers, in this lodge, and were blessed in waiting upon God in the wilderness. We awoke on Sabbath morning somewhat rested from the weariness of the previous day. At ten o'clock, A. M., we met again for worship. I preached from Isaiah iii, 10, 11. It was quite windy, and forced the smoke back into the lodge so that it was almost suffocating. I spoke with great difficulty, and did not know but I would be forced to follow the example of some other missionaries and preach in a sitting posture; but felt as if I could not be reconciled to this apparently indolent way of preaching.

A SCENE IN DOMESTIC LIFE.

As night approached I could not but look thoughtfully on what was passing around me contrasted with civilized life. I was seated upon a mat, Indian fashion, at supper. Before the fire were some fish spread out on a stick, stuck in the ground, roasting. Any one approached and took a piece at pleasure. On each side of us the Indians were eating corn soup with wooden spoons. In the company were two dogs and a cat, which made themselves perfectly at home, and seemed to be objects of amusement to the inmates approaching veneration. Overhead were suspended, on poles, some of the fish caught the preceding day. On the end of one of these poles sat a chicken, very gracefully surveying the interesting scene below. Here, thought I, is life, in patriarchal simplicity, sure enough—every one seeming to do what is right, in his own eyes, with no one to say, What doest thou?

At night we met again for religious worship. I spoke from Ezekiel xxxiii, 11, and a few prayers closed the public exercises of the Sabbath. Afterward I had some conversation with the chief about the religious belief of the heathen Indians. What I gathered, from a poor interpreter, was, in substance, as follows: They believed there were four gods in heaven. One was the Great God. When they worshiped him they used to prepare their wigwam very nicely. They worshiped him with music and dancing. They looked upon him as the god of medicine, who gave health to the people. Besides these, they believed that there is one under the earth, which is *Mah-je-mon-e-doo*, the devil, or evil spirit. They frequently fasted, and some, who were very wicked, sometimes fasted eight or ten days. They were also the worshipers of idols.

Monday, the 5th, we left the encampment about

nine o'clock, A. M. The weather was moderate. It was heavy and tedious walking. The wind, on Sabbath, had also entirely obliterated the track. But by half-past twelve o'clock we reached home, inclined to the belief that walking on snow-shoes would be the best possible athletic exercise for modern dyspeptics.

FISHES AND FISHING.

From the time that we had reached Mackinaw we had often shared in the luxury afforded by the delicious fishes abounding in those waters. In the spring and fall the far-famed *white fish* are caught plentifully in scoop-nets, just at the foot of the Rapids. *Trout* are also abundant, including the *speckled*, or *brook-trout*, a rare pan fish. Pickerel are caught in the spring and fall, and barreled in large quantities, at Muddy Lake, several miles down the river from the Saut. Another excellent fish is the *herring*. These run in schools at certain seasons, winter and summer, and are caught either in gill-nets or with the spear. The latter method furnishes great amusement to the natives in the winter season. Some of the mission boys exhibited much dexterity in this line, and, in the season, kept us in fish.

CLOSE OF WINTER.

Our winter proved to be a mild one for that climate. Only occasionally was the thermometer below zero. One or two of the coldest days it fell as low as 24°

below. Toward the close we had snow from three to four feet deep on a level. Spring began to open gradually, the last of March and through the month of April, by the close of which the river was open, and the way clear for boats from below. It is not uncommon for the river to be closed up with ice till the tenth, and sometimes as late as the middle of May. It was cheering, after being closed in by so long a winter, and shut out, to a great extent, from the busy world, to see the dreariness of winter gone, and all things wearing the cheerful aspect of a lovely spring. It was not long before the noble steamer was seen stemming the rapid current, as the sailors say, "with a bone in her teeth." To the inhabitants of that region the arrival of the first boat in spring is a season of intense interest. Crowds collect at the landing to witness the new arrival, and obtain the latest news.

SUMMER.

This was to us a busy season, and passed rapidly away. Our duties were too monotonous to require minute description. The day school and Sunday school have been before described. There was little variation during the summer months. There was much hard work done on the farm by brother Brockway and Indians hired by him for this purpose, in clearing, fencing, plowing, planting, and cultivating the crops. Here we found abundant exercise for all the time that could be spared from other duties, and such work was a part of the daily training of the boys belonging to the mission.

We were favored, during the summer months, with the visits of many persons from abroad, who seemed to feel a lively interest in whatever appertained to the Indians. I believe our mission stations generally are—they ought to be—what Paul calls "given to hospitality." It often fell to our lot to entertain our brethren, sometimes for days and weeks together, who were bound to more remote parts. The following note was penned July 6th: "For a few weeks we have had a good deal of company, which, by the way, is no new thing. For several successive Sabbaths we have had more or less Indians from abroad. Besides these brother Johnson and family, the Government carpenter for L'Anse, stopped with us more than a week. In addition to these we had a number of visitors. Several Indians are now down from Grand Island, and some from *Te-quah-me-non*, who are now at the Fort, and will probably be with us to-morrow. There are also here three lodges from *Mah-shkoo-ta-sah-ga*. These visits, though, for the most part, very agreeable, add not a little to Mrs. P.'s domestic cares."

We felt at times greatly tempted that the visible effects of our efforts were not more striking and apparent. Then we were comforted to toil on, and leave the event with Him who sees the end from the beginning, and has promised that our "labor shall not be in vain in the Lord." An extract or two from my journal, about this time, will illustrate what is here alluded to, and show something of the state of religion at the mission:

"Sunday, May 26th, preached a plain, practical discourse from, 'If I regard iniquity in my heart, the Lord will not hear me.' I felt happy in endeavoring to discharge my duty. At half-past one we held a class meeting, and are soon to meet for our evening prayer meeting. Have had some peculiar trials of mind the past week; but out of them all the Lord hath delivered me, and to his great name be all the praise. Have this day felt a divine consolation and peace in my heart. How much consolation there is in that one word IMMANUEL, GOD WITH US! Often when my soul has seemed to be tossed on life's stormy deep, as a ship on the ocean, a consciousness of God with ME, the unworthiest of all, has hushed every rising apprehension, and spread calm over my soul. John Wesley's living and dying motto was, 'The best of all is, God is with us.' Surely this is the best of all. Heaven never made a more gracious promise to Israel than that God 'shall be their God, and shall dwell among them.'"

SABBATH DESECRATION.

"We are here at times called upon to witness som of the crying sins of our land, among others that of Sabbath-breaking, as was the case here to-day. Boatmen are frequently seen passing and repassing, singing their boat-songs, and calling for vengeance upon themselves by profane swearing. A fishing-boat went down this morning, and one up this afternoon, laden with fish, towing an empty boat. The boatmen had to wade and pull the boat up the Little Rapids. But they comforted themselves by swearing that they would get drunk at night."

"*June* 2. This morning preached from Hebrews x, 22–24. Was much blessed in attempting to urge upon the people the important consideration in the text. A fixed attention and deep solemnity pervaded the congregation. At two we met again, and partook of the sacrament of the Lord's supper. Brother Brockway came down, but was so unwell as to be unable to attend the meeting, much less administer the eucharist; so this duty devolved on me. But God was with us in the breaking of bread. Some wept; one woman was so affected that she left the room weeping aloud; others rejoiced; and a deep solemnity characterized the whole scene. This evening had a very lively and interesting prayer meeting. The members of the Church were much blessed."

Enough has been said to show, at least, that the Angel of the covenant was with this little Church just emerging from the night of pagan darkness.

NOTES OF STUDY.

The missionary appointed to labor among the Indians has it in his power to shape, to a good degree, his own course. He can let himself down to the condition of the Indians, or, by habits of diligent study and an adherence to the customs of civilized life, raise the Indian to the sphere in which he moves. He can at least aim at this and realize its gradual accomplishment. The latter course we chose. In the school and in the field, as well as in the kitchen, our aim was to teach the Indians to live like white people. But to throw aside our books and spend the long winter nights in chatting, and smoking, and laughing with the Indians, in their wigwams—a course some have pursued—was to us any thing but tolerable. In that far-off land, deprived, to a great extent, of civilized society, the missionary can only atone for this loss by communing with his books. It may be added, that to preach acceptably among either Indians or white people a man must study.

As illustrative of the manner in which we endeavored to husband our time, this brief record is made, which, if not generally edifying, it is hoped may serve as a source of encouragement to some young brethren in the ministry, who, like the writer, were deprived of early advantages, and have had to force their way up the rugged defiles of knowledge, mostly unaided and alone, beset with all the obstacles of itinerant life, in the "backwoods." My daily reading was the holy Scriptures, the Old Testament in the English, by course, and a portion of the Greek New Testament. Among the miscellaneous reading, for the year, were, added to our periodicals, Dr. Olin's Travels in Egypt, Arabia, etc.; and, in connection, Dr. Robinson's Biblical Researches in Mount

Sinai, etc.; Stephens's Central America; Lanman's History of Michigan; Bancroft's History of the United States, the first two volumes, etc. Some attention was paid to the Indian language, sufficient to enable me to read, with readiness, their hymns and the Scriptures translated into the Ojibwa, so that the Indians could understand. After a short time the services of an interpreter were dispensed with in this work. Most of what was acquired of the language, otherwise of practical benefit, was in colloquial intercourse.

"*Feb.* 7. This morning I finished reading through, by course, the Greek Testament. Though a small thing in itself, it is what, at one time, I hardly expected to accomplish—was in my twenty-fourth year before I knew the Greek alphabet. All the assistance I have received from a teacher, has been some fractions of four or five weeks, by an ordinary linguist. Since that I have passed through some of the severest conflicts of my life, and, on account of other pressing duties, and the difficulties and discouragements of mastering a dead language, alone, I have, several times, for months together, laid my Greek entirely aside. But I have scarcely entered this delightful field of literature, and feel like 'forgetting the things that are behind,' and reaching on to further attainments. I am reviewing my Latin, and find I can make more rapid progress than at any former period."

To gain time to prosecute these studies I usually rose at four or five in the morning, and endeavored carefully to redeem the passing moments.

CLOSE OF THE YEAR—APPOINTMENT TO THE KEWAWENON MISSION.

No note was made in my journal, from the sixth of July to the twenty-fifth of September. It was with us a very busy season. In the absence of Rev. W. H. Brockway, to visit the upper missions, it became necessary for me to take my scythe and help to cut and secure the hay. During the year we had gained some members and lost some, so that the returns to conference were about what we found them. Though we could not rejoice over any special revival, we could at least perceive that the Church exhibited signs of healthfulness and improvement.

We lost, by death, a very amiable and interesting Christian youth, named Beverly Waugh, who died of lingering consumption, in great peace and triumph. It has not been our lot to witness many brighter examples of Christianity, in life and in death, any where, than was seen in this child of the wilderness.

Amid the ever-recurring changes incident to mortals, it fell to our lot to dissolve the relation which we sustained to this mission. It was the superintendent's desire that we should take charge of the Kewawenon mission, distant two hundred and fifty miles, on the shore of Lake Superior. To this arrangement we cheerfully submitted, although we knew that it would subject us to privations and perhaps sufferings, to which, as yet, we were strangers. The season was advancing, and it would not do to await the sanction of conference. Accordingly we had our things boxed up, and. in part, sent up to the Fort, ready for shipping on the *Astor*, a noble brig, then up the Lake, and expected soon to return. She was then to sail for Kewawenon, with winter's supplies for the traders, Government officials, missionaries, and others. Mary Jane, sister of Mrs. P., was to return to her friends, accompanied by brother Brockway, who left on the twenty-third of September, to attend the annual conference. We now had all things in readiness to leave, at short notice, for our new home.

CHAPTER III.

VOYAGE TO KEWAWENON.

WRECK OF THE ASTOR.

THE Astor had been due, from Lake Superior, about ten days, while we were waiting in anxious suspense. Meantime the Algonquin arrived with intelligence that, in a terrible gale, while she lay in Copper Harbor, she dragged her anchor, and was wrecked, on the rocky coast, near Fort Wilkins. It was melancholy to think of the loss of such a craft, especially at a time when it must subject many to privation and suffering, for want of food, during the long winter just at hand. The Algonquin was now the only boat, on Lake Superior, that could be depended on, and she had more than she could do to get supplies to Fort Wilkins. No boat could go to Kewawenon. What were we to do in this strait? Our missionary at Kewawenon, we knew, must be out of provisions. To hire hands and go, in open boat, or canoe, at that late season, must be attended with considerable expense, and subject us to great exposure. Who should bear all this responsibility? The superintendent was absent, and our funds were low. There are times when missionaries must assume responsibility, and, in justification, point to the necessity or wisdom of their course. We felt this to be just such a time. Our first endeavor was to procure a large Mackinaw boat. But we soon found that the Fur Company had chartered every one that we could hear of, to send supplies to Copper Harbor, and to carry on their fisheries. Our last and only alternative was to buy a large bark canoe, for which we paid twenty dollars. We rigged it with sails and substantial oars, paddles, and other necessary appendages.

Mrs. P. was afraid to venture in so frail a craft, and could hardly have been persuaded to do so only on being assured, by one of our voyagers, that we should keep near the shore—by the way, at times, an impossibility, without the greatest hazard. This is especially the case in coasting along a rocky shore, when the sea is all commotion, and a landing could not be effected. The only safety, then, is in keeping off from the shore. How this promise was fulfilled will be seen in the sequel.

OUTFIT.

Our books and goods, except clothes and bedding, must be left to be forwarded in the spring. We must take provision enough to supply us till the next spring, and also to serve for our journey. We had three hearty Indians, besides our own family, who, at such work, can always eat a full allowance. Took with us a tent, four barrels of flour, in sacks, one of pork, also in sacks. Besides the articles named, we took a keg of butter, one of lard, a box of candles, one of soap, a small cheese, one hundred pounds of sugar, etc. Long slim poles were laid in the bottom of the canoe to give it strength and firmness, and all this lading stowed in, as few, except Indians, could do it. Brother John Kah-beege was our main dependence, whose skill, as an accomplished *voyageur*, we had abundant occasion to prove.

THE JOURNEY.

September 30th, we took our leave of the Saut Ste. Marie mission—went to the Fort and passed our things over the portage, and the canoe over the Rapids, at the head of which we camped.

October 1. We were up at three o'clock, A. M., and would have been off very early, but one of the men had returned to the mission and detained us. But at eight o'clock we were all ready, and left, with a beautiful day, and a light wind aft. At ten o'clock we passed *Pointe au Pin*, or Pine Point, six miles distant. The current here is very rapid. In an hour more we had reached Gross Cap, sixteen miles from the Saut, on the Canada side. We had now an opportunity to test our Indian's readiness to keep near the shore. To do this we must have coasted round a deep bay, fifty or more miles, to reach White Fish Point. Directly across it was only thirty miles, and now the wind had increased, and promised, in a few hours, to waft us over.

So favorable an omen was not to be slighted.

Kah-beege proposed to make the traverse. Mrs. P. remonstrated, reminding him of his promise, but was overruled. Parisian Island lay a little out of our course, to the north-west. We steered directly for this, eleven miles distant. Here we landed a few minutes, and again hoisted sail, and were off for White Fish Point. When out miles from land, in every direction, the huge waves rose higher and set in stronger, in the direction we were bound. But our canoe mounted them, and skimmed over the deep like a bird of passage. About four o'clock, P. M., we neared the Point, passed on about six miles farther, and pitched our tent on a beautiful mossy beach; rejoiced that the first day had landed us more than fifty miles from the Saut. While at supper a little snake came into our tent and crawled into a tea saucer. We rested comfortably, and arose much refreshed the next morning.

October 2. We did not start early. Our canoe had sprung a leak the day before, and must be gummed. But we were ready again by eight o'clock. Wind was from land, and we kept near the shore, and made slow progress by rowing. At one o'clock we reached Two Heart Rivers, and took a lunch. Afternoon we gained a few miles by towing and rowing, alternately. All of a sudden the heavens, in the north and west, became very dark, accompanied by a roaring, indicative of an immediate storm. We made all possible haste to get to the shore, at a suitable landing. We had scarcely reached it before the waves were dashing with such violence that, with difficulty, two men could hold the canoe, while the others waded in and out to take out our things. I stood in one end and held it with an oar. It was about as hard work as I had ever attempted. We succeeded to get all on shore, and our goods covered, before it commenced to rain. We took shelter under umbrellas till it abated sufficiently to pitch the tent. The night proved to be a very rainy one, but our tent sheltered us. The lake roared terribly all night. The next day we were wind-bound all day. To add to our comfort we cast up a breastwork of boughs, to break the storm from the tent, which we had pitched in a ravine. One of the men went out hunting, but caught nothing. The following night wind continued from the lake, and the roar of the waves, dashing against the shore, was like the noise of distant thunder. About midnight we became quite uneasy, lest the waves should dash over our provisions, covered up on the beach. We waked up one of the men to examine their condition. He returned, exclaiming, *Ka-gah*, that is, *almost.* So we arose and carried the things farther back from the water.

October 4. We were still chained to our encampment by adverse weather. Our men went out hunting, and returned, in the evening, with four partridges, and each a handkerchief full of cranberries, the largest we had ever seen.

Saturday, October 5. We were still wind-bound, till eleven o'clock, A. M., when we once more left our encampment. It was hard rowing against the wind. We had not gone far when Kah-beege aimed at three ducks on the wing, and shot two of them. We coasted along till four o'clock, P. M., making only about nine miles. Wind increased so that we were obliged to land, which we did with difficulty, on account of the heavy swells setting in to the shore.

We went back some distance, and found a most delightful spot for our tent in a pine grove. Kah-beege took his gun and went to the woods; the other men and myself pitched the tent, secured the stores, and prepared wood for the Sabbath, while Mrs. P. got the supper in readiness. The evening was spent in drying our wet bedding, the effect of rough seas occasionally breaking over the canoe. Kah-beege returned with a partridge. After family worship, which we had regularly morning and evening, we laid us down to rest, feeling that God's banner over us was love.

Sunday, October 6th, was a most delightful day. Every thing about us wore the garb of loveliness. We rested, unmolested, in our camp, spending the time in reading, meditation, and prayer; feeling, in truth, that God is every-where present to bless,

"In the void waste as in the city full."

Monday morning we were up by one o'clock, and at three were in our canoe, bidding adieu to our quiet Sabbath retreat. We passed, before noon, the "*Grand Sable,*" or celebrated sand cliffs, lifting their summit more than three hundred feet above the level of the Lake—a natural curiosity only inferior to the neighboring Pictured Rocks, so renowned in the annals of Lake Superior. These we passed during the afternoon. As the Lake was calm, we coasted along close to them, and had a complete view of the ever-varying phases they presented. Their hight is from fifty feet to about two hundred above the water, from which they rise boldly and perpendicularly. Now they present a smooth wall, supporting trees and shrubbery; then a beautiful cascade is formed by a stream leaping from the summit. Here is a magnificent tower cut loose from the main wall by the action of the waves; there we pass numerous deep caverns and beautiful arcades, supported by gigantic pillars and columns. We passed into some of those caverns and under some of the arches with our canoe. The rocks in many places are striped and tinged with various colors, which is supposed to have been the origin of the name Pictured Rocks. But a subsequent view of this wonderful object led me to conclude that it could not have been this close view that suggested the name. In the summer of 1852 I saw those rocks in the light of the setting sun, some miles from land. They appeared like a magnificent city, with vast blocks of brick buildings, several stories high, presenting bold pillars, columns, and arches, relieved with patches of green shrubbery, cascades, etc. The picture loomed up in the distance, with constantly-varying tints of light and shade, presenting the appearance of a most gorgeous panorama. Such a picture as then seen, spread out on canvas by a good artist, would be of rare value. But mine is not the pencil to give any adequate conception of this grand display of the wisdom and power of God. This wall of rocks extends about twelve* miles, and in the whole distance there is, as I have been credibly informed, only two or three places where a landing could be effected, to afford protection from the angry surges. While passing over the last four miles before we camped, the wind began to breeze up ahead, giving us a rather rough sea. About ten o'clock at night we landed on a sand-beach, opposite Grand Island; and by the time we had pitched our tent and were ready to retire, we were well-nigh exhausted, having traveled about forty miles, rowing and towing all the way except about a mile, where we sailed.

Tuesday it was ten o'clock before we were ready to leave camp. We crossed over to Grand Island, against a strong head wind. The Bay became quite rough. Touched a few moments at Mr. Williams's, a trading-post, and procured some potatoes, and were again on our way. We kept under the island for some distance, sheltered from the wind. Sailed about a mile, in making for the main shore. Here our

---

* Messrs. Foster and Whitney say, in their reports, "about five miles," embracing doubtless that portion which may more properly be called "Pictured." It is common, however, for the natives and others in that country to speak of this whole extent of rocks as Pictured Rocks.

way led us along an exceedingly rocky and dangerous coast. The wind increased so that we could not land, and we did not dare to put far out to sea. We toiled hard at the oar, the swells occasionally dashing into the canoe. About four o'clock, P. M., we were thankful to reach a fine sand-beach, and a small river, into which we ran, and found safe harbor from the noisy billows of the deep. We had only traveled about ten miles that day. Found here the frame-work of several wigwams, and the bones of deer and bear, strung up on the bushes. Our leisure was taken up in baking bread and cooking something for the journey yet before us.

October 8. We arose very early, and by five o'clock had breakfasted and were ready to start. We had the Huron Mountains in view much of the day. Reached Dead river, where we camped for the night. A bay is formed here by the jutting out of a bold, rocky coast, called Bald Head. This is only a few miles west of the now flourishing town of Marquette, where nothing could then be seen but the solitary wigwam. We caught two fine trout on our way, which relished well as a change of diet. Here were two deserted log-houses, built by Mr. Williams, of Grand Island.

October 9. We were wind-bound all day, and interested ourselves as much as possible among the craggy rocks along the shore.

October 10. We were off a little before noon. Made a good run for the day, and *sailed* about five miles. As the Lake had calmed down, we kept on all night till about three o'clock, A. M., when we went ashore, struck up a fire, and, without pitching our tent, we just spread our bedding on the ground, and slept a short time. It had been a severe night of toil with us. With blistered hands, and painfully-weary limbs, and heavy eyes, we could have slept almost any where.

Saturday, 11th, we were off again soon after light, and stopped once during the day to take a little refreshment. We ate our sad cake before it was fairly baked, resumed our oars, and, by the blessing of an ever-watchful Providence, we reached the Kewawenon mission just at dusk in the evening, rejoiced to end our wearisome journey and enjoy the society of brother Brown and his family around the cheerful hearth. The Lord had dealt with us in great mercy, and our hearts were filled with grateful emotions. After twelve days and nights exposed to the warring elements, and subjected to an extraordinary degree of fatigue, rest was to us sweet and refreshing. This was true especially of the rest of the holy Sabbath, which soon dawned upon us. I preached in the morning. Brother Brown preached his farewell sermon in the afternoon. He had labored three years at that station, and was beloved by the Indians as a devoted Christian and faithful pastor. All of Monday and part of Tuesday we were busily employed in assisting brother Brown in his preparations to go to the Saut. He, his wife, and a little babe, about three months old, were to take our canoe and men for this voyage. Out of the small quantity of provisions we had brought, we paid back half a barrel of borrowed flour and some borrowed pork, and furnished brother Brown with provisions for his trip. He took leave of the mission October 14th, was sixteen days on the way, encountered severe storms, and his provisions failed before reaching the Saut. This may be added to the numerous instances of privation and suffering connected with the missionary work on Lake Superior.

CHAPTER IV.

FIRST YEAR AT THE KEWAWENON MISSION.

THIS mission is situated near the head of *Ke-we-naw* Bay, one of the finest in the world, on a sightly spot, about forty rods back from the water. Near the house bursts forth from the side hill a living spring, an invaluable treasure any where. From the shape of the Bay, this region, for miles around, is called by the French *L'Anse*, which may apply to any thing shaped like an arch. Should we use this word occasionally, instead of the longer Indian name, it will be understood as designating the same place. The Indian cabins lined the shore, and were mostly those built by order of Rev. John Clark. They bore evident marks of age and decay. The mission-house was of hewed logs, about twenty-four by sixteen feet, one and a half stories high, covered with cedar bark, and a little shanty appended, which some of the missionaries had used for a study.

We had on one side of us, near by, the Government blacksmith, and on the other side the carpenter, and off some distance, in another direction, was the farmer's family. These constituted our white neighbors. Across the Bay, directly opposite, was the Catholic mission, three miles distant.

PREPARATIONS FOR WINTER.

The roof on the mission-house was old and leaked badly. We therefore purchased cedar barks of the Indians, and put on a new roof. Then we took out the old mortar, and pointed the house anew with good lime mortar, and whitewashed it inside, which very much added to its appearance as well as comfort. This cost us a week of hard toil.

BROTHER AND SISTER MARKSMAN.

At this time Peter Marksman was not a member of the Church. A wily snare had been but too successfully laid for his feet, and he became entangled and fell. He was shorn of that strength which had characterized him as a youthful preacher among the Indians of Saginaw, where he had been instrumental in turning many from heathenism to God. Our mission sensibly felt the force of such a shock. But brother Marksman had the magnanimity to own his fault, and he deeply deplored his fall; and, in process of time, that look which had broken a faithless Peter's heart moved him to genuine repentance, and he was restored again to the favor of God and to his former standing in the Church. Mrs. Marksman had been educated at the mission of the American Board at La Pointe, and was, in every respect, an intelligent Christian lady, and a very neat housekeeper. This union proved to be a very happy one. During the winter they occupied a part of the mission building. Brother Marksman was my interpreter, and generally took charge of the school.

PRODUCE FROM THE MISSION GARDEN.

Brother Brown had raised and stored away about fifty bushels of excellent potatoes, and left some fine turnips in the ground, which, with our scanty supplies, and the unusually hard winter which was just at hand, afforded us great relief, and enabled us to feed many hungry persons, who looked to us when other sources failed.

OUR FURNITURE.

There was one old, rickety table; several stools; two splint-bottom chairs in their decrepitude; one rocking-chair, made of materials taken from the woods by one of the missionaries, without form or comeliness; and a lounge, the frame of which was bass-wood puncheon, and rough enough at that. What other furniture we found was about ditto, excepting a cooking-stove and a box-stove.

SCHOOLS.

In our day school we had from thirty to forty scholars. Like most Indian schools, the attendance varied much according to circumstances. When the Indians were all at the mission, the school was generally well attended; but often, in the season for hunting, making sugar, etc., the children would accompany the parents to the woods. This was especially so in sugar-making, when the whole family usually removed, and the school for a time had to be discontinued. The Indians are not fond of confinement, and missionaries, uniformly, experience much embarrassment in conducting schools among them, from their restless and unsettled habits. In the school at Kewawenon, we found that the scholars did not acquire the English language so readily as the children boarded at the mission at Saut Ste. Marie. The reason, every person will perceive, was that, in the one case, they heard scarcely any thing at home but their own language—in the other it was mostly English. Like most people they prefer their mother tongue to any other. When the school could be kept up, we did all in our power to advance the children in the elementary studies adapted to their capacities. And we were permitted to see them make commendable progress.

As indispensable to every mission, we had also a Sabbath school. Besides the children of the day school, we sometimes had married persons and such as were far advanced in life in attendance. These were taught to read the hymn-book, and also the word of God in the Ojibwa.

The Sabbath school, as well as the day school, was a work of *time* as well as of *faith*. We could not look for any marked immediate results. This remark holds true of most missions among the heathen. And such as can not be satisfied, except with a great show of statistics, will meet with disappointment in looking at results; they are but gradually, often slowly developed.

SCARLET FEVER.

In the early part of November, the scarlet fever broke out in the settlement. Several of our nearest neighbors were attacked—some were quite sick, but it did not prove fatal in any case. Brother Marksman and wife, and A. W. B., a young man boarding with us, all were prostrated by it, and as they began to recover our Carrie was taken; but in her case it was light, and soon passed off. We were thankful to escape with no farther injury.

MANUAL LABOR.

No person is fit to be a missionary who is not willing to labor with his hands. The apostle Paul was not ashamed thus to labor. But there is another extreme into which some of our missionaries are driven, from necessity—too much and too severe manual labor. Ours was a remote station. Hired help was, at that time, scarcely to be obtained. And if it could, we were out of funds to pay workmen. There was much work to be done, and the missionary must do it mostly, or every thing must be at loose ends. The repairs about the mission have been mentioned. An old hovel had answered for barn and stable. This must be torn down and a better one built, which was not done without some labor. Our fire wood must be chopped in the woods, then drawn and prepared for the fire by the missionary—no small chore in that cold region. He must also aid in procuring wood for the school and the meetings. His hay was several miles distant, at a marsh, and must be drawn in on a single ox-train, over a narrow, crooked trail, through the woods. Considerable fencing must be done in the coming spring, and it was necessary to go into the cedar swamp, cut and split the rails, and draw them to their place. When summer came the potatoes must be planted, and the sowing done, and the growing crops cultivated, to afford us supplies for the coming winter. From such numerous and pressing duties we were often in weariness and pain, and deprived of time needful for study and pastoral duties. Our white neighbors afforded us much relief in such emergencies; we changed work, and so assisted each other. As an illustration of the severe labor it was found necessary to perform, the following note, made December 7th, may serve:

"Since we have been here I have been but illy prepared to preach. Have been under the necessity of laboring so hard in the week, as not only to interfere with time necessary for study, but so that, on the Sabbath, I have felt jaded down. Have not been able to set apart one whole day to study since we came. And nearly every week-day have labored hard from morning till night with my hands."

It is not here intimated that such continued to be the case all the time; but it is a fair sample of what must often be done, for days and sometimes for weeks, in succession. In the early part of the following summer, aided by the Indians, who, in this instance, did themselves great credit, our school-house was renovated. It had been daubed inside and outside with red clay. This had fallen out in places, and the house was dirty and uncomfortable. Besides, the roof leaked badly. We put on a new roof of cedar bark—took out the old mortar; and washed the logs clean inside—then pointed it with lime-mortar, and whitewashed it inside and outside. After the women had finished the scrubbing, we had a place of worship that we had no reason to be ashamed of.

RELIGIOUS ASPECT.

There had been a time of great religious promise at this station. This was soon after the foundation of the mission was laid, by the lamented John Clark. Then the Indians were collected about the station, several hundred in number. Instead of being fortified by a strong force, it was subsequently, for years, placed under the charge of single men, who often did their own cooking, and who, in that far-off land, felt, at times, as if they were expatriated. Generally, they would return to visit their parents toward the close of the year—perhaps to remain. At such times the mission would be left, for two or three months, to take care of itself. Taking advantage of such circumstances, Catholic emissaries, headed by the priest, brought about a division in the band, and induced a large portion to cross over to the west side of the bay, where a flourishing mission was established at an expense and sacrifice worthy of a better cause. The tide of prosperity had changed, and our little society was called to pass through sad reverses.

The Indian membership we found generally attached to the institutions of the Church. They were remarkably punctual in attendance on the public worship of God—were attached to the class, and met in the prayer meeting. If they were disposed to neglect any means of grace it was the *eucharist.* In this solemn service there was something which inspired them with such feelings of awe, accompanied with such a sense of unworthiness, that, at times, they would look on with amazement, as if the very scenes of Calvary were enacted before them, not daring to approach. Exhortation and entreaty had often to be used to enforce the observance of this duty. The whole congregation kneeled in time of prayer, and stood up while we sung. Storms seldom kept them from the house of worship, so that our congregations were not half as fluctuating as among our own people.

During the early part of the winter no extraordinary religious interest was manifest. Preaching once, sometimes twice a day, on the Sabbath; class meeting and prayer meeting were our usual services among the Indians. Once in two weeks I preached to the whites, on Sabbath afternoon. About midwinter we commenced prayer meeting at five o'clock Sunday mornings, and kept it up the remainder of the winter, and part of the summer. These meetings were mostly confined to the whites, including brother and sister Marksman, and were often seasons of great spiritual profit to us. New-Year's eve we held a watch meeting, which was attended with the Divine presence and blessing. The services commenced at nine o'clock, and continued till the close of the year. The new year was ushered in with the voice of prayer. The little society covenanted together to live nearer to God; and several expressed, by rising to their feet, that they desired to be Christians.

During the month of January we had frequent evening meetings, sometimes occupying nearly every evening in the week. The Church was greatly quickened, but we were favored with no general revival.

As usual, about the first of March the Indians left for the sugar bush, and our meetings, till they returned, were thinly attended. We visited them several times in their encampment, and broke to them the bread of life.

In the early part of May our little society was favored with a refreshing shower of grace. The following facts were recorded the 5th: "The Lord appears to be favoring us with an outpouring of his Spirit upon the Church here. This commenced with brother J., who stated, in meeting yesterday, that, for some time past, he had lived much in unbelief, and at a great distance from God. Last Wednesday he was peculiarly drawn out in prayer to God, and while in an agony, these words came into his mind, 'Only believe,' and he exclaimed, 'Lord, I will believe,' and instantly his burden was removed, and ever since he had been so blessed that he felt like shouting and praising God aloud, wherever he went. He immediately told his wife what the Lord had done for him, and exhorted her to look for the same blessing. From her acknowledgment, she also had been in a backslidden state. She stated that instead of feeling happy at what her husband had related, it appeared to make her angry at the Lord, saying that she had done all she could. Her husband still pressed the case—she yielded—gave herself anew to Christ, and has since rejoiced in the liberty of the Gospel. Brother J. was the carpenter.

"Some others of our white brethren and sisters have been greatly blessed since. My own soul has shared in the general blessing. To-day *Peter Marksman* was brought into the liberty of the Gospel, from which he fell last year, and which he has again been seeking for some months past. I trust this flame will spread not only among the whites but among the Indians. They are still, most of them, absent in the sugar-camps. This evening was our monthly missionary prayer meeting, and it proved a truly-refreshing season.

May 25. Things appear more promising in regard to the spiritual interests of the mission. For some two months and a half the Indians have been scattered; they are now together again. Our day school commenced last week. This morning our Sabbath school opened with some promise. We had five o'clock meeting this morning, both among the white people and the Indians. At 10½ o'clock, A. M., I preached from Isaiah lii, 1. Had the largest congregation we had seen for some time. Was blessed with great enlargement in preaching. Had not experienced such an overwhelming sense of the Divine presence before since our arrival. My faith in the power of God to accompany the preaching of the Gospel, by however weak instrumentality, was increased, and my soul went out in longing desire for the Indians. God was present to bless his people."

In the afternoon, in the midst of our meeting, the alarm of fire was given. It had been raging fearfully in the woods, and found its way into an old slashing close to the mission, and the rest of the afternoon and evening we were forced to fight the fire desperately to preserve our fences and buildings.

Many of our meetings during the summer season possessed much interest, but, in the midst of many pressing duties, no accurate memoranda were kept. As our work was here mostly confined to one spot, there was, necessarily, much monotony in the routine of our duty.

Brother Carrier, the farmer, and his excellent wife, exerted a most wholesome influence among the Indians. They were Congregationalists, educated at the Oberlin School, Ohio. They felt that their mission was not simply to teach the Indians how to plow and plant. Sister C., who possessed a more than common degree of intelligence, studied the Indian language, and, taking sister Marksman for interpreter, she used to visit the Indians in their houses, read God's word to them, pray with them, and instruct them how to live as Christians, and as white people. A female prayer meeting was established, and a moral reform society organized for the benefit of the Indians. If the Government should send such families among the Indians, instead of supplying those posts with men, as is often done, who have no higher claim than that their political creed accords with the party in power, they would shed light and happiness on the pathway of the Indian. If any Government officers should be persons of sterling moral character, they are those sent among the natives.

SEVERITY OF THE WINTER.

The ground was covered with snow about the middle of October. This left us, and we had several days of very fine weather. The 14th of November several inches of snow fell, and winter was soon upon us in good earnest. The coldest weather commenced about the last of January. We had no thermometer to show the exact state of the weather. January 31st, the bay was frozen over, and as it had been calm it was perfectly smooth for miles. This was a source of joy to the Indians. They had caught but few fish for a month or two before—now the prospect was that they could set their nets to advantage. Most of the settlement were out on the ice skating and fishing. But in less than a week a terrible gale from the north-east broke the ice all to pieces, and drove it together edgeways, and in all forms, six or eight feet deep, destroying a number of nets, and rendering it impossible for the Indians to set others. In a time of such scarcity as then existed in the provision line, every thing looked gloomy. From that on till the last of March, very few fish were caught. The potatoes had been mostly consumed, and the game taken from the woods was inadequate. There was, necessarily, a considerable amount of suffering before the winter closed. During sugar-making some lived almost entirely on sugar. But God mercifully preserved both whites and Indians till the opening spring afforded us plenty of the most delicious fish, and the whitened sail was seen in the distance, which brought us a new recruit from below. In this time of want and hunger we set apart a day of fasting and prayer among the whites, and met during the day for public worship.

PROVIDENTIAL DELIVERANCE.

Toward the latter part of March, in company with some other men, I was helping to remove some hay from a marsh to the shore, near the head of the bay. The marsh was about a mile back through the woods. Just at the bay our trail crossed a very deep creek. We had drawn most of the stack. I had just passed over the creek with an ox and train, threw off the hay, and was returning for my last load. The ice gave way and the ox fell through. Fortunately the bow-pin came out, and the ox was disentangled from the yoke and train. I caught a rope which we had for binding the hay, and, in an instant, made fast to the horns of the ox, which must soon have gone under. By this means I kept his head out of the water. I next called aloud to the men at the marsh, who heard me, and came speedily to my assistance. We released the ox without loss or damage to any thing; but it was not till after all was done that I realized my own imminent danger. Some may regard this as a mere instance of good luck; I rejoice to trace in such events the hand of a kind Providence, and to ascribe to his name the glory.

STUDIES.

Our opportunity for study was, at best, but limited. My library had been left at the Saut during the winter. In this interval we had received but one mail, and that we had hired an Indian to bring on his back from *Saut Ste. Marie.* The Bible and Greek Testament were constant companions. In the spring I added a copy of the Septuagint to my course. When our books arrived we endeavored, as far as practicable, to obey the apostle's injunction, "Give attendance to reading," and strove, meanwhile, at least, not to *forget* the use of the pen. Would that our profiting had been more apparent!

CHAPTER V.

TRIP TO LA POINTE TO ATTEND THE INDIAN PAYMENT.

OUR Indians were to receive their annuities at La Pointe. It was agreed that a few should go and receive the pay, and the rest remain at the mission. I had arranged to accompany them.

Tuesday, August 12. We left in a large bark canoe which the chief, David King, had made for the purpose. There were four stout Indians, besides David, who himself possesses a herculean frame. We crossed over to the Entry, into Portage river, and camped at night on the shore of Portage Lake. We had fallen in company with several canoes from the Catholic mission. The next morning we were up by three o'clock, and left our camp a little after four. Went eight miles and breakfasted. David and G. were quite unwell, and took an emetic of alder bark, drinking a large quantity of warm water. It did the work effectually; for in a few minutes they were ready to take down as much bread, pork, potatoes, fish, and coffee as any body. We soon reached what is called the Portage—a mile and a half of land carriage, where the canoe and all our effects must be carried over. One-third of the way we had to wade in water and mud. To me this was quite new business. But we were all over before noon to the shore of Lake Superior. Here we were wind-bound the remainder of the afternoon. A little after midnight we were off again—the day was fine, but the sun scorching hot at noon, and the Lake calm. We coasted about seventy miles and camped. Friday morning we were on our way again by half-past four o'clock; but we were baffled most of the day by contrary winds. About five o'clock, P. M., we ran into Carp river, where we found safe harbor. Shortly after James Schoolcraft, sutler from Fort Brady, came up with a large canoe and camped. I felt concerned lest we should be caught out over the Sabbath, and determined to urge our men off as soon as the Lake was sufficiently calm. Instead of camping on shore with them, I took a blanket and laid down in the canoe, which was made fast in the river. At eleven o'clock I aroused the men, and urged them to start. The chief said, "*Ka-gah Ne-shko-de-ze;*" that is, "I am almost mad. You know but little about the Lake." To this I readily assented, but was well assured that we could go, and told him we could try. I succeeded in getting them off about midnight. When we first started heavy dead swells were rolling, but the Lake soon became quite calm, and we had coasted about twenty miles by the time it was fairly light, and stopped for breakfast at the mouth of Black river. Here we found a tent and three copper hunters. Breakfast over, we put out again to sea, rowed about four miles from shore, and a most favorable breeze sprung up from the north-east. Now we had up main, fore, and top-sail, but the wind increasing, all were taken down but the fore-sail, and that closely reefed. Here was a traverse of about forty miles, directly to La Pointe. The heavy seas, which soon set into the bay, made it dangerous to effect a landing any where short of this. So, heading directly for La Pointe, we sailed at a rapid rate. The sea became very rough when we were in the midst of this great traverse. Now the high land to the left of us was in full view, and the Montreal river, dashing and foaming over falls of about eighty feet in hight; then all was hid in that direction but the blue sky. How frail was our craft, and what atoms we ourselves, compared with the billows around us! But God was with us, and held us in the hollow of his hand. Here we felt how good it was to trust in the Lord. By about noon on Saturday we landed in safety on Madeline Island, at La Pointe. I was very kindly received by the missionaries of the American Board, composed of Rev. S. Hall and family, Rev. Mr. Wheeler and Mr. Sproats and their families. Met here, also, Mr. Ely, a missionary from Pokegama, brother P. O. Johnson, from Leach Lake, several Indian preachers, and Rev. Mr. Rosseal, from the state of New York. Here were, also, traders and visitors from the Saut, Detroit, and other parts, and the place swarmed with Indians who had come hundreds of miles, out of the dense wilderness, to receive their annuity. We were de-

MONTREAL RIVER FALLS.

tained here thirteen days before we could leave, during which our time was spent very agreeably and profitably with the resident and visiting missionaries. It was to us a kind of missionary conference, and made up for many of our past privations. With those devoted missionary brethren we lived much in a few days.

RELIGIOUS EXERCISES.

Each Sabbath we had four services, two in English and two in Ojibwa, in which the resident and visiting brethren participated. We had also a morning prayer meeting each day in the week. Among our most hallowed seasons were those spent under the mission-roof at family worship. Two of the mission families, with their visitors and boarders, met around one altar. Among them were several charming singers. All present took part in reading the holy Scriptures. The persons who led the devotions made brief remarks on the lesson. This was followed by a devotional hymn, in which the different parts were carried. Then followed the prayer. The Spirit's divine influence seemed to fill the room. We felt as Peter, on the Mount of Vision, that it was good to be there. These delightful exercises were conducted with the spirit and with the understanding also. Such a bright spot was like an oasis in the desert. We hope never to forget those sacred hours. Our seasons of public worship were attended with the divine blessing.

THE MISSION.

Rev. S. Hall, the superintendent, had resided here about thirteen years, with an interesting family of children growing up around him, who were about as familiar with the Indian as with their native tongue. Mr. Hall has been, in every sense, a laborious missionary, working hard with his hands, preaching, translating, etc. With the aid of native interpreters, he had translated the New Testament into the Ojibwa, a work which is invaluable to the missions all through that region. Rev. Mr. Wheeler, of whom we could say many good things, spent considerable time at Bad river, where he has since succeeded in establishing a flourishing mission. Two schools were under the direction of the mission at La Pointe—one taught by Mr. Sproats and the other by Miss Spooner, a well-qualified Christian lady, who, like the others, had, for Christ's sake, volunteered to leave friends and home in the east, to be a missionary. The schools were reported as in a flourishing condition. Most of our missionaries, about Lake Superior, have occasionally found shelter under the roof of that mission, and there is but one voice from the whole, in regard to the unaffected hospitality and dignified Christian bearing of those missionaries and their families. In comparing the mission here, with our Methodist missions among the Indians, I gained the impression that these missionaries excelled us in their schools, and endeavored to train the Indians intellectually; but that we were far in advance, so far as making converts from paganism is concerned, and in promoting their civilization generally. Each, however, has marked out its appropriate sphere of influence, and is accomplishing the one great work.*

INDIANS FROM THE WOODS.

Their condition appeared deplorable enough. Many of them were disgustingly filthy—they looked as if they never pretended to wash either their persons or their clothes. Some of them had scarcely a tatter of even a filthy garment about them, and were almost destitute of provisions. They were painted and disfigured, and decorated in the most grotesque and ludicrous manner. Their outward appearance was only the counterpart of their minds—ignorant, morally polluted, and debased to the level of the brute. Their insolent pride gave the finishing stroke to their morally depraved condition. They were much addicted to gambling—some of them would part with all they had, in their strife to win the game. All that was wanting to complete their wretchedness was, to let them have whisky, which, fortunately, at this payment, by untiring vigilance, was kept from them. In looking at our Christian Indians, by the side of those,

* It is due to us to observe, that a large proportion of those in attendance upon those schools were of a mixed population—few full-blooded Indians. They were consequently more settled—less dependent on the chase, and better prepared to excel in their studies. Under the direction of such teachers they could not but succeed.

I wanted no further proof of the power of the Gospel to elevate the red man.

WAR-DANCE AND HEATHEN BURIAL.

On the evening of the 19th the Indians had a war-dance. They made dull music on two drums of their own construction. This was accompanied by singing and an occasional whoop. They commenced in a large lodge and marched out, when they were joined by others, till they formed quite a procession. Two of them had flags of divers colors. They marched in a kind of dance. In those dances some one usually makes a speech in which some great exploits are recounted.

On the evening of the 29th we observed a funeral. An aged Indian, after he had received his pay, was returning to his lodge, and dropped down dead in the road. This was about noon. Just before dusk he was buried, according to heathen custom. A kettle of provision was put in the grave by the head of the departed, on which it was supposed his spirit would feed. After the grave was closed, the relatives feasted on a kettle of boiled pork and "*dough-boys*," that is, pieces of dough boiled with the pork—a rare treat among the wild Indians. They were thus, as they supposed, feasting with their departed brother. They often place tobacco at the head of their graves, to serve for the departed. How gloomy such a burial! Is it wonderful that heathen Indians blacken their faces for the dead, and often spend hours of incon-

HORSE-SHOE HARBOR, NEAR COPPER HARBOR, L. S.

solable grief over the graves of their deceased friends! Their grief is that of frenzy and despair. *No Christ, no hope in death!*

RETURN.

After much delay the payment was made, and we took our departure August 29th. It was not convenient to return in the canoe with our Indians, on account of the goods, provisions, etc., they had to carry. Brother Marksman and his wife, who had preceded us to La Pointe, and myself, took passage on the Algonquin, which was to take us directly to Copper Harbor, where a trader was to wait for us with his canoe, and take us to L'Anse. Contrary to agreement, and to the great disappointment of several traders aboard, the captain steered directly for Isle Royal, to pick up some miners, who wished a passage down. We were becalmed, and did not reach the island till Monday morning, when we ran into the delightful harbor, called Rock Harbor. Dropping down about three miles to an old fishing post, we were disappointed again to find, by a card left, that the miners were on the opposite side. A gun was fired, which they heard, and they reached us just before dark. We had the day to hunt agates, and stroll among the wild scenery. Here we were forced to lay all night, and till one o'clock the next day, before we cleared the Harbor. We were then favored with a good wind, which brought us into Copper Harbor Tuesday, about midnight.

Landing in the morning, we learned that the trader, who was to take us home, became tired waiting, and left us. We were now in a *fix*, mostly among entire strangers, our money nearly spent, and, to human appearance, no way to reach home, seventy-five miles distant. After taking breakfast at a boarding house, and before taking any step, I retired to the woods and spread out our case before the Lord, and returned fully assured that some relief would be afforded us in our trying situation. We looked about and found a small canoe, for which the owner asked us twelve dollars. It was too much, but we did not know any better course to pursue, and bought it. Having learned something about our disappointment, he came afterward and refunded two dollars. A Mr. Hopkins, who was, probably, at the head of this movement, gave us two dollars. Mr. M. gave us one dollar, and some pork for our journey; and two merchants, Messrs. Barbeau and Chapman, gave us a bag of hard bread, worth about three dollars. We fell in with the lamented Dr. Houghton, who kindly furnished us with a tent. Thus were all our wants met by a merciful Providence.

Copper Harbor was, at that time, the central point of attraction for all concerned in the mines, which had just begun to excite attention. The shore, all about the Harbor, was lined with tents, and every thing was on the move as if the people were driving on to a speedy fortune.

We were detained here, in our camp, till Thursday afternoon. The wind blew a gale most of the time, and the Lake was all agitation. We left the Harbor in our frail bark attached by a rope to the large boat of Dr. Houghton. The breakers were rolling in, angrily, when we left, and it was not without risk of running under that we had to resort to this expedient. The Doctor would have given us a place in his boat, but his own lading was sufficiently heavy. After passing fairly out of the Harbor we were in little danger, and, with a fine breeze, soon reached the end of Point Kewenaw. Rounding the Point we came into smooth water, and dropped loose from the Doctor's boat. He stopped with his men, and we kept on till some time after dark, when we reached the opposite shore of *Bate du Gris*, commonly called Bay Degree. Here we camped in company with some Indians, who had left Copper Harbor before us. The tent we had left with the Doctor. Here we ate our homely meal, and, as was our uniform custom, sung and prayed, and laid us down, under the open canopy of heaven, and slept sweetly till the dawn of day. The morning light was saluted also with the voice of prayer and praise. We craved the watchful care of God over us, exposed, as we were, to the perils of the deep. And the day had not passed before we saw our need of this. Early in the day we met a canoe from home, which had been dispatched to look after us. Finding that we were all "right side up with care," Mr. B. went on to Copper Harbor on his own business. When the wind would allow we carried a small sail, such as our craft could bear, and sailing some, and using the paddles briskly, we proceeded very well till toward night, when a fine breeze sprung up, which was bearing us along nicely. But gradually it gathered strength, and now the white caps began to appear, and wave succeeded wave, till the scene about us looked frightful. A short distance before us was a point, and on from that, for a distance of about eight miles, was a high wall of rocks, where we could not have landed. As night was approaching it added to the risk of any attempt to pass them. About a mile to our right was a beautiful sand-beach, but a terrible sea was rolling in to the shore. A moment was spent in deciding what to do. We agreed that our only hope was to try to land. Marskman had the stern of the canoe, and I managed the bow. We wheeled for the shore, meanwhile throwing off our coats, shoes, and stockings, to be ready to spring into the water before the canoe should strike. The steersman was to give the word of command. As we approached the shore we paddled with all our might to ride in upon one of the huge waves. Just now said Marksman, "make ready." No sooner said than I found myself on my feet, firmly grasping the bow of the canoe. In an instant he was out at the stern, and taking advantage of the wave, we ran her as high as possible on the beach. Now a large swell broke over the stern, but doing us little damage. With the utmost dispatch we had every thing safely landed. Our feelings of thankfulness may be more easily imagined than expressed. We kindled a fire, and, as it had commenced to rain, constructed a tent out of our sail and a coverlet. Then singing a hymn of praise, we implored God's blessing upon us, and were drawn out especially in behalf of the Indians we had camped with the night before. Having a larger craft they put out further to sea, and the storm was now ahead for them. The night was dark and rainy, and much doubt hung over their prospect; so we worked about half of the night, to keep up a bright fire to serve as a beacon. It is enough to say that they found a shelter from the storm, and reached home in safety. We rested but little that night—the howling of the wind—the roaring of the lake—the chilliness of the atmosphere—the thought of home—the uneasiness of my dear wife and daughter, all conduced more to reflection and prayer than to sleep. Saturday the wind was in the east, and a heavy sea continued to set in to the bay. The following was penned on the spot:

"Unless the tempest should soon subside we shall not reach home this week. Blessed be God, I trust that this journey, which has been adverse at almost every turn since I left La Pointe, has taught me many important lessons. I have seen the hand of God strikingly exhibited in several instances. My soul is fixed trusting in the Lord. I will not fear though the sea roar, and the mountains shake, with the swelling thereof."

After noon the lake measurably calmed down, and we might have gone on, but for the heavy breakers which still rolled up against the shore. We made an ineffectual attempt to get off. Pushing the canoe to the water's edge, we put in our things, shoving it out gradually as far as we dared. We stood in water about half an hour watching a favorable swell. At length we shoved off, but were met about as soon with a huge wave, which broke over the canoe, filling the bow half full, submerging a box of Indian Testaments and badly wetting our things. We were now in danger of losing the canoe, as from its weight it was unmanageable. But making fast to a tree by means of a rope, we got out our effects and secured the canoe. Making ourselves as comfortable as we could, we were compelled to wait more favorable auspices.

We arose early the next morning to hail the light of a lovely Sabbath. What should we do? Our bread had become damp and musty. Our other provisions were nearly exhausted. Our situation was very uncomfortable. With our small canoe we could not go when it was rough, and should we neglect the present opportunity, we might have to stay for days on that dreary shore, when a few hours would take us home. We thought of the anxious suspense of our friends, to know what had become of us. These and other similar reasons led us to think that it was our duty to go, especially in the light of Christ's declaration respecting the observance of the Sabbath: "I will have mercy and not sacrifice." We therefore coasted leisurely along on the placid lake, till we came within about six miles of home, when we caught a favorable breeze, which soon bore us across to the mission, where we landed a little after noon—finding all well and rejoicing in God at our deliverance from the perils of the deep.

CHAPTER VI.

SECOND YEAR AT THE KEWAWENON MISSION

THE conference, which had recently been in session, saw fit to continue us at this station. We shall aim to group together what is worthy of notice during this year, in as brief a manner as possible. Our work was mostly at home, and therefore was more monotonous than some other periods of our connection with the missions.

The summer before we had succeeded in raising a good crop of vegetables. Several days were spent in digging and taking care of our potato crop. We had not only enough for our own use but a surplus. Those I took in a large batteau to the Eagle River mine, where I was paid for them, in gold, about forty-five dollars. This was the first surplus the mission had produced. The avails greatly aided us in our work. The batteau had been sold by a Mr. B. to the Mining Company, and was to be left at Eagle river. We took a small bark canoe in tow, to return home with. The tour was the shortest and most successful coasting-trip I ever made. We reached Eagle river, *via* Kewenaw Point, in a little more than two days and a half. The same afternoon we disposed of our vegetables, unloaded the batteau, gummed our canoe, and by dark were ready to start for home. I was dubbed *captain*, for the first time, by the receiver of our cargo. I had an interview here with the late lamented Dr. Houghton, and passed that night—Friday—in our frail bark over the spot where he was drowned, in a terrible gale, the Monday night following. The Lake was calm, and we reached the Portage, twenty-five miles, by midnight. The next night, by ten o'clock, we reached the mission in safety. The whole journey, a distance of one hundred and seventy-five miles, was performed within four days.

We were embarrassed, during the fall and winter, by the serious illness of brother Marksman, by which he was laid aside from the work.* This threw the school on my hands, in addition to the onerous duties which already claimed my attention. And till the middle of December we had no regular interpreter. In this interim we had to depend mostly on two females, who spoke both languages well, and rendered us good service. G. Bedell arrived from a more distant station the 13th of December, and was hired to interpret the rest of the winter. With our limited help we endeavored to have all the interests of the mission cared for to the best of our ability. The day school and Sunday school were kept up, except

---

*Toward spring sister Marksman was brought to the confines of the grave by a most painful affliction. It was a time of fiery trial to brother M. and his family. But they found their help in God.

in absence of the scholars for sugar-making. But, as there was little change in the inhabitants, our schools were made up of nearly the same scholars as the year before, and the description before given may suffice.

Our religious meetings were attended with many discouragements, as well as our educational interests—perhaps not proportionately more than among our own people. Our native population at the mission was less than one hundred and fifty souls, including children. Most of the adult population had, at some time, professed religion. Backsliding is a sin among Indians as well as among white people. Take a community of the same size and character, religiously, among white people, and then ask, would it be reasonable to expect sweeping revivals of religion from year to year, in which scores would crowd the altar as penitents, and go on their way rejoicing as new converts? It is no uncommon thing in a community of hundreds of white people for the Church to have only an occasional revival. Spiritual declension is by no means a rare thing. I speak of this not to justify want of revival in either case; but, simply, as an existing fact in both cases, and no less notorious among whites than Indians. It is a false view of this very thing which operates to the prejudice of our Indian missions. Many are wont to expect results, which will tally with successful efforts in a dense population, where no hinderance is placed in the way by a strange language. The question, whether we ought to abandon such posts because of the paucity of numbers, is another thing, which I shall not stop here to answer. All we ask is, that, as long as the Church, in her wisdom, shall think best to cultivate such ground, our people should not look despairingly at the results so long as they equal those among the same number of white people. But we were not left without witness that God was with us. The Church was often quickened, backsliders were occasionally reclaimed, and, in some instances, we were enabled to rejoice in the conversion of sinners.

The following was noted December 8th: "After mentioning some of our discouragements, on account of brother Marksman's illness, etc., I was led to say, 'Man's extremity is often God's opportunity.' In the midst of all these discouragements he has been pleased to visit and bless us. Our meetings among the Indians have never been so interesting since I came here, as for some time past. A week ago last Sabbath was our communion season, and a more melting time I have never witnessed any where. My own soul was so peculiarly drawn out in behalf of the Indians, as seemed to dissolve me in tears. My interpretress became so deeply affected that she had to make occasional pauses to give vent to tears. A divine influence seemed to pervade the house, so that nearly the whole congregation were melted into tenderness. So far as I was concerned it was not merely the effect of the moment, but, for some time before, I had communed intimately with God in secret."

At night of the same day a backslider was reclaimed and united again on trial. Confession was also made by others who had been in a backslidden state, who expressed a determination to lead a new life.

The next Sabbath I took for my text, "*Therefore will the Lord wait that he may be gracious.*" Our meeting was very similar to those of the preceding Sabbath. The Church was evidently rising to newness of spiritual life.

Christmas eve was, with us, a season owned of God. We had our house neatly trimmed with evergreens furnished to hand in such abundance, and well lighted. The meeting was attended by our own and some of the Catholic Indians. We met again the next day and had public worship, and baptized two children.

December 27. After laboring hard all day with my hands, I visited, at night, eight families. I found, in conversation with them, that, for a time, most of them had been in a low state of religion, but that, in most cases, of late, they had been making renewed efforts to love and serve God. Two or three spoke of having the load of sorrow removed from their hearts, which were now filled with peace and joy. Some who were not yet brought into this liberty expressed a determination to continue seeking. I was rejoiced to find, in the midst of much backsliding, a hungering and thirsting after righteousness.

We held a watch meeting New-Year's eve as usual, which was well attended and blessed to those present Two backsliders expressed a determination to return again to their Father's house, and most of the professors renewed their covenant with God. After the meeting was dismissed a young man desired to speak with me. He was so deeply affected that he could scarcely speak for sobs and tears. He stated that he had been reminded of his unfaithfulness the past year. He was troubled on that account. But the Lord had been near him during the watch meeting, and he was resolved to serve God better for the future.

Just as we were about leaving the house a person came to tell me that my daughter was quite ill. On returning to the house I found her severely attacked with croup. Using the best means at command we were thankful to see her soon convalescent.

In one of our meetings about this time, the chief, David King, arose, so deeply affected that he could say but few words at a time. Among other things he said, that "while he was talking with his family in the morning, and telling them how they should live, he thought of his brethren, some of whom were cold in their hearts. This overpowered him. He sung and prayed, and now exhorted his brethren to be more faithful." While he spoke I saw some others weeping freely. The Indians are taught to believe that it is the greatest weakness for a *man* to weep. Nothing but the love of Jesus can open the fountain of tears. In their heathen state they can look on, apparently with stoical indifference, when their dearest friends are torn from them by death. They often have deep feelings bordering on despair, but it would be unmanly to betray them. To weep would be to act like women. But the strong man armed is brought to bow, and the adamantine heart to melt, under the power of the cross.

As we were about leaving the house of prayer we witnessed a scene in striking contrast with the one just mentioned. Several white men in a boat came to the shore, singing the song called "The Flowing Bowl," and hallooing at the top of their voice, evidently influenced by liquor. They appeared perfectly reckless of all order and decency. They went from house to house with their jug, but found no one to drink with them. Even our Indians despised them, and they soon left for the settlement across the Bay.

The 4th of January was our communion day. It was an occasion of much interest. Christ was present to bless in our love-feast. Thirteen, principally youth from ten to sixteen years of age, united with the Church on trial, most of them as seekers. The scene was delightful and truly affecting, to see those children give their hand to the Church while tears trickled down their cheeks. Among the parents and older members of the Church, some were overcome with joyful emotions, and others were agonizing for a blessing. Two of those who joined us had been members of the Roman Catholic Church, one a member that they prized highly. In the afternoon I baptized a young man, who had also been a Papist; he united with our Church on trial. At night we had a manifest display of the power and mercy of

God. At an invitation for persons cold in religion and seekers to come forward, two benches were soon filled. As they came to the seats prepared, they fell upon their knees, and each seemed deeply engaged for himself. There was some noise, but no extravagance. The agonizing sigh and groan were heard to escape the burdened heart; the prayer of the believer mingled with that of the penitent seeker; an occasional burst of praise was heard, and at times the hearty *amen*, which seemed to speak from the heart, "*Lord, even so let it be.*" One, at least, of the seekers obtained pardon, and we had reason to believe that several cold professors were reclaimed from their backslidings.

FIERY TRIALS.

Not long after those precious showers of grace our spiritual horizon was overcast with dark and threatening clouds. Almost every thing had changed as it respected the little company of white members who had enjoyed such refreshings from the presence of God the previous year. One of those brethren had removed to Pittsburg. The farmer and his wife, who had been such a help to us, had left. His successor made no pretensions to religion. A most unhappy difficulty arose among several of the white residents, involving two members of the Church, and resulted in the expulsion of one and the withdrawal of the other from the Church. The dispute was so connected with the affairs of the Indians as to involve them also. For a time it really seemed as if the powers of darkness would prevail. These were to us hours of sadness. Our faith in God was put to the severest test. But the cloud at length passed over, and the bright Sun of righteousness again shone upon us.

In the early part of the summer the society was arranged in three classes—one a juvenile class, consisting of those who had recently united with the Church. I took charge of this class as leader.

The following facts were noted as occurring on Friday, July 10th. It was observed as a day of fasting and prayer, preparatory to our communion. We met at five o'clock, A. M., for prayer meeting. Had a general attendance and a good meeting. In the evening I met the juvenile class, most of whose members joined the Church last winter. There were ten present, and I was glad to find them all entertaining a hope of heaven and a determination to live a Christian life.

I have been thus particular to show that, with all the difficulties and discouragements we had to meet, we were still enabled to say, "The best of all is, God is with us."

TRAVELS.

Though my work was mostly confined to Kewawenon, I traveled some during the year. Some account of a trip made on snow-shoes must suffice. It was in some respects one of the most laborious and painful journeys of my life. On the 6th of January I left the mission, accompanied by two able-bodied Indians, to visit a band of Indians at Grand Island, a distance of a hundred and twenty miles. The chief Monomonee and his family had embraced religion and united with our Church under the labors of Rev. George W. Brown. They belonged properly to the mission at Saut Ste. Marie, but were farther from that station than from us, and were thus mostly deprived of the labors of a Christian pastor. The Catholic priest told some of our Indians that he had received an invitation from Monomonee to come and Christianize those Indians. I doubted the correctness of the report; but, as I was informed that the priest was intending to go immediately to Grand Island to accomplish this end, and was prepared to make the Indians liberal offers, if they would consent to settle near his mission and become Catholics, I felt it my duty to go before him, and, with the help of God, defeat his proselyting attempts. The desired end was accomplished. The priest followed me, and made but a brief stay with the Indians. Years after this I was permitted to see the chief and his family settled with our Indians at Naomikong, firmly attached to Protestant Christianity, and constant worshipers with us.

OUTFIT.

Our outfit for this journey consisted of snow-shoes, two small axes, a gun, a cedar snow-shovel to clear away snow for our encampment, a small sail to stretch over our camp for covering, blankets, about sixty pounds of provisions—mostly pork and flour, tea, coffee, sugar, etc.—a camp-kettle, frying-pan, tin-cups, etc. This load was all carried by my guides except my two blankets, Bible, hymn-book, etc., which made up my pack. We had no dog-train—an article seldom used in that region.

Our journey led mostly through a dense forest, with not even a trail, and little to guide us, except some indistinct marks recognized only by Indians. Sometimes we crossed a chain of little lakes, and occasionally we clambered along the rocky shore of Lake Superior, and then made the *detour* of deep bays, over a sandy and less rugged shore. We forced our way through several cedar swamps, where we had often either to climb over or creep under fallen brush and timber. We usually traveled from twenty to thirty-five miles a day; once about forty miles. At noon we stopped just long enough to take a cold lunch, near some place where we could obtain water, and then we continued our march till after sundown. The last day on our way down we traveled till midnight by the light of the moon. Our labor was by no means ended when we stopped for the night. The snow, two to three feet deep, must be shoveled away to make a place for our camp; boughs must be cut and spread down to serve the double purpose of floor and bed; wood must be chopped to keep a good fire all night—and, if very cold, we usually burnt a huge pile. Next our supper must be prepared. It was generally nine or ten o'clock before we were ready to wrap up in our blankets and give our eyes to sleep. The next morning we must be up at four or five o'clock, cook our breakfast, and perform the same arduous toil.

On the evening of the fourth day we reached Carp river, near the *now* flourishing town of Marquette. Here was then one solitary wigwam, occupied by an Indian family. I had worn my moccasins through; my feet were both badly blistered, and my limbs so wearied that I could scarcely drag my snow-shoes along. The sight of a human habitation, though but an Indian lodge, gave me such joy that I was involuntarily moved to tears. Here we were warmly received. One of the men had just taken a deer. *Mah-je-ge-zhik's* wife made us a warm cake, cooked venison and some potatoes, and made us a dish of tea—all neatly and well served, and which had a relish not common at sumptuous feasts. Our hostess then dried and mended my moccasins, and seemed to take pleasure in doing all she could to minister to our wants. The next day was Saturday. We reached the Island, by traveling forty miles, about midnight. This hard day's work was too much for me, and I was quite unwell during the Sabbath.* I remained at the Island till Tuesday

* Sunday afternoon we crossed over the Bay, and staid for the night with Mr. Williams, of whom we purchased provisions the next morning for our return voyage.

noon, held several meetings with the Indians, and found them in a low state of religion; but they made new vows to lead a more devoted Christian life. We were kindly received, and they professed unwavering attachment to our Church. I gave them a copy of St. John's Gospel and a hymn-book—both in the Ojibwa language—exhorted them to faithfulness, and set out for Kewawenon.

By the severe exercise on the way down I had lamed my ankle. It was what the Indians call snow-shoe-lameness, arising from overstraining of the tendons. It is very painful when the limb must be exercised, and permanent relief can hardly be obtained only by rest from the labor that causes it. We had traveled only a few miles when I had not strength in my ankle to carry the snow-shoe, and yet could not walk without. In this emergency I tied a string to the fore-end of the snow-shoe, which at every step I raised with the left hand. A hard way to walk, but it must be that or nothing. The next morning, after going about five miles, I was compelled to stop. We had scarcely made our camp before the priest passed us on his way down. I had a short interview with him, and told him that the Indians had not sent for him. He was resolved to go on and see them, which was his privilege. Here I went through a course of Indian treatment. My ankle was lacerated with a sharp flint, and rubbed with liniment. I was somewhat relieved the next morning, and we were off by five o'clock. We followed the priest's track, by moonlight, till the day dawned. After the first two or three hours of each day I could walk only by aid of the string as before. Thursday we made about twenty-five miles; Friday about thirty; my lameness abating but little. Saturday morning we were off before day. One of my men now served me a perfect Indian trick. W. B. was a great walker. Early in the morning he passed G. and me, and traveled that day within twenty miles of home. He went into the mission early on Sabbath morning, and told Mrs. P. that he had left us about sixty miles off—which was true—that I was so lame as hardly to be able to walk, and that we were just out of provisions. The impression was made that we were in a sad predicament, sure enough.

Saturday evening found us about thirty miles from our morning camp. Here we stopped early, and chopped wood to last us over the Sabbath, and resolved to rest and await the result.

The flour we procured of the trader was sour, and we had sour, heavy bread all the way, which would have been indigestible but for our hard exercise. But this was nearly spent, and for meat and drink we were on short allowance. We rested in our camp till two o'clock, Monday morning, when we were again feeling our way through the forest by the aid of a bright moonlight. By sunrise we had reached Huron Bay, having traveled over half a day's march on our way down. About eight o'clock we met two Indians, who had been dispatched with a supply of provisions for us. Short as was our allowance, we had still a cold lunch left, and could have reached home on the strength of that. I felt provoked that W. B. should have occasioned my family and friends such unnecessary anxiety and trouble. After a wearisome forced march of about thirty-five miles, we reached home by two o'clock, P. M., having traveled at least two hundred and forty miles in less than two weeks, including all our delays. We often have accounts of the herculean labors performed by our pioneer ministers, who have had to travel three or four hundred miles *on horseback* in as many weeks. If our northern missionaries should only relate their unvarnished story, they might at least claim to know something respecting the toil and sacrifice of itinerant life, not on horseback, but on *foot*. Speaking from experience, we must be allowed to speak with a degree of confidence.

HANDICRAFT.

The missionary at so remote a post must be able to adapt himself to almost any exigency. We had, the previous fall, ordered a box of clothing from Detroit, including shoes for the family. The box came as far as the Saut, and was there detained all winter. Meanwhile Mrs. P. and Carrie were becoming almost destitute of shoes. I procured sole-leather of a neighbor, cut uppers out of some boot-tops, made my own lasts, and, being mostly confined to the house with lameness for several days, I made shoes for my wife and daughter, modeled after the "latest fashion" of Lake Superior.

During the summer the country swarmed with surveyors, geologists, and men of all ranks and grades, in search of fortunes in the minerals which just began to be developed. Several of the Indians were employed as guides, packers, and *voyageurs*, which materially abated our forces at the mission. Three miles from us, near the head of the Bay, a saw-mill was in process of erection—an improvement greatly needed. On the third day of August the first election for the town of L'Anse was held at our school-house. The officers were J. B., moderator; B. F. R., J. K., and A. W. D., inspectors; and, in their scarcity of material, I was chosen clerk. Thirty-two votes were polled. Most of the voters came out of the woods, and returned after the election. Elections were held also at other places in the mineral regions; but, from some failure to meet the requirements of law, the elections were rendered null and void, and the country was left again, as it had been, literally without law.

At the close of the summer we left the mission to attend conference, and make some transient visits among esteemed friends below. We coasted in open boat to Copper Harbor, thence were conveyed to the Saut Ste. Marie by the propeller Independence, and by various public conveyances reached our friends in Ohio. After a short stay we returned to Michigan. Mrs. P. and Carrie remained with our friends in

Adrian, and I proceeded to Marshall, the seat of our conference. Many interesting circumstances were connected with those visits, but I must not tax the patience of the reader with them.

CHAPTER VII.

PERILS ON THE DEEP.

HAVING for three years been deprived of the privilege of meeting in conference, the interview I had enjoyed with my ministerial brethren was one of interest and profit. I was reappointed to the Kewawenon mission, with a roving commission from Bishop Janes to explore the mining region, and do what I could to establish religious worship among the miners. Rev. J. W. Holt was appointed as my assistant to teach the school, and attend to the wants of the mission in my absence. Conference ended, I repaired to Adrian, where I was joined by my family. Mrs. P.'s father accompanied us. After a short stay at Detroit we soon arrived at the Saut, *via* Mackinaw. During the several days in which we were detained at the Saut, embracing one Sabbath, it was our privilege to enjoy the genial sunlight of missionary life with other missionaries.

On the morning of the 15th of October the ground was covered with snow; but as the sun arose it soon disappeared.

In the afternoon the wind was fair for going up Lake Superior. After dark we were called on board the schooner *Fur Trader*. A very rainy night ensued. We had soon weighed anchor, and were disputing our way with the rapid current of the St. Mary's.

Friday, 16th, two o'clock, A. M. Strong wind driving us at the rate of ten knots per hour. All were cheerful at the thought of a quick trip. But how illusive are some of our most joyous hopes! Like the *mirage*, seen in the distance, hope is only begotten to add weight to disappointment. We had passed White Fish Point, fifty miles from the Saut, and all was well. We sat down in the morning to breakfast, on homely sailor fare. It was about eight o'clock. No one dreamed of being interrupted before breakfast was over. Just now one of the sailors cried out, "Captain, it looks rather squally!" No sooner said than Captain R. dropped his knife and fork, and was on deck. Order was given to *reef the mainsail.* It was promptly done. Captain R. cried again, "*Reef the foresail.*" "*Ay, ay, sir.*" And the foresail was reefed. All interpreted these signs to have an important meaning. At ten o'clock the storm had greatly increased; hard rain and cold withal. Wind had hauled round more to the north. At twelve the seas ran very high, raging as if some angry spirit had troubled the mighty deep. Our schooner rose upon the waves, and then plunged her bows into the foaming deep, groaning at every plunge.

She was heavily freighted. Forward she had on a quantity of hay, a horse, and other live stock. The hay soon became filled with water, from the seas which swept over us. *Abaft*, her deck was stowed with barrels, two deep, even on the top with the railing. When a hard squall struck her, it would lay her over "*on her beam ends*," and, much of the time, the upper tier of barrels on the *larboard deck* was under water. She consequently made bad weather. Meanwhile one of the *davits*, or tackle, to hold up the boat, gave way and dropped one end of the yawl. Order was given to cut the boat loose, which was done, and for some time it was towed with a large rope. But soon the rope broke, and now our yawl was seen floating, bottom up, with the hay which had just been thrown overboard. The pump was kept in operation most of the time. Captain R., who stood at the helm all the time, was in a most exposed condition; sometimes in water up to his knees, and then forced, with the violence of the waves, from side to side of the steerage deck. We were now in the vicinity of the *Grand Sable*, a little east of the Pictured Rocks, about thirty miles from Grand Island. We had hoped to reach the Island, where there is a harbor secure from all winds, but this was now found to be impossible. It only remained for us to be driven ashore, with all the peril to which this would expose us, or to make the *attempt* to get back under the lee of White Fish Point, about fifty* miles distant. The latter alternative the Captain chose. We *wore ship*, as the

* In mentioning distances perfect accuracy must not be expected. In the Repository this was set down at sixty miles. The last mentioned is probably nearer correct.

sailors say, and succeeded in clearing the shore; and, sailing at a rapid rate, we rounded White Fish Point in safety, and, getting into comparatively smooth water, by ten o'clock at night we were very much rejoiced to hear the Captain give orders to let go the anchor.

I have given only a faint description of the scene without. If all was storm without, all was far from being calm within. Most of the crew and passengers were irreligious, and the voice of God, which spoke amidst the warring elements, was not in soothing accents to such as were at enmity with him. It was a sober time to all on board. The most daring and profane seemed awe-struck. One man who was not in the habit of praying in a calm, said he "guessed there were none on board but that prayed." Another said, "I think I shall not be found at the billiard-table very soon again." The cook, a colored man, was frightened nearly out of his wits. A female was terribly alarmed. "We shall all go to the bottom," said she, frequently. Bitterly did she lament having left a comfortable home, to suffer such hardships and dangers. "O, Mr. ——," said she, "do pray for us." Many silent prayers ascended to heaven, but it was rather inconvenient to hold a public prayer meeting, when each was so sick as scarcely to be able to hold up his head.

Our boat was long, narrow, and flat, setting at defiance the symmetry and proportion of the ship-builder's art, but, withal, was an admirable sailer.

Her cabin, if such it may be called, was small—only four berths, and not any too neat. The table was without legs, and shoved up and down a center-post, supported by a wooden pin. When not needed it was shoved overhead. A small stove stood in the corner near the hatchway. Such was the boat into which we were crowded. Two Indian girls had gained admittance into one of the berths, the others were resigned to those who had women and children. The floor as well as the berths was stowed full. And those who could find no room here, found such accommodations as they could in the hold.

The storm came on so suddenly that there was not time to clear away the breakfast dishes; these were huddled down on the floor by the stove. Scarcely had the storm struck us, before the stove tumbled, bottom upward, among the breakfast dishes. The violent tossings of the boat, the scent of bilge-water, which escaped through a hole in the floor, the strange sights and sounds all around us, gave every one a disposition to part with his breakfast; and a scene ensued so ludicrous as to excite our risibles in the midst of all our peril.

Our situation was extremely uncomfortable; we could have no fire, and could not keep dry. With an overcoat on I was wet throughout. Several large waves poured down upon us through the hatchway. The large seas dashing against the side of the boat, forced water through the berths, from one side to the other. We were literally drenched, and became much chilled before we could have fire again—not till after ten o'clock at night. But praise to an overruling Providence for our rescue from the dangers to which we were exposed! Several causes conduced to this under the blessing of a good God. Our boat had recently been fitted up with new sails; about the time we began to *wear ship*, the wind hauled about two points to westward, which enabled us to clear the shore; but added to these were the self-possession and fidelity of Captain R. and his crew. They will ever have the gratitude of the passengers for their conduct during this severe storm.

We lay at anchor till the next morning after breakfast. Having lost our boat, it was agreed to run back to the Saut and get another. Wind being in our favor, we set sail and dropped anchor at the head of the Rapids just after dark. We now landed and walked through the mud to Fort Brady, a mile distant, and put up with the Chaplain. All were surprised at our speedy return. It will not be thought very strange that, after the perils and exposures on the deep, just named, the following day, which was the holy Sabbath, was to us one of the best Sabbaths of all our life.

While at the Saut, Captain B., of another boat, came aboard, either on business or from curiosity. He had the audacity to charge our mishaps to the preachers and the women. He might also have included the cats, for there was one aboard during the storm. He said that he "never knew it to fail—with women and preachers aboard, sailors were sure to have storms." It seems that, since the sad affair of poor Jonah, preachers must be made the scape-goats, to bear off the sins of the *Tars*. Why the fair sex should influence the spirit of storms against our friends of the deep, it is hard to conceive, unless it be for the many long and painful neglects they have suffered from those who have followed the sea. Be this as it may, Mr. B. himself, who was a fearless sailor and a daring sinner, was not proof against storms. He was one of the unfortunate company who perished on the schooner Merchant, in the summer of 1847.

After a detention of another week at the Saut, trudging back and forth over the muddy Portage, now called aboard by the captain, with a prospect of fair wind, and then debarking in disappointment, really fearing that we must winter at the Saut, we left port once more, and till we landed at Grand Island encountered another storm but little inferior to the one above described. Nearly all the passengers became desperately seasick. The greatest sufferers were, perhaps, my wife and daughter.

GRAND ISLAND.

This is a large island, as its name imports, situated near the southern shore of Lake Superior, nearly midway from the Saut to Kewawenon. The soil is generally good. It is well timbered, principally with birch, maple, and beech.

Mr. W. came here in an early day and took up his residence. He had a numerous family growing around him. One of his daughters had married and settled by him. In the fall of 1845 she came, accompanied by her lover, in a small boat to Kewawenon, a hundred and twenty miles, to be sacrificed on the hymeneal altar. The writer felt himself not a little honored by this visit from his neighbors of the Island, especially as he was called upon to perform the solemn rite.

At this island is one of the most beautiful and commodious harbors to be found any where.

Wednesday, 28th, was a beautiful morning, enlivened by a bland south breeze. After a good rest on shore, where we shared the generous hospitality of Mr. W.'s family, at twelve o'clock, M., we were again called on board. At four, P. M., we were nearly becalmed. At sunset the wind was slightly ahead. During the night we beat with some success. Thursday morning Presque Isle was south, in sight, and Granite Island several miles ahead. We could now lay our course for Kewawenon. We had a rough sea all day. But by the blessing of a gracious Providence, the same evening we dropped anchor in the Bay, near the Methodist mission. We were now soon surrounding our own cheerful fire, to recount, with gratitude, the goodness of God to us during a long and perilous voyage. Never before did home seem so sweet.

November 1st, the Sabbath after our return, was

a memorable day to us. The Indians came out in the morning, and brother H. preached them a good practical sermon. In the afternoon I preached to the few white residents, from Hebrews xiii, 12–14, dwelling particularly on the latter part, "Here we have no continuing city." I was blessed with great freedom, and considerable enlargement in speaking. The congregation were melted into tears. The subject, applicable as it is to men at all times, was especially so at this time. Death had, during our absence, invaded our ranks among the Indians. He had dealt a terrible blow upon our small white settlement in the very sudden death of Mr. J., the carpenter, who was cut down in the prime and vigor of life. He died, we trust, not without hope in Christ. The text did not tend more to impress us with the past than to admonish us of the future. In the congregation was a Mr. B., a respectable and worthy member of a sister Church. He was the agent of a mine at Silver Mountain, as it was called, about fifteen miles off. His leisure time he spent at our place. He seemed to enjoy much the privilege of worshiping with us. The following Sabbath he spoke in our class meeting of his strong confidence in God, and of his determination to stand, at all times, as a witness for the Savior. That week was not half gone before I saw the dead body of Mr. B. taken out of Sturgeon river, where he had been drowned. He had loaded a small bark canoe with vegetables. Accompanied by two men he attempted to reach Silver

Mountain by water. He had crossed the Bay, entered Portage river, passed thence into Sturgeon river, where he had gone only a short distance before, running upon a large snag, he broke a hole through the canoe, and, in attempting to escape, was drowned. The two men made their escape, got out the canoe, and came down the river in one end, after having cut it in two. Such was the sad fâte of Mr. B. Nor was the fate of the Company any less disastrous than that of their worthy agent. The succeeding season they rallied afresh to prosecute the work at Silver Mountain. They sent on a new agent, and new recruits of men and means. They all reached the Saut de Ste. Marie in safety. They left the Saut, bound for the mine, on the schooner Merchant, and have never since been heard of. A small fragment of the wreck is all that has been discovered of this sad catastrophe. Mining has not since been prosecuted at Silver Mountain. Indeed it has never been a mine, only *in prospect.* The location was a bone of contention when first made, and has ended in disappointment to all, and in irreparable loss to some. Thus does wealth often elude the grasp of those that would be rich, and the glory of the world passes away.

CHAPTER VIII.

WORK AMONG THE MINERS—KEWAWENON MISSION.

THE week after our arrival at Kewawenon we succeeded in securing our crop and in arranging affairs at the mission preparatory to my expected absence among the miners.

The great show of native copper, at the Cliff Mine, had but recently been discovered, which was looked upon as one of the world's wonders. Mining at that locality was prosecuted very briskly. The brightening prospect here gave a new impetus to mining all through the mineral region. Companies had been formed and mining forces concentrated, in various places, scattered over Point Kewenaw, and also in the vicinity of the *On-to-na-gon* river. As yet the foundation of Christian institutions had not been laid. It was to plant the Rose of Sharon among the craggy rocks of that desolate region that such a mission was contemplated.

FIRST VISIT AMONG THE MINERS.

November the 10th, I left home in company with two young men from Point Kewenaw, to visit and preach among the miners, as opportunity offered.

Took with me a heavy Indian blanket and a pair of snow-shoes. The young men with whom I took passage, had a small Mackinaw boat. In this each took his appropriate station, one to steer, the others to row. The first day, which turned out to be rainy and disagreeable, we crossed over to the mouth of Portage river, twelve miles and a half. Here we found a number of miners encamped, all looking serious as the grave; word had just reached them that Mr. Barber, before mentioned, was drowned. We tarried here for the night, and the next morning pursued our journey up Portage river into Portage Lake, thence to the mouth of Sturgeon river, where we aided in the search for the body of Mr. Barber. It was soon found, and taken to Kewawenon. Turning away from this affecting scene, we made our way through the eastern arm of Portage Lake; thence by Torch river into and across Torch Lake. A mile and a half by land, brought us to the Douglas Houghton Company's Works. These were situated in a narrow chasm, between two precipitous bluffs, on the banks of a delightful brook, like the fountain of life itself, ever flowing and clear. A little above it forms a beautiful cascade, leaping down from the top of the southern bluff, dashing and foaming over its uneven bed, keeping up a perpetual roar. Much labor and money were spent here to no purpose, and the works have since been abandoned. We were comfortably and cordially entertained.

Thursday, the 12th, we traveled on foot to the Cliff

Mine, a distance of about sixteen miles. Part of our way was a passable road, newly cut through the dense forest; the other was a rough trail over hills and valleys. It led by several locations where comfortable log-houses had been erected and mining briskly prosecuted. But several of these locations have been abandoned, and the moldering ruins admonish us how often men draw blanks from the lottery of human fortune. I might mention each of the stations visited, and at each find something profitable for reflection; but this would perhaps tax unnecessarily the reader's patience. Let it suffice that I traveled over Point Kewenaw to nearly all the locations, making, in this circuit, about one hundred and ninety miles—fifty-five by water, and the rest by land. I had the privilege of proclaiming the Gospel eleven times—in some places where the cross of Christ had never before been preached. Every-where I met the warmest reception and many marks of favor, which I shall always remember and prize.

On my return home from this trip I lost my way in a dreary wilderness, which was to me an occasion of much fatigue and peril. As I can not but own the hand of a kind Providence in my deliverance, I will give a brief account of the circumstances. The night of the last day of November I slept at the Douglas Houghton location, on my return home. Already the ground was covered with snow some inches deep. Torch Lake was yet open; but the river forming its outlet was frozen over for three miles and a half. Water communication to Kewawenon was thus interrupted, and I was compelled to go by land most of the way. Had hoped here to procure company, but no one could be spared from the mines to go any distance. Mr. F. D. and another person consented to go with me across Torch Lake, and down the river where it was frozen, to a place where some of their stores had been left.

We left about eight o'clock, A. M. It was snowing very fast, and continued most of the day. We had soon crossed the Lake—about three and a half miles wide—in a boat; then we walked on the ice till we came to the Company's stores. Here my friends loaded their hand-train and returned. I went into the woods, and attempted to cross the strip of land between Portage Lake and Kewenaw Bay. Directly across it was only about eight miles; but there was neither road, nor trail, nor footprint of a human being to be seen. My first search was for a surveyor's line. Found several trees blazed, but could trace no regular line. I had a small pocket-compass—at best an uncertain guide in a mineral region; but it was not long before the glass came out, and it was useless to me. I was now left to *guess* out my way, without even the semblance of a guide.

The snow was now about six inches deep, and continually falling—enough to make walking hard without snow-shoes, but not enough for walking with them. To carry them was an incumbrance; but I dared not leave them, not knowing how soon I might need them. These, together with my blanket and other parts of my outfit, weighed about twenty pounds. My eatables consisted of six biscuits. I had also a small hatchet—too small for any thing but to blaze trees and to cut off small limbs. So armed I plunged into the forest, climbing hills and plodding through valleys and swamps. At noon, seated on a log, I dined on a biscuit and a half—not such biscuits, by the way, as our good sisters often get up when visited by the itinerant. Those bisquits had never seen a lady's fingers; they were sorry food, suitable to the occasion. But they were the best our poor bachelors could afford—such as they were accustomed to eat, freely given, thankfully received, and eaten with thanks to Him who has assured us that "man shall not live by bread alone."

Thus refreshed, I addressed myself anew to the task before me. From this time I was governed by the distant roar of waves ahead. The trees and bushes were heavily loaded with snow, so as to make it very wet overhead, and the low and swampy land was not yet frozen. With my clothes and moccasins literally soaked, I had very *sensible* impressions, if not the most agreeable.

Night overtook me in the midst of a cedar swamp. One who has never traveled through such swamps can scarcely have an idea with how much difficulty this is attended. He must climb over fallen brush and timber; often creep on his hands and knees under logs and limbs, and press through the thick underwood. Such traveling is fatiguing in the best weather and with every possible help; but with the obstructions I met it was almost impossible t6 make headway. I looked about for some time for a suitable place to camp. At length I came to a small spot of comparativly dry land, on which stood a large hemlock, surrounded by smaller trees, mostly balsam. With some effort I made a fire at the roots of that hemlock. I then cut small poles, and leaned them against the tree, covering them with balsam boughs, so as to afford temporary shelter; spreading boughs on the snow within for floor .and carpet. I now endeavored to provide wood for the night, which gave me no little labor, as good wood was hardly to be found, and worse to be cut into pieces with a poor tool. It was ten o'clock at night before I finished this task, and even then I had not a supply. Before morning I had to chop more or be without fire.

By this time I was forcibly reminded that my supper hour had arrived. But I was so exhausted that I felt little inclined to eat; half a biscuit served my turn. As night closed in it commenced raining, and continued, with little abatement, through the night. The wind howled among the tree-tops, and the roar of distant waves fell on my ear. I tried to dry my wet clothes; and, commending myself and my all to God, wrapped me up in my blanket, and laid me down to sleep. But this was nearly out of the question. Without constant attention the rain would put out my fire; otherwise I could have slept soundly.

I had now a good opportunity to test the support religion can give when all other help is cut off. In the possession of that which

> "Gives even affliction a grace,
> And reconciles man to his lot,"

I was enabled to

> "Give to the winds my fears,
> Hope, and be undismayed."

I felt not the least doubt concerning the *final issue;* nor did the raging elements disturb my inward tranquillity.

Early on the morning of the 2d I arose, and, after offering up praise for past mercies, and imploring divine protection for the coming day, I partook of such luxury as the place would afford for breakfast—a biscuit, ready baked. Now shouldering my pack, I left this temporary abode, scarcely knowing whither I was bound. The sun was obscured by clouds, and considerable rain fell during the forenoon. I bent my course toward the roaring of the waves. What was my surprise, when I came out, to find that I was on the shore of Portage Lake, instead of Kewenaw Bay! In bearing too far to the west, I added much to the distance and had more swampy land.

Retracing my steps back into the woods, I endeavored to steer my course more to the south-east. But it was, at best, mostly guess-work. Let me turn which way I would, almost impassable cedar swamps seemed to beset me. After some time I came in sight of a broad sheet of water, which, at first glance, I took to be Kewenaw Bay, but soon discovered my error. At any rate, I concluded to go to the water, if possible, hoping to be able to follow along shore, and come out somewhere. But a bad swamp was between, which I made three ineffectual attempts to cross. It was miry, and matted with brush and timber.

My situation now became very perplexing. I was drenched thoroughly with rain and snow-water. Being much exhausted from constant and severe exercise, I became very thirsty, and drank several times of water which stood in hollow places. But this increased rather than allayed thirst. At one time I made a circle, and came again on my own tracks. Said I within myself, "What Indian has been along here?" for I took it, at first, to be the track of an Indian hunter; but a moment's attention showed me that it was the print of my own moccasin. I was obliged, at frequent intervals, to stop and rest; found it quite burdensome to drag myself along. Lest I should become faint and stupid, and perhaps chill to death, as many others in similar situations, I stopped to make a fire and rest awhile. But, first eating a biscuit, I felt somewhat revived, and went on again. Now, for the first time since I had entered the woods, the sun, for a few moments, looked down on me through the opening clouds. It was about two o'clock, P. M. I was enabled by this means to lay my course.

Walking a little longer brought me to Portage river, not far from Kewenaw Bay. I followed down the shore till I came to a Pine point, from which to the Entry—mouth of Portage river—it was only a mile straight across. The beautiful Bay was in full view, and the high land in the rear of the mission at Kewawenon. With the fine prospect ahead, my muscles seemed to gather fresh elasticity.

But I was not yet out. Between me and the Entry was a low marsh, at that time full of water. To go round this would cost me about four miles' walking. Which would be best—to try to wade through, or to go round? I chose the first. But I soon found hard wading; proceeded perhaps thirty-five rods, by stopping several times to rest. At length I came to a full stop. The further I went the worse it became, and I despaired of getting across. Was about to turn back, and do the next best thing, but, casting my eyes down toward the Entry, I saw two sails. With a stiff breeze *aft*, they were making up the river. Hope again revived; help appeared to be approaching at a time most needed. I had waited only a few moments till two boats arrived. James Tanner was in one; his wife and children in the other. They were going up the river after wood. They came to my relief. I went aboard the small boat, and exchanged wading for rowing, while Mrs. Tanner managed the helm. James went on and procured his wood. We soon reached the bark-covered cabin, and had a good fire. Dry clothes were furnished, and some warm food soon provided. My appetite returned, and I began once more to feel like myself. The past scarcely looked like reality. The night following it snowed, and the wind blew as if to unroof our cabin. And this might have been done, had not my host gone up and nailed the barks two or three times. I need make no remarks respecting my own feelings, in view of the difference between my situation in that humble dwelling, and what it would have been out in that storm.

The next day I had a pretty severe walk of about thirteen miles, over a rough trail, to the Catholic mission, where I arrived at four o'clock, P. M. Soon obtained an Indian and his son, who took me in a small bark canoe, and carried me across the Bay, where, just at nightfall, I set foot into our own door, and realized once more what the poet meant when he said,

> "Home, sweet home!
> Be it ever so homely, there's no place like home."

If the writer of this imperfect sketch, and those into whose hands it may fall, shall at last gain *that sweet home* in the skies, we shall never find reason to regret the roughness of the way.

TABLE NUMBER I.

Date—1846.	Miles Traveled	Sermons Preached	Name of Company or Place.	Agent or Occupant.	No. of Families	No. of Children under twelve years of age.	Total Inhabitants	Profess'rs of Religion.	Protestants	Roman Catholics	Remarks.
Tuesday, Nov. 10th.	14	..	Entry	James Tanner.	1	3	5	..	..	..	For these statistics I was indebted to agents and mining captains. They are, no doubt, an approximation to correctness. They err from deficit, rather than from excess.
Wednesday, 11th.	20	..	Douglas Houghton Co.	F. Douglas	..	..	2	..	..	..	
Thursday, 12th.	16	..	Cliff Mine	John Hayes	9	10	122	11	8	3	
Friday, 13th.	2	1	Albion Co.	Mr. Stevens	..	..	60	..	..	..	
Saturday, 14th.	2	..	Cliff Mine		..	..	..	..	..	..	
Sunday, 15th.	..	1	" "		..	..	..	..	..	..	At Albion, the Cliff, Eagle River, Eagle Harbor, and several other places, preached the first sermon ever preached in those localities.
" "	3	1	Eagle River	Martin Coryell	9	11	53	6	..	6	
Monday, 16th.	8	..	Eagle Harbor	David French	5	5	33	6	6	..	
" "	14	..	Copper Harbor	D. D. Brockway	5	7	27	6	2	4	
Tuesday, 17th.	3	..	Vicinity of C. Harbor.		..	..	..	..	..	..	
Wednesday, 18th.	3	1	Copper Harbor		..	..	..	..	..	..	At several places it was not convenient to have public worship. When several mines were near each other, the people usually collected from all to one place.
Thursday, 19th.	5	..	Boston Co., No. 15.	Mr. Bernard	..	..	6	..	..	..	
" "	8	1	Bohemian	S. Mendlebaum.	..	..	22	14	..	14	
" "	¼	..	Lac Labelle	Mr. Sibley	..	..	28	..	..	..	
Friday, 20th.	¼	1	Bohemian		..	..	..	..	..	..	
" "	4	..	Chippewa	Mr. M'Carty	..	..	13	11	..	11	
Saturday, 21st.	14	..	Eagle Harbor		..	..	..	..	..	..	Generally I was obliged to make appointments on the way, to fill on my return.
Sunday, 22d.	..	2	" "		..	..	..	..	..	..	
Monday, 23d.	2½	..	Copper Falls	Joshua Childs	6	8	43	..	..	..	
" "	7	..	Eagle River		..	..	..	..	..	..	
Tuesday, 24th.	3	..	Cliff Mine		..	..	..	..	..	..	
Wednesday, 25th.	..	..	" "		..	..	..	..	..	..	

TABLE NUMBER I, CONTINUED.

Date—1846.	Miles Traveled.....	Sermons Preached..	Name of Company or Place.	Agent or Occupant.	No. of Families....	No. of Children under twelve years of age.	Total Inhabitants....	Profess'rs of Religion	Protestants........	Roman Catholics...	Remarks.
Thursday, 26th.	3	1	Eagle River	..	..	..	..	..	..	..	Thanksgiving sermon from Psalm
Friday, 27th.	..	..	" "	..	..	..	..	..	..	..	cvii, 1.
" "	3	..	Cliff Mine	..	..	..	..	..	..	..	Several companies visited afterward,
Saturday, 28th.	¼	..	North American	John Bacon	..	..	..	..	..	..	and some not visited, are not in this
Sunday, 29th.	¼	1	Cliff Mine	..	..	..	..	..	..	..	enumeration. The total number of
" "	2	1	Albion	..	..	..	..	..	..	..	persons on Point Kewenaw must have
Monday, 30th.	14	..	Douglas Houghton Co.	..	..	..	..	..	..	..	been about five hundred, besides those
Tuesday, Dec. 1st.	15	..	Cedar Swamp	Wild beasts	..	..	..	..	..	..	at the Ontonagon. There were prob-
Wednesday, 2d.	8	..	Entry	..	..	..	..	..	..	..	ably one thousand white inhabitants
Thursday, 3d.	16	..	Ke-wa-we-non	..	..	..	..	..	..	..	about Lake Superior.
	190½	11			35	44	414	54	16	38	

SUBSEQUENT VISITS AMONG THE MINERS.

December 23. Left Kewawenon to visit the miners the second time, and returned in just three weeks, having traveled two hundred and twelve miles, nearly all on foot—preached twelve times and delivered one temperance address, to a crowded and very attentive audience, at the Cliff Mine. Quite an interest was here waked up on this subject, and rising of thirty persons signed the pledge of total abstinence. A small class of eight persons was organized at the Cliff, with which we enjoyed some precious seasons during the year.

Made three other visits, one in the winter and two during the following summer. The first visit I left home without scrip or purse, and, unasked, sundry persons contributed twenty-four dollars and a half for our support. The second visit they raised, of their own free will, sixty dollars and twenty cents. And so on, in subsequent visits, till it amounted to about two hundred dollars. And besides, they contributed above sixty dollars toward the erection of our new church at Kewawenon.

The names of agents and mining captains, mentioned in the accompanying table, were among the foremost in these acts of generosity. In addition to persons already named, I was much indebted to Mr. Taylor of Albion Mine, Mr. J. Senter of Eagle river, Mr. Shaply of Copper Falls, Mr. D. D. Brockway of Copper Harbor, and Judge Hawes and his estimable lady of Fort Wilkins, with others too tedious to name. Such large-heartedness is worthy of permanent record, as characterizing the hardy pioneers of that vast wilderness. May their inheritance be that "which maketh rich and addeth no sorrow!"

Brother Holt visited the miners twice during the year. The first time he was taken sick and confined to his bed about eight weeks.

I may add, in substance, what was published at the time, in the Western Christian Advocate, that, "after many a weary walk alone, through a dense wilderness, supported by snow-shoes, on a depth of three or four feet of snow, at times wading through swamps, then climbing mountains, crossing lakes, or following the meanderings of a river, on the ice—often, after such seasons of toil, and sometimes of danger, my soul has been exceedingly blessed in preaching Christ crucified to the people. And although little fruit has as yet appeared, I trust it will be found, in the great day, that our 'labor has not been in vain in the Lord.' This circuit, as it might be called, is over two hundred miles in extent, counting the zigzag trails across Point Kewenaw. Each tour was generally performed in three weeks, sometimes less. This made it necessary to travel more or less almost every day, often twenty-five or thirty and even more miles a day, on foot, carrying a pack weighing from twelve to twenty pounds. It cost me, in all, about twelve hundred miles traveling, nearly eight hundred on foot and the rest by water. Such are some of the characteristics of Methodist itinerancy in this region. These things are mentioned, not boastingly, but with the most grateful recollections of that Providence who gave me such power of endurance."

STATE OF THINGS AT KEWAWENON.

So far as the white residents were concerned important changes had taken place. An entire change had been made in the Government men—the old ones had all been displaced by others. Those newly appointed, with their families, were kind and obliging neighbors, but made no pretensions to religion. The saw-mill near the head of the Bay was now in operation, and several white men were there employed in lumbering, who often came to the mission to hear preaching. Two or three were persons of strict morality, and well-wishers to the cause of religion; but the others had little of the fear of God, and, by their example, exerted an influence hostile to piety.

Brother Holt taught the day school and kept up the Sunday school and the religious meetings in my absence. When at home the other duties, except the school, were shared between us. There was much manual labor to be done during the year, which devolved mostly on me. In the various departments of labor and responsibility, we had evidences of gradual improvement, if not of very marked success. And, in their place, the gently-distilling dew, the kindly shower, and the genial sunlight, are as necessary as the drenching rain and scorching sun. Many of our meetings during the year were seasons of refreshing from the presence of the Lord. In the month of February we were made to rejoice at the apparently-marked conversion of J. T. and his wife, who had once been Papists. On the 21st I baptized him and his family, and received him and his wife into the Church on trial. Mr. T. promised great usefulness to the cause of Christ. Physically he was equal to almost any emergency. He had also strong powers of mind, but affording at times pretty clear evidence of partial insanity. Such was the opinion of some expressed at this time. He spoke fluently Ojibwa, French, and English. His experience appeared to be deep, and his whole deportment most exemplary, as was also that of his wife. One of his little sons also furnished good evidence of conversion. I have never witnessed any where more genuine evidences of deep and heart-felt piety than were to be seen in this family. And yet I regret to state that, two or three years afterward, at a remote station, he sadly fell, so as to bring great reproach upon the cause of Christ. But the details, as involving several persons, whites and Indians, I must omit, as affording nothing either edifying or profitable to the reader. The fact should remind us of the inspired caution, "Let him that thinketh he standeth take heed lest he fall."

ERECTION OF A CHURCH.

One of the most important movements connected with the Kewawenon mission this year, was the building of a church. The log school-house, which had answered our purpose, had been rendered tolerably comfortable by frequent repairs. But we felt that the time had fully come when the mission needed a better house. Our limited missionary appropriation afforded us no help in this direction, and the prospect of securing the necessary means to accomplish such a work was at best doubtful. But we determined, with the help of God, to make the attempt.

The few white people at our station, together with the Indians, pledged something more than a hundred dollars toward this object, to be paid mostly in work. But this was a small beginning. We called for help from abroad, but to this call there was no very liberal response, and we were thrown upon our own resources. But this imposed no little hard toil and care on us, in getting out and drawing the timber, making the shingles, drawing on the ice and boating the lumber from the saw-mill, planing and putting on the siding, and putting on the roof, much of which work was done with our own hands. But with the aid afforded us by the miners, and those at home, and a little help from abroad, most of which was sent to us by brother A. W. Brockway, of Pittsburg, we erected the frame and inclosed and secured it for the winter by the time we were called to go to another field. When we went to the pinery, three miles distant, to cut the timber, before we struck a blow, the little company kneeled down upon the snow, and, by fervent prayer to God, invoked his guidance and aid, which we as fully believe he afforded as that we exist. It was estimated that one hundred and fifty or two hundred dollars would complete the house, when it would be worth five or six hundred. Thus far it was free from debt.

While we had reason to believe that the society connected with the mission was generally in a healthy and prosperous state, two circumstances occurred at the close of the year which gave us great pain and sorrow. We were obliged to lay aside two of the old members of the Church, but in their case there was yet hope—they might repent and be restored to God, and to the bosom of the Church. But the other evil was beyond remedy. On the night of the 27th of October three of our Indians went across the Bay to a trader's, purchased liquor and became intoxicated. They returned late at night, and one of them, too drunk to know what he was about, was left in the boat. In the morning he was found lying on the ground, on his face, near the water, *dead!* This story is soon told; but O, the dreadful end of the drunkard! and the curse that must fall on the head of him who was instrumental in the death and ruin of this young man! His name was Joshua Soule. He was a youth of fine appearance and promise, and an exemplary Christian till he was led into this fatal snare. In this fact the reader has one of the leading causes why the Indians are a doomed race.

During our stay at this mission the superintendent, Rev. W. H. Brockway, visited us once a year. Those visits, few and far between, and necessarily short, were highly prized by us, and the more so as, for most of the time, we were cut off from the society and salutary counsel and help of our ministerial brethren. This remark is due also to our esteemed superintendent, who had been so long in labors more abundant to evangelize the Indians, and who never failed to make his mark.

CHAPTER IX.

APPOINTMENT TO EAGLE RIVER MISSION—PERPLEXITIES—OUR NEW FIELD.

THE Michigan annual conference met this year in Ypsilanti, on the 15th of September. It was more than a month after before we heard any thing about our appointment, and, even then, nothing official. We had never before been so comfortably fixed to winter at that station as now. On account of our new church, which had progressed thus far under our supervision, and some other matters not so easily managed by strangers, we had hoped to remain another year; on other accounts we had no special reason to regret a change.

It was near the close of October, when blustering winds and occasional snow squalls warned us of the near approach of a long winter, that a breeze from a warmer clime, chilled in its long passage over the lakes, reached us, uttering, in language not to be misunderstood, "Arise, for this is not your rest." But many and formidable were the obstacles in the way of removal. The lateness of the season, the dangers of the Lake, rendered appalling by late and serious disasters, particularly that which happened to the steamer Julia Palmer, which for sixteen days had been at the mercy of storms—all these, aggravated by a report directly from Point Kewenaw that, in consequence of the great loss* on the Julia Palmer, many of the miners were almost exposed to starvation, and that provisions were not to be obtained; added to the fact that our own funds were nearly exhausted—these and other circumstances gave a gloomy appearance to our future prospect. But while reflecting on this aspect of things, I was rebuked by that passage from the Savior, "Behold the fowls of the air, for they sow not, neither do they reap, nor gather into barns, and yet your heavenly Father feedeth them." This is enough. Will God feed his birds and not his children?

The want of religious society in our prospective field was a serious drawback on our feelings. But we had always made it a matter of conscience to go, if possible, to an appointment; and, therefore, resolved to venture our all on the goodness of THE APPOINTING POWER, and, at least, throw our length that way.

For a long time we had looked, in vain, for some vessel to bring winter supplies to the mission. For nearly two months, up to the 6th of November, we had lived on borrowed provisions, and yet none came, and no way seemed to open for us to get away.

The schooner *Fur Trader* was expected by the

---

* For want of fuel they were obliged to burn the pork, hams, etc., on board, to make steam to propel the boat.

10th of November, on her way from the *Saut* to the Ontonagon. We put all things in readiness, and awaited her arrival with solicitude. November 10th came, and true to expectation the old schooner came in sight. Night had just dropped her dark brow over the face of day, when a rap was heard at the door of the mission. Who should be there? Who but one of the hardy pioneers of Lake Superior, who knew not what it was to shrink from toil and danger? Yes, it was a missionary, brother P. O. Johnson, and his delicate wife, who had come about two hundred miles, in a bark canoe, to labor in the place of the old incumbents. This does not look like an assertion I saw some time ago in a Catholic publication, that Protestant missionaries did not penetrate into this country till "*feather beds,*" *etc.*, had been provided for them. No missionaries have labored in the true spirit of sacrifice more than some of the Protestant missionaries of this region. I need not say that they came unexpected, as it was the first hint we had of the new arrangement, only so far as we were concerned.

November 11. The *Fur Trader* came to anchor opposite the mission. But imagine our disappointment when we learned that she had been driven out of her course by adverse winds—had been to the Ontonagon, and was on her downward course for Saut Ste. Marie. Nothing could induce the captain to take us to Point Kewenaw. The only alternative now left us was to coast. We were now subjected to a series of perplexities and disappointments in procuring men, a canoe, etc., which it would be tedious to name.

By the evening of the 15th of November we succeeded, with the blessing of a kind Providence, in finding a good bark canoe, and two able-bodied *voyageurs.* Now our goods, which had been packed for shipping, must be overhauled, and the bare indispensables packed ship-shape for a canoe, and the remainder repacked and left till spring. The whole constituted no great bulk, as we had no furniture of any kind. What little we had once was disposed of on leaving the work below. And whether we could get chairs, bedsteads, tables, stoves, crockery, etc., where we were going, without any thing to buy with, was a question that it would not do to try to solve. The truth is, means should have been sent us on the start. The Missionary Society had appropriated one hundred dollars toward our support on condition we failed to get our pay from the miners. But had the rigors to which we were constantly exposed been fully known, the appropriation, small as it was, could have been subject to no such contingency. With eight dollars loaned us by a friend, after a rough journey of four days, in which we were buffeted by the elements, having, in one place, for some distance, to force our way through ice which had closed up Portage river, we succeeded in reaching our new home, adoring that kind and merciful Providence which had kept us and guarded our way at every step.

OUR NEW FIELD.

After being very uncomfortably situated for some time for want of a house to live in, a place was at length provided for us by the Company. This would have been ready for us on our arrival, but our long detention at Kewawenon led the Company to think that we were not coming, and all the buildings had been leased. On the 29th of November, much to our comfort, we took possession of our new home. This was a cabin built of round logs, a story and a half high, divided below into two apartments by a board partition, with a wood-shed made of rough boards. There was no cellar, or other conveniences about the concern, except what were included within the building. During the winter, when a large body of snow lay on the roof, as was often the case, the heat of the two stove-pipes, passing directly through the roof without chimneys, and the rarified air under the roof, caused the snow to melt, and the water running down the walls on the outside became congealed, which, on thawing, often forced its way inside, and made the house wet and uncomfortable. Our utmost vigilance could not wholly guard against this difficulty. But our cabin was a much better one than some of our neighbors had, and we have always felt grateful to the Company for giving us possession of such a home. It is simply mentioned here as a specimen of backwoods life. Added to the house, the Company kindly furnished us with a cooking-stove and other heavy furniture, which we were to use free of charge, and return when done with them. They also filled our bill of supplies in the provision line, and charged to my account till it could be canceled. Mr. Taylor, of the Albion Mine, kindly loaned us a box stove and some crockery. Thus all our wants were met in a way we had not anticipated.

The scenes surrounding us were different from any to which we had before been accustomed. Mining must go on day and night, the constant din and bustle of which is often annoying to one unused to such business. If you retire at nine o'clock the bell ringing for a change of *shifts*, at *ten* o'clock, will awake you. This will be accompanied with the bustle of men coming from the mine, and fresh hands taking their place. Perhaps before you are fairly asleep again, you will be aroused by a car rumbling on a track, from the mineral shed to the stamp-house, where the mineral is precipitated into a large box, the bottom of which is an inclined plane, and thus conducted to the stamps. And then here are these six ponderous stamps, propelled by steam, which are crushing the mineral all night. Meanwhile you may hear the hammer and anvil and the incessant creaking of the old *whim*—a machine for raising copper from the mine—and the report of an occasional blast like that of cannonade. All these things make some noise, but the frequent fighting of several mules, in a barn near our dwelling, added to all the rest, completes the "confusion worse confounded."

Such, in substance, were our impressions penned on the spot.

In the period of a year, matters had materially changed on Point Kewenaw. The two previous years the "copper fever" had raged to a great extent. The country swarmed with persons who were exploring it, and "laying permits," or "making claims." If *trap rock* could be found in any locality, having veins of *quartz* or *spar*, with or without copper, it was thought to be a "good indication," and forthwith a permit was laid, a company formed, and the stock divided up into shares, and these were thrown into the market for the highest bidder. Sometimes gentlemen from the cities, a little flush with money, but green enough, as it regarded the geological formations of that region, at the sight of a few rock "*specimens*," without ever having seen the prospective mine, would eagerly catch the bait thus thrown out. Perhaps, on more close inspection, the mine which presented such "good indications," was located in some cedar swamp or lake.

But in many places the prospect was sufficiently flattering to induce the proprietors to erect buildings at considerable cost and prosecute mining. But these prospects becoming overhung with doubt, such locations had, in many instances, been abandoned. The ill-directed attempts of persons who came there and expected to grasp an immediate fortune, without either capital or labor, and the extreme into which speculation had been carried, were now reacting, most severely, upon the interests of the country. Sc much so that many persons abroad seriously thought mining operations on Lake Superior to be all a "humbug," undertaken on purpose to swindle men out of their money. This change in the condition of the country tended materially to circumscribe the sphere of our missionary efforts. Several locations were visited at different times during the year, and meetings held among the miners as opportunity offered. I made one trip about midwinter, to the Kewawenon mission, and administered the ordinances to the people at the request of the missionaries, neither of whom was ordained. In my absence Rev. J. W. Holt, from this mission, supplied my place. These trips were all made on foot, as was the customary mode of traveling by land. Excepting those occasional excursions abroad, our efforts were mostly confined to the Cliff Mine and vicinity.

The mixed and unsettled character of the inhabitants was not very favorable to evangelical effort. The English miners were principally from Cornwall, England, and were familiarly known by the title "Cornish." Their dialect, though not so barbarous as the Yorkshire, is so different from the Anglo-Saxon of our own land, that an inexperienced ear is often at a loss to determine what is said, especially in rapid speech. The letter h, especially, is so much in the habit of straying away from home that he is seldom found where he really belongs. He usually finds about the following connections: "*Hi will give the orse some hoats and ay.*" In a school which I taught at the Cliff, during the winter, there were some scholars that I could hardly make give the simple sound of i, without the h going before. This must serve as a specimen of the manner in which the Queen trains her subjects to "murder the King's English."

Many of the miners were German and Irish. Among the former a few were Lutherans; the others, with the mass of the Irish population, adhered to the Romish Church. There were also a few French who were Romanists. Several of the agents, clerks, or employes were our own countrymen, and, in general, were well educated and shrewd business men. To make money was the object which induced most of the inhabitants to forego the blessings of home, in a better land, and endure the privations and hardships of the wilderness. Many favored the institutions of religion as a matter of policy, as connected with mining, who, so far as their own life and practice were concerned, lived in entire neglect of their spiritual interests. It is tacitly acknowledged, even by the most skeptical, that without the moral and religious restraints of the Church, it would be hard to control such men as are generally employed to work the mines.

Many of those miners had families in a distant land, some across the great Atlantic, whose society they had not enjoyed for years. A few knew what it was to rejoice in the liberty of the Gospel. But several had found their way into that region who had once tasted of the sweets of redeeming love, but like the prodigal had left their Father's house. In this wilderness many snares were but too successfully laid for their feet. The influences around them tended to harden them in their career of backsliding. Some abandoned themselves to drinking and gambling, hunting and fishing, and other amusements on the Lord's day. To such the warning voice of the Gospel seemed lifted in vain. Vice and wickedness of various kinds and degrees obtained here a luxurious growth.

Our religious meetings were conducted with great inconvenience for want of a suitable place. The only place we could obtain at the Cliff was a small schoolroom. The class formed the year before had been broken up by removals. Soon after our arrival we collected another class of about a dozen members, with whom, during the year, we enjoyed many precious seasons. Our public meetings were often seasons of interest and profit; and, in the midst of a far too general neglect of divine things, we have reason to believe that the efforts put forth at that station, in the name of the Lord, were owned by him to the edification of his people and the advancement of his cause.

As is the case in many parts of the country, it was customary to have dancing parties as an expedient to avoid the tedium of the long winter nights. While living at the Cliff arrangements were made to have a Christmas ball at Eagle river. The managers, several of whom, as men of the world, the writer and his family had every reason to respect for their kind and gentlemanly bearing, sent him a note politely inviting him and his wife to attend. The case was disposed of by the following answer:

"TO THE MANAGERS OF THE CHRISTMAS BALL, TO BE HELD AT EAGLE RIVER:

"GENTLEMEN,—I received your compliments to myself and wife, together with an invitation to attend the proposed ball. The following considerations compel me to decline:

"*First.* As it would be a *beginning* with me I should cut an awkward figure in a ball-room.

"*Second.* In the earlier stages of my religious experience I conscientiously abstained from such amusements, as in no way conducing to a life of godliness; it could hardly be expected that, after professing to be a disciple of Christ more than twenty years, I should be *less* scrupulous.

"*Third.* In addition to the solemn vows of a private Christian, the increased responsibilities of a Gospel minister have entirely unfitted me for such scenes.

"*Fourth* and last, though not least, I have been a great sinner against Christ; it is, therefore, befitting in me to hail the anniversary of his lowly advent with sincere and deep penitence for the past; with humble and devout acknowledgments of my present want of conformity to his will, and with increased resolutions, accompanied with prayer for Divine aid, to *finish my work* as a *Christian* and a *minister*, that when death comes to my release I may have no bitter reflections on the past, and no cloud to dim my prospect of the future. Whether I could or could not thus salute the approach of Christmas at a ball, judge ye. With an unaffected regard for your best good for time and eternity,

"I am, gentlemen, yours,
most truly and affectionately, etc."

During my residence among the miners we found many large and warm hearts to throb under the rough exterior. And while the facts compel us to speak of many evils, many things were found worthy of high commendation. For frankness, warm and generous sympathy, and liberality to relieve the suffering, to support the Gospel, to aid the cause of Sunday schools, or the missionary cause, we have seldom known this people to be excelled. They have been trained to acts of liberality and hospitality from children. Convince them that a noble charity is in want, and it will here find a ready and generous response.

One practice as connected with the public worship of God among them we could wish was generally in use; that is, congregational singing. No people in the world are so familiar with the Methodist hymns as our English brethren. And they nearly all sing. The praises of God as thus sung by the whole congregation, in which the several parts are generally well sustained, come nearest to our notion of the anthems of heaven of any thing we can conceive. Some of the singing we have heard at the Cliff Mine is often brought to our remembrance. With those dear brethren we hope by and by to sing "the song of Moses and the Lamb."

CLIFF 'MINE, LAKE SUPERIOR.

CHAPTER X.

SCENERY ABOUT EAGLE RIVER AND THE CLIFF MINE—SKETCH OF THE MINE.

What is embraced in this chapter, with slight variations, was penned on the spot in the summer of 1848, and published in the "Christian Visitor."

Eagle river is an inconsiderable stream, except at its mouth, emptying into Lake Superior about twenty-five miles west of Copper Harbor. It derives its name from the Indian *Me-ge-zeh*—an eagle—and *se-beh*—a river. The small town at the mouth bears the same name. The site is an immense sand-bank, and has no attractiveness. The special want is a good harbor, as it forms the depot for the Cliff Mine and several others, is a central rallying-point for all parts of the Lake, and necessarily a place of much business. A good pier, built at great expense, supplies, in a measure, the want of harbor. Here is a regular preaching-place; but no society has been formed, and no immediate prospect of one. Mr. Atwood kindly opened his dining-hall for religious worship, and, with his family, has shown us many marks of favor. A mile and a half up stream is what is called Eagle River Diggings. Here are the Lake Superior Company's works—now abandoned—our place of residence.

From the Lake, going nearly south to the Cliff, we ascend gradually till we reach the top of the hill, five or six hundred feet above the level of the Lake, two and a half miles inland. A road has been constructed at much expense—still very rough and uncomfortable. The wet places are bridged with round logs, technically termed *corduroy*. The hill-side is stony and uneven. From the top we have a fine view of Lake Superior to the north. When the atmosphere is clear, Isle Royal can be seen, at a distance of fifty miles. The land is heavily timbered with birch, maple, hemlock, etc., and well watered with numerous springs. The soil is alluvial, and adapted to farming purposes. Many people get their living by farming in as rigid a climate and on poorer soil. Still it is granted that farming can never become a chief source of industry or revenue in the Lake Superior region.

Passing through a defile, we gradually descend, by means of a road which winds around the side of the bluff, to the south. The natural scenery is here highly picturesque. As you descend, to your left is a deep chasm, which forms the valley of Eagle river. Here you look down on the tops of tall trees, and far beyond the land rises to view in mountainous ranges. Here a cold spring gurgles from the Cliff, and crosses the road; there a delightful little stream tumbles down the precipice, and makes music on the ear. To your right the Cliff now rises above you in majesty and grandeur. At the works the top of the Cliff is two hundred and twenty feet above the west branch of Eagle river. Here one would suppose that nature in one of her freaks, had attempted to shake down the mountain; for in every direction lay broken masses and heaps on heaps of the trap rock thrown down from the top. Some of these masses are as large as good-sized cabins, and have lain in their present position sufficiently long to support the growth of good-sized trees. As you look up to the masses which *crop out** at the summit, you would naturally imagine that some were just ready to leap from their fastnesses. And should they do so, woe betide whatever was beneath them.

On the side of this convulsed and rocky cliff, in the midst of some of these huge rocks, are situated the houses, shops, and works of the miners. There is here no appearance of pleasantness for a village, environed, as it is, with lofty woodland, which intercepts the view in all directions. The office and store joined together is a pretty good building. Some of the dwellings are tolerably comfortable, but not built with regard to convenience, or external neatness and order. Necessity has been the rule, and was a good one to begin with, but the Company has opened on a rich treasure, and will probably be disposed to bestow more taste on their future improvements. On our arrival here we found one hundred and forty persons at work at the Cliff Mine, seventy to eighty under ground, and about sixty *grass hands*—a miner's term

* This geological term was incorrectly printed in the Visitor, *cross out.*

for surface workmen. Captain Jennings, a master at mining, was Agent, but succeeded the next summer by Mr. L. Hanna, a gentleman well qualified for so important a charge. Captain J. still managed the principal mining operations, while Mr. H. took a general oversight of the whole business.

The workmen are generally robust and hardy, but rough in their appearance and manners; yet, under the rough exterior are some noble minds and generous hearts. To get a good view of them as they issue from the mine, you should be at a prominent place at the ringing of the dinner-bell. You may see them coming from the mine, covered with mud and dirt, and often drenched from head to foot. Sometimes they leave their light behind them, but often you will see a small tin lamp fastened to the hat, or a piece of candle in a lump of wet clay attached to the hat—all burning. The workmen now, generally in single file, make a straight wake for their boarding-house, crossing each other's path in nearly all directions. If one did not know better he would suppose them to be inhabitants of a world where the sun's rays never reached; and they are, eight hours out of twenty-four.

THE CLIFF MINE AS SEEN IN THE SUMMER OF 1848.

If the kind reader is disposed to take a peep into some of the wonders that are disclosed beneath the surface of the earth, he may please accompany me through the Cliff Mine. But before doing so we will go to the office and form the acquaintance of the

Agent, Mr. Hanna, Captain Jennings, and others. Thence you will be desirous to visit the stamps, where you will see a large bank of mineral, stamped through the winter, yielding from ten to twenty per cent. of copper. Several persons are here employed in washing copper. The stamps have lately been somewhat improved. They now stamp about two hundred and thirty tuns per month. In one month eighty-six barrels of this copper were washed and barreled ready for shipping.

Let us now go partly up the bluff, into a large mineral shed, where the stamp-work is first burned in a huge fire, then broken to pieces, and conveyed to the stamps. Here are also several men engaged in cutting huge masses of the pure copper into blocks sufficiently small to admit of being transported. This part is attended with great labor and expense. A wagon is driven along side this shed, where these masses are raised by a crane, and thus swung into the wagon, and drawn to the Lake. From eighty to one hundred tuns of copper, including that which is barreled, are taken to the Lake monthly.

We will now go up a flight of stairs to another large level, formed of broken stone taken out of the mine. Here is a machine, worked by two horses, to pump out the mine. Adjoining this is what is called a *whim*—the Cornish say *wim*. This is a large perpendicular cylinder, turned by horse power, as tanners grind bark. A large rope is wound around this cylinder, with a large bucket at each end, which connects with shaft No. 1, to raise the rock and mineral. To your right is a blacksmith-shop, used mostly for sharpening drills. To the north is another machine connected with shaft No. 1, called a *sheer;* it should be sheers. (*Vide* Webster's Dictionary.) This machine gives a power sufficient to raise ten tuns weight. With this the large masses of copper are taken out of the mine. A little to the left, overhead, is another whim, which connects with shaft No. 2, twenty-eight yards north of No. 1. You may now turn to the right, and follow a rail-track through another mineral shed, where all the broken rock of a poorer quality is taken, and the precious separated from the vile. As we turn about to see whence all this treasure is taken, you will naturally cast your eyes up the bluff, where you may see a large opening which once contained a great mass of copper. You will notice also a slide of greenstone, dipping to the north at an angle of perhaps 45°. This occasions a *fault* in the vein, at which the mineral ceases.

Before going into the mine we must return to the office to get a change of apparel. If you are at all careful about your velvet or broadcloth, you must doff it before you go under ground. You want a complete miner's suit from head to foot. Then you must have the safe conduct of Captain Jennings or Boss Jones, who will see that each one is furnished with a candle, and a lump of wet clay to put around it, which you must keep moist. Thus equipped we will now go into drift No. 1, which is on a level with most of the works we have been viewing; only be careful, in passing by No. 2, not to step off the plank into the depths below. Here you may go in several hundred feet, where not much is to be seen, except the empty space where the mineral has been removed.

We will now return to shaft No. 1, and go below, sixty feet, into the *Adit.* This is a drift extending from the river nine hundred feet north, and is used for draining the mine. Let it now be remembered that we must descend by ladders, several of which are nearly perpendicular, and one quite so. You must now pull off your gloves—if you have any on—and do not be afraid of soiling your hands as you hold on to the muddy rounds of the ladder. As you follow your guide, you must learn this lesson, and not forget it for a moment: "*Hold fast with your hands—never mind your feet.*" As we go down we occasionally come on to a small platform, and, by simply turning round, we take hold of another ladder. But you must not let go one ladder till you see where you are; a single misstep may precipitate you down the main shaft from one hundred to two hundred feet. We now find ourselves safely in the *Adit.* This is called the ten fathom level, or drift No. 2. The course of the vein is nearly north and south, dipping slightly to the east.

From shaft No. 1 we will now go north, passing over a pit fifteen or twenty feet deep, where the mineral has been removed. Soon we shall reach shaft No. 2, which we will cross on planks, on one side, holding on to an iron bar fastened to the rock on each side. At the north extremity of this drift is a mass of copper which has been thrown down by a sand-blast, which will probably weigh from thirty to fifty tuns. This must be cut to pieces with chisels before it can be taken out. Overhead you will see, in many places, what is called a *stull*, or *pent-house*. This consists of heavy timbers placed across the mine so as to form a scaffold. In this way the *lode* is all approached, and removed from one drift to another, ten fathoms, or sixty feet. This *stulling* is often torn down by heavy blasts, and is one source of the danger of miners. In going south we will see nothing very different from what is to be seen north, except that there the lode is not so rich as here.

Finding our way to shaft No. 1, we will again go down sixty feet to drift No. 3. The appearance here is very similar to that in drift No. 2. Every-where you have evidences of an inconceivably rich mine. In places you will find the lode entirely removed; then you will pass huge masses of mineral not yet disturbed. North of shaft No. 2 we pass a chain-ladder, which, if you are fond of adventure, you may ascend five or six fathoms into a large opening in the mine. A little farther on we cross over a *winze*, which is a communication from one drift to another to air the mine. This is soon to be used for a third shaft. The whole length of this drift, from north to south, is about one hundred and ten yards. If your curiosity is not yet satisfied, we may go down sixty feet further, into drift No. 4. In the extreme end north, after crawling on your hands and knees for some distance, over what miners call *deads*—that is, broken rock—you find yourself in a large opening, where is the appearance of a large mass of copper. The mine in this region is very rich. In this drift, among the many things too tedious to name, we notice what is called the *sump-shaft*. This is only a continuation of shaft No. 1, eighteen feet below the lower level. This, as the others, is to be sunk sixty feet before drifting again. The Captain is much elated with the prospect here, and promises for the next sixty feet to show the richest part of the mine. In what is called the *country*—that is, by the side of the vein—a mass of copper has been taken out weighing fifteen hundred pounds. The material is here raised to the lower drift by a windlass. A short time since I was visiting the mine, and, being desirous to see the bottom, my friend J. let me down in a bucket. But the miners having stopped work, water had collected two or three feet deep in the bottom. The first warning I had of this was the impression of wet feet as the tub was filling with water. This Boss Jones called *sumpen*.

The most agreeable time to go into the mine is Monday morning when the work commences, or Saturday afternoon after the miners quit work. The mine is then free from smoke. But if you choose to go when all are at work, you will see more. Here you may see a person holding a huge drill, and another with a large hammer, making every stroke tell on the hard rock. There you may see several men, with levers, at work at a mass which has been torn loose by a *sand-blast.* Here you may see one wheeling the rock, and throwing it down through a *mill*, where it is taken by others, put into buckets, and raised to the surface. In different parts of the mine you will hear the blast, the report of which rolls like thunder through the subterranean vaults. A dismal gloom seems to pervade the whole region, and at every turn you will be impressed with the fact that few men are so exposed to danger as miners. But what above every thing else should impress every one is the evidence of the wisdom, goodness, and power of God, above, beneath, and all around.

Doubtless you are as ready now to leave the mine as you were to enter it. We have now one hundred and eighty feet of ladder to climb; but, by perseverance, stopping a moment occasionally to take breath, we shall soon be at the top. Now we emerge from a world of darkness into a world of light. We may now return to the office, and assume our own attire, by which time it would be no very strange thing if a good meal would relish well. If the reader thinks this description of the Cliff Mine too minute, it may be a source of relief that this must suffice for all the other mines of Lake Superior—to explore one thoroughly is to see the leading features of all the rest.

CHAPTER XI.

INTERVAL OF CONFERENCE—APPOINTMENT TO THE INDIAN MISSION DISTRICT, AND REMOVAL TO THE SAUT.

August 18th, we found ourselves at the close of another conference year, and on board the propeller Independence. I had left to attend the annual conference which was to meet at Kalamazoo on the 6th of September. My family accompanied me as far as Copper Harbor, where, at midnight, we parted. They would have continued with me but for the extremely delicate health of Mrs. P. Mr. D. D. Brockway had kindly invited them to remain under his roof, where, with Mrs. Brockway, they were sure to have not only a hearty welcome, but every necessary attention. I feel called upon thus publicly to acknowledge the kindness shown to my family in the few weeks of their stay at Mrs. Brockway's.

A DELIGHTFUL SABBATH AT SEA.

August 20th, Sabbath, was a clear and delightful day. The following minute was made at the time: "Wind dead ahead ever since we started, but not enough to make a rough sea. We are in sight of White Fish Point, about twelve miles off. This has been more like Sabbath to me than any I have before seen on the Lake. I have seen no ungentlemanly behavior among either crew or passengers. I felt desirous, and prayed yesterday and this morning, that some door of usefulness might be opened to me on board. Have put a number of good tracts in circulation, which, in several instances, were thankfully received. At about ten o'clock, A. M., I had the privilege of conducting divine worship on board. We sung first,

'From all that dwell below the skies.'

After prayer and the reading of part of the hundred and seventh Psalm, we sung the second part of the hymn, 'to be sung at sea,' beginning,

'Infinite God, thy greatness spann'd.'

I strove as well as I could to preach Christ crucified, to present the cross in its spiritual import and bearings. I opened my mouth and the Lord filled it. By the serious attention paid I trust it was a word not spoken in vain. We then joined in singing the celebrated missionary hymn,

'From Greenland's icy mountain.'

Rev. J. W. Holt, from Kewawenon, made an appropriate closing prayer, and the congregation, consisting of about thirty souls, were dismissed and quietly retired.

"In the afternoon I had an interesting conversation

with W. H. B., one of the sailors. He is one who was rescued from the wreck of the Barbara. He has sailed twenty-five years on salt water and three on fresh—has witnessed many perils and dangers. He had sailed under Father Taylor, and sat with delight under his preaching. He says he is not destitute of the comforts of religion. An old backslider, who once belonged to the Methodists, B., opened to me the state of his mind, while tears ran down his wrinkled and care-worn cheeks. I gave him such instruction as I thought best suited his case. O that God may lead him to the foot of the cross! Beside my regular Bible lessons, I was edified in the perusal of a tract and three of Bishop Morris's sermons. Judge Hawes and his excellent wife are on board, who exert a commanding influence, happily, in favor of religion." For such a Sabbath at sea I felt that I could not be sufficiently grateful, especially as I had, in several instances, witnessed such shocking desecration of the Lord's day on similar occasions.

On reaching the Saut, I was urged by the superintendent to remain here, instead of going to conference, to look after the interests of the mission. There were good reasons why the missionaries should not all be absent at this time; and, though at the sacrifice of inclination, I abandoned going to conference, and remained at the Saut. The families of brothers Brockway and Barnum remained at Little Rapids during this interval, where I found a most agreeable home.

My time was spent very pleasantly in reading, writing, visiting, and attending to such duties as grew out of my calling. Several of those pastoral visits among afflicted and poor families on both sides of the river were seasons of edification to my own soul; for here I saw, in one or two instances especially, the support that our holy religion can give when earthly refuge fails.

I spent four Sabbaths here, during which I preached to the white citizens of the village part of the day, and the other part to the Indians at Little Rapids. Much of the time, as is often the case here at this season, we had very driving and cold easterly rain-storms. The weather was very disagreeable, and our meetings were thinly attended. I here formed the acquaintance of Colonel M'Nair, the mineral agent, Dr. Patterson, Judge Hunt, Mr. Whiting—all connected in some way with the business of the land-office—and Colonel M'Knight, at whose quarters in Fort Brady I was made welcome.

The following thoughts were suggested by our meeting at Little Rapids on the evening of September 10th: "Much is said about the poor Indians; their slowness in making improvement. But I was led to contrast the actual condition of the natives with the whites of this region. At the village the Gospel has been preached by different missionaries for the last twenty years—some of them talented and powerful preachers; but at this time there is not a Protestant society in the place, and only a few scattered members to represent several Churches. If the Christian desires a spiritual feast, let him turn in and visit the mission at Little Rapids. Here is a little band decently clad and neat in their appearance; but we see no external pomp or parade—no artificials or studied decorations to please the eye or attract the notice of spectators. Each one, with a solemn and reverential step, comes to the house of prayer, exhibiting by his demeanor that he is entering a place where God manifests his presence. A seriousness becoming the time and place is seen in each countenance. It is a rare thing to see a smile, much less that airy vanity often witnessed in white congregations. They sing with the spirit, and pray with great simplicity and earnestness. That saying of the Savior was forcibly brought to mind, as applied to the Jews: "Ye shall see Abraham, and Isaac, and Jacob, and all the prophets in the kingdom of God, and you yourselves thrust out. And they shall come from the east, and from the west, and from the north, and from the south, and shall sit down in the kingdom of God."

On the 16th of September I received intelligence from conference up to the 11th inst., but no hint as to our future destiny. The same day, by an arrival from above, I received word from my family. Their situation rendered it necessary for me to return to Copper Harbor by the first boat. And this I must do, still in the dark as to our appointment.

Tuesday, September 19th, by propeller, I left the

Saut. We were out two days, and had to return again on account of adverse weather. Friday we again went aboard, and were off once more. Our boat was heavily laden, and a large number of passengers aboard, of almost every description. The night following was to the sober part of the company a most unpleasant night, on account of some "lewd fellows of the baser sort," whose obscene and disorderly behavior was scarcely endurable. And this the more so because there were aboard gentlemen and ladies whose presence, if nothing more, should have commanded respect and decent behavior from the most abandoned.

Among the passengers was Mr. Richmond, the Indian Agent, and his brother, on their way to La Pointe to make the Indian payment. Here was Mr. Ramsay Crooks, a noble-looking man, who figures largely in Irving's "Astoria." After all his perils in and beyond the Rocky Mountains, he appeared to possess the vigor and sprightliness of youth. On board were the editor of the Lake Superior News and lady, and numerous others bound for La Pointe; also brother K. and wife on their way to the Ontonagon, with Mr. S., pale and blanched with the ague. It had given him a cruel shaking on the lakes. Here was also Mrs. L. Hanna, wife of the Agent of the Cliff Mine, with her three little children, going to meet her husband after a long separation. She had just buried her aged mother and her youngest daughter, and was to be the bearer of this mournful news to her companion. How sad such a meeting in view of the missing ones!

Saturday night we had a very rough sea, and the boat rolled and tumbled amazingly. But the roughness of the Lake quieted, in a good degree, the turbulence of some of the passengers. The Christian can much easier endure the raging of the sea than the raging of those who are "foaming out their own shame." This trip was, in almost every respect, in perfect contrast with our downward trip. But just at daybreak on Sabbath morning we arrived at Copper Harbor, and found all as well as could have been expected.

October 5. We had an arrival at Copper Harbor, bringing word that I was appointed superintendent of the missions in the district, and was urged by brother Brockway to come immediately to the Saut. But, on account of the situation of Mrs. P., this was impracticable.

Though not without risk, I took passage for Eagle Harbor, where I was landed with difficulty on account of a strong south-west wind. The next morning I walked nine miles, to the mouth of Eagle river, before breakfast; thence to the Diggings, where we had resided during the summer; packed up our things, and had all down to the Lake, marked and ready for shipping, by nine o'clock at night. Much fatigued, I relished the kindly influences of

"Tired nature's sweet restorer,
Balmy sleep."

Saturday I obtained a horse, and rode as far as Eagle Harbor, and walked the rest of the way to Copper Harbor. My feelings in view of the future were thus expressed at the time:

"In looking ahead I see a world, in miniature, of labor and responsibility. In God alone is my trust. Aided by him I shall succeed. And how can I fail of his aid, if I hold on to his word and promise! Our way looks dark in some respects; but how often have I been consoled by that passage, 'All things work together for good to them that love the Lord!' I hold on to this promise. Though I can not see the end, I am sure it will turn out for the best in some way. Here then I rest, and find an inward tranquillity which I would not exchange for an earthly crown.

"*Monday* 9. This morning Mrs. P. was delivered of an interesting little son. I think we have realized an answer to many prayers. She came out of this trial beyond our most sanguine hopes. May we ever magnify and praise thee, O our heavenly Father, who art our ever-present, ever-sufficient help in time of need!

"*October* 10. The Chippewa arrived from the *Saut*, bound for *Fond du Lac*, with brother Holt and wife, the missionaries for that station; and brother P. O. Johnson and family, bound for Saut Ste. Marie, to be helpers with us there."

This was providential, as I could not yet leave for the Saut. Brother Johnson acted as my deputy, in receiving the papers and other things belonging to the mission from brother Brockway.

A sad affair occurred at the Harbor the same day. A young man came there a few days before, from the mines. He had in his pocket about seventeen dollars, which he spent in gambling and drinking. Monday night he came from a liquor-shop, near by, to the Brockway House, where we were stopping, crying murder, and calling to Mr. B. to let him in, saying that C. was going to kill him. He was brought in and sent up stairs to bed. But he raved, as most any other person would do under the influence of *delirium tremens*. He quieted down toward morning, and nothing unusual was seen in his appearance during the forenoon. But about noon he started, in front of the Brockway House, and ran with all his might, and plunged into the Harbor, into deep water, and went to the bottom like a stone. Efforts were speedily made to rescue him, but, before he could be taken out, his spirit had fled to the retributions of eternity!

October 11th the Fur Trader arrived, bound for the Saut, *via* Kewawenon. Brother Marksman and wife, who were to be our associates at the *Saut*, were aboard, and a number of our Indian brethren residing at Kewawenon. Most of the afternoon was spent in conversation with them. Brother Johnson left the same day for the Saut.

During the time I was detained here I went again to Eagle river, and spent a Sabbath at the Cliff Mine, preaching and administering the sacrament of the Lord's supper.

October 24th the Independence arrived at Copper Harbor, on her downward course to the Saut. Two weeks had just elapsed since Mrs. P.'s confinement, and it appeared hazardous to commit ourselves to the mercy of storms; but trusting that a good Providence would "temper the winds to the shorn lamb," we went aboard and bade adieu to the Harbor, and reached the Saut in safety on the 27th instant. Here Mr. J. R. Livingston kindly furnished me with horse and a comfortable buggy, with which I conveyed my family to the mission at Little Rapids, where, for the present, associated with Rev. P. O. Johnson's family, we made our home. Shortly after Mrs. P. was taken suddenly, and, as we then thought, dangerously ill. But she was soon relieved and gradually recovered her strength.

The change of missionaries all round, as might be expected, tended greatly to derange matters for a while. But we hoped, with God's blessing, soon to bring some kind of order out of the confusion around us. Our winter's supplies must yet be ordered from Detroit, and we found much to do to prepare for winter.

It seemed not only desirable but indeed necessary, in view of the situation of the work, that we should reside at the village. The Fort was now without troops. Sergeant Gent, to whose care Fort Brady was consigned, kindly offered us quarters, rent free, during the winter. We gladly embraced his offer, and took possession of our new home on the 27th of November, when I made this note: "How transient is our stay in any one place! Well, we shall soon be done with earth, and it matters but little, so that we have 'a house not made with hands, eternal in the heavens.'"

We had just become settled in the Fort when a most sad event occurred near us. An Indian by the name of Nahbenaosh, whose residence was at Little Rapids, who had never abandoned his heathenism, and who had been accustomed to become intoxicated, came at last to a dreadful end. On the last night of November, a cold wintery night, he had turned away from the place where some one, who had the physical form and carriage of a man, had filled his bottle with the liquid poison. He found his way to a deserted wigwam, on the road to Little Rapids. Here, in some way, he set the wigwam on fire, which burned down over his besotted frame, crisping and shockingly mutilating it. The next morning a bottle was found by his side, telling, truthfully, the cause of this wreck and ruin of another deathless immortal! On the 2d of December, a windy and snowy day, I saw the Indians deposit his remains in the grave, while a son, a devoted Christian, wept tears of inconsolable grief over one he had once been wont to call *father!* Such melancholy facts are most painful to record, yet they are *facts*, in the midst of which we were called to move, and of which we were, at times, eye-witnesses, and without their mention the reader can hardly appreciate the influences that operated to impoverish and ruin the Indians, soul and body. In the light of such speaking facts it is easy to perceive who are the true friends of the red man.

CHAPTER XII.

TRAVELS AMONG THE INDIANS DURING THE WINTER.

I MADE one visit, during the winter, to the Indian settlement at Garden River, Canada, now under the care of Rev. Mr. Anderson, of the Episcopal Church. My old friends appeared very glad to see me; and, at the request of the missionary, I preached to them.

I made two very interesting trips to Naomikong, Lake Superior, some thirty-five miles from the *Saut*, which I think deserving of a more particular account.

January 5th, 1849, in company with brother Marksman, I left home after noon. Rode in a one-horse cutter eight miles. P. G. returned with the horse and cutter, and with our blankets, camp kettle, and provisions, we went on afoot. Faced a cold and blustery wind, and the ice was very smooth, so that we could scarcely keep to our feet. A poor Dutchman, on the same route, with boots instead of moccasins, came near perishing, as we afterward learned. He turned aside and spent the night in the woods, without fire, and but thinly clad. He made out to reach a house the next day, and was thus saved. We arrived safely at Waishkees Bay just before dark. Found here a tolerably-comfortable cedar-bark wigwam. The two men who had left the Saut in company with the Dutchman were here, and had a fire for our accommodation. We immediately went to work with our hatchets and provided wood for the night. Notwithstanding the cold we should have slept pretty well, but for the smoke which drove into the lodge.

January 6. After a hard walk of five hours, through woods most of the way, and on snow-shoes, we reached Carp river. Here was a saw-mill, a French family, two or three Americans, and a few Indians—the Waishkees. As they were old acquaintances they were very glad to see us, and we must drink with them some *shah-gah-mit-ta*—hot drink, either tea or coffee. To this proposal we readily acceded, eating with our tea some bread and pork. Then we had a season of prayer, and resumed our journey. A stiff cold wind was in our faces, and the ice, most of the way, was jammed together, nearly perpendicular like knives, and made it hard walking and trying to our feet. Reached Naomikong before night, and put up with my old friend, *Monomonee*, the chief, lately from Grand Island. Here were two other quite good log-houses, and the Indians, generally, appeared comfortably situated. Several called to see us, and kept us talking till the evening was spent.

Sabbath a good congregation collected to hear the word of the Lord. They were well clad, and very attentive while I preached them a plain, practical sermon from "the grace of God that bringeth salvation to all men hath appeared," etc. The Lord was present to bless. After noon brother Marksman preached on the parable of "the barren fig tree." This was also called a season of spiritual profit. The prayer meeting at night was a season owned of God. There was no flagging; both the singing and praying were in the spirit. I gave out an appointment for the next morning, at the close of which I had designed to leave for home. But on dismissing the congregation I was urged to go on to Te-quah-me-non, some five miles farther. It was said that the Indians there were very desirous that we should visit them. We had three or four members there—several persons were sick—one or two desired to be baptized, etc. To this call we felt constrained to yield.

On returning to Monomonee's from the meeting, we had an illustration of the manner in which the Indians prize a writing. Three years before, when I had visited his family at Grand Island, with a copy of John's Gospel, I gave him also a small class-book, with his own name and the names of his family written with pencil. Both of these he had preserved neat and clean. He took them out of his trunk and showed them to me. The class paper, though now of no use, was kept as a kind of memento.

Accompanied by five Indians, we went the nex morning to visit *Te-quah-me-non.* The second house we entered we had a specimen of the supreme selfishness of a heathen Indian. As usual, I passed round the house to shake hands with the inmates.

I offered my hand to an old woman, who was making snow-shoes. She continued her work as though she did not see me. After giving her a fair opportunity to reciprocate this token of friendship and civility, in vain, I turned away, in disappointment, while she muttered, "I see your hand, but there is nothing in it. that will benefit me. I am poor, and you might bring me something that would do me some good."

We next went to the wigwam of *O-ge-mah-pe-na-sa*, or the *King-hawk*. Here the people who were disposed collected together, to whom I preached a short sermon from "behold the Lamb of God," etc., and baptized an infant. The erysipelas was prevailing—a bad type of it, and kept several away.

Kah-ba-no-den, the old chief, sent an invitation for me to visit him in his wigwam. We went immediately after meeting, and had an interview with him and his family. He said that "he was very desirous to have us come and preach to his people, and that this was not merely his desire, but the general wish of the people there. He said that the preacher that occasionally preached to them,* was a kind of scolding preacher, and the people would not hear him." Again, "he said some of the young people were not members of any Church, and if we should labor among them we might do them good." I gave him all the encouragement I could, and before I parted with him remarked, that I was glad once

* A native preacher of another persuasion

more to meet with his family; that the last time I met with them was five years before at Saut Ste Marie, when his son, Beverly Waugh, lay sick in his wigwam. Till now he had not recognized me, and, looking up, he exclaimed, *Me-suh owh ka-get? Is this the very one?* Seeming to start up as from a reverie, he reached out his hand to me saying, *Bushoo, bushoo*—the word they use as equivalent to our *how do you do?* Poor old man! he had just lost one of his fingers from the disease before named. But he had a worse disease; he was sometimes overcome with intemperance. He was a shrewd, intelligent-looking Indian, and, perhaps, but for this besetment, would long before have been an active Christian.

Without stopping for any refreshment, eating simply some crackers which we carried in our pockets by the way, we returned immediately to Naomikong, where, at night, we had another interesting meeting. Tuesday went six miles to Carp river, and at ten o'clock, A. M., preached to the little band there. About noon we left, and, after a walk of about fourteen miles, we reached Waishkees Bay and camped in the wigwam, which gave us shelter on our way up. Two of the Waishkee boys had been here, and a small fire was still left. We found here some fine, fresh pike, a pretty good pile of wood, some flour in a barrel, etc. We commenced getting supper, but before it was ready the boys came in with a lynx and a rabbit. We all messed together, and spent the night very comfortably by keeping a good fire. But the weather was intensely cold, and a very cold day followed, but walking on the ice from this was good. At ten o'clock we reached T. S.'s, within six miles of home. The family were just at breakfast, and urged us to partake with them. This we did; and, after prayer and conversation on the subject of religion, we left, and were at home by noon. Our visit was made in an auspicious time—we saw nearly all the Indians together, had six public meetings, none of which were barren seasons, besides religious exercises in several private families. We were persuaded that we were in the work of the Lord, and that the angel of mercy had accompanied us. To his name alone be the glory forever!

A TRIP DURING THE CRUST-MOON.

The Indians have no months nor years in their calendar. They count by moons and winters. The month of March is called by them *O-nah-bun-a-ge-zis—the crust-moon.* The name is derived from the fact, that during this *moon* the snow is usually crusted over so hard that persons can walk on the crust without the aid of snow-shoes.

The first day of March, accompanied by brother Marksman, I left home to visit the Indians at *Na-omikong.* Our team took us six miles, where we staid all night with the family of T. S. The next morning we left by eight o'clock. Brother M. thought we could trust the crust-moon, so we left our snow-shoes. We did not need them any of the way. The day was delightful, and walking good, except where the ice was too slippery. We had soon passed *Pointe au Pin.* Before us some eight miles, across the ice, was *Pointe Iroquois.* Still further ahead was, in sight, an island called by the Indians Nod-o-wa-we-gun-e-min-e-sha—literally, the island of the bones of the Nod-o-wag,* a warlike tribe of Indians, who were deadly enemies of the Ojibwas, and who, as tradition says, were massacred by the latter on Pointe Iroquois.

Their story is that "those Indians had been at war with the Ojibwas, and whenever they killed an Ojibwa they roasted and ate him. The Ojibwas had at that time a large village at Saut Ste. Marie. They had heard of the coming of this tribe, and took their departure from the Saut, with their wives and children, whom they took to *Parisian Island,* and there concealed them. They sent three Indians to see where the *Nodowag* should camp. These the *Nodowag* caught on the way, killed them, and took them to Point Iroquois. Here they made a huge fire, roasted the men they had taken, and feasted and danced nearly all night. Their fire was seen by the

* By Nodowag the Chippeway Indians doubtless meant the *Dakotas* or *Sioux,* who from time immemorial have been deadly enemies to each other. The term *nadowessi* has from an early date been applied by the Chippeways to the Sioux. Nodowag is probably only another form of the same word. Governor Ramsay, of Minnesota territory, thinks that the Chippeways used the word *nadowessi* as synonymous with the term *enemies,* of whatever tribe. See a very elaborate and able document from his pen, on the various Indian tribes under his supervision, in the Annual Report of the Commissioners of Indian Affairs, for 1849–50, p. 68.

Ojibwas, who made preparations to fall upon them. Just before day the *Nodowag* all lay down, and fell into a sound sleep. The Ojibwas surrounded them, and so arranged that two persons should seize on each tent simultaneously. By this means, at a given signal, each tent was thrown down on its inmates, who were all captured and slain, except one, whose ears they cut off, and then sent him home to bear the news to his friends." Brother M. said that his father had often seen the bones which had covered this place of slaughter. Hence the name of the little island just at the end of the Point. This was one subject of conversation as we crossed this long icy bridge.

Another topic of discourse while making this long traverse was about Indian *medicine men*. Brother M. said that "his father had designed him for a medicine man, and, till he was fifteen years of age, he was more or less instructed in those mysteries. He was taught that the instruction thus given was to be kept as a profound secret—that it should be known by none except those who were members of the fraternity. At their great *Mittas*, or *medicine feasts*, persons were initiated into these mysteries. They usually had six persons, males, called elders, who performed the services of the gods of medicine, and one female, for the goddess of medicine. The ceremonies were performed in a large wigwam, in the shape of the horizon as it appears to the eye. This was to resemble the earth, which they considered a great wigwam, with the sky for a covering. Their songs were a kind of praise to the Great Spirit for the good effects of the medicine. And without this praise to the Great Spirit they consider that he would be angry, and the medicine be without its desired effect. They must handle every kind of medicine as something sacred, and never use harsh language in addressing any god. Old men they were taught to respect. They must never be trifling; 'for,' said they, 'the eyes of the Great Spirit are as large as the sky, and he sees all that we do.' These medicine men must be well dressed and appear respectably."

Thus employed time passed pleasantly, and we had soon reached the Point, and then the island, near which we seated ourselves on a large piece of ice, and ate a lunch of crackers and cold pork. So true is it that "there is but a step between the sublime and the ridiculous."

A little after noon we reached Carp river, and were warmly received by the Waishkee family. They went to work immediately to prepare us some warm victuals. One of the viands was a great treat—it was *Caraboo* meat, tender and sweet as any venison. We could not avoid thinking of patriarchal simplicity in eating of a good warm cake and "savory meat" taken from the forest. Here we rested awhile, worshiped together, and were again *en route* for *Naomikong*, where we arrived after a walk of twenty-eight miles, but not without weariness.

We stopped with Monomonee, who, with the other Indians, met us cordially.

I never witnessed a more beautiful appearance of the sky than as seen just about sunset. Not a cloud was to be seen, except in the north-west one of milky appearance. The sky above and around was of transparent blue. To the westward it was of a mellow golden hue, with a purple tinge. As the sun was receding from view, the reflection was like a lambent blaze in the tops of the intervening trees. The scene was a reflection of the glory of God. "How manifold are thy works, O Lord: in wisdom hast thou made them all!"

March 3d, accompanied by Monomonee, we left to visit *Tequahmenon.* We had not gone far before brother Marksman was obliged to turn back. He had lamed his feet the day before by walking on the hard ice. So I went on without an interpreter. Here we visited several families, and had a season of worship at the lodge of O. We also called on *She-gud*, a very devoted Christian Indian, a *deacon* in the Baptist Church, but in a declining state. After a short conversation with him I left, craving the blessing of God upon him; to which he responded, "*Ah pa-gish ka-gate*"—"*This is what I sincerely desire.*" One such monument of the saving power of the Gospel is worth years of missionary toil and sacrifice. Deacon *She-gud* has since gone to his reward, loved and lamented by all who knew him. We now returned to *Naomikong*, fatigued from our walk on the smooth ice. My feet were blistered and sore.

Just before night the dogs commenced barking and running toward the Lake, announcing an arrival from abroad. It was old sister Waishkee, from Carp river, with her two daughters-in-law, come to enjoy the communion with us the next day. She was probably sixty or seventy years of age, large and fleshy, and could not walk far on the smooth ice, though vigorous for her years. Her daughters drew her most of the way on a hand-train. This looked like old-fashioned Methodist meetings, when people could work a little to attend them.

In the meeting at night we read and explained the General Rules of the society. Sabbath morning was most lovely—a fair emblem of what it was to be to us spiritually. Early in the morning two of sister Waishkee's sons arrived. At nine we met for love-feast. After the introductory services a most interesting relation of Christian experiences followed. No time was lost. I could with difficulty close the delightful exercises by eleven o'clock. Others were still ready to speak. Nearly all seemed to feel that God was in our midst. My attention was attracted more particularly by an aged widow, an aunt to brother Marksman. She lived about a mile from the settlement, in the woods, and could seldom get out. Brother M. had visited her on Saturday. She expressed great desire to meet with us on Sabbath; but she was in charge of two little children, and did not know how to leave them; besides her daughter and little boy had gone to the Saut for provisions. How she managed to be there I did not learn. At any rate she was in the love-feast in season. She was plainly but well clad. She had on a good broadcloth shawl and a clean checkered apron. Her face was furrowed with age, but her hair not much turned. The expression of her face indicated a serene frame of mind and deep devotional feeling. I occasionally noticed the moving of her lips; then with her handkerchief she would wipe the tears from her eyes. After the meeting had progressed at some length, she arose. A brother arose at the same time, but gave way. She then commenced, in a subdued tone, to relate what God had done for her soul, occasionally pausing to give vent to her overflowing heart in tears. Among other things, she said that "*she had not language to express what she felt in her heart of the goodness of God.*" When done speaking she fell on her knees, with her face on the mat on which she had been sitting, and continued for a time as if engaged with God in prayer. Thus passed away this most interesting love-feast. It was good to be there.

The public meeting was one not soon to be forgotten. We administered the sacrament of the Lord's supper to twenty-three. The hearts of most, if not all, were deeply affected.

At night brother Marksman preached to a full attendance on the "one thing needful." The people heard the word gladly.

After the evening meeting, which closed about eight o'clock, we accompanied our friends from Carp river to their homes, and tarried with them for the night. I was led then to remark: "I sometimes wonder how I can endure such continued and hard exercise, and yet feel no inconvenience, only occasional weariness."

Monday morning, about nine o'clock, we left for the Saut. We passed over the first eight or nine miles quite comfortably. But after we rounded Point Iroquois we encountered a severe snow-storm, driving full in our faces the rest of the way. But we reached home before night, finding all comfortable but our little son, who had been quite unwell during my absence. Thus ended our trip during the *crust-moon.*

17

CHAPTER XIII.

SUMMER'S TOUR AND THE MISSIONS EN ROUTE.

On the 8th of June I left the *Saut*, on the schooner ——, to visit the missions. There were on board some eighteen, including crew and passengers—rather a motley mixture of Cornish, Belgians, Irish, and Americans. Some soon rendered themselves conspicuous by their profanity. Several were seated astern, to whom the captain remarked: "Gentlemen, we have a very pious man on board; I hope we shall hear no profane language." He was not aware that the person to whom he alluded was in hearing, who immediately responded, "I hope the gentlemen will bear in mind that they are in the presence of God;" taking the liberty at the same time to expatiate on the evil of swearing, even as a social wrong, to say nothing of its moral turpitude. All readily acquiesced in what was said. But several afterward forgot themselves, among whom was the captain himself.

We arrived at La Pointe on the evening of the 14th. We had alternate spells of fair sailing, head wind, rain, sunshine, and fog. A sudden squall struck us before we came into harbor, which gave all hands on board as much as they could attend to for a short time. As we were on the Lake during the Sabbath,

I endeavored once to preach to those on board. Whether any good was done or not, both the messenger and his message were treated with respect. At La Pointe I was kindly welcomed and hospitably entertained at the mission of the American Board.

TRIP TO FOND DU LAC.

I was obliged to lay over one day at La Pointe, to procure men and an outfit. We now exchanged a schooner for a three-fathom birch-bark canoe. Saturday, the 16th, with two good voyagers, I left at half-past six, A. M., one of the men prepared with two small oars, the other and myself with each a paddle. Went about eight miles and stopped for breakfast. While the men were preparing our repast, I took out my old and well-tried Bible, and commenced reading, with a little surprise, as it was my lesson in course, Isaiah xliii, 1, 2: "But now thus saith the Lord that created thee, O Jacob, and he that formed thee, O Israel: Fear not; for I have redeemed thee, I have called thee by thy name; thou art mine. When thou passest through the waters, I will be with thee; and through the rivers, they shall not overflow thee," etc. I had afterward, several times, occasion to rely on this cheering promise.

The Lake was calm most of the day. Toward night wind was from the north-east, and a heavy sea rolling in toward the shore. We were obliged to camp rather early on this account. For this purpose we found a convenient nook, sheltered by a high sand cliff. In this wild and desolate spot we rested during the holy Sabbath. At times we were much annoyed by musketoes and black flies. My men were not Christians; I, however, sung and read prayers to them in Ojibwa. Fanned by the Lake breeze, and cheered by the music of its surf, I spent the day happily in reading, meditation, and prayer.

June 18. It thundered, lightened, and rained very hard during the past night. Early in the morning a torrent was rushing down from the cliff, just before our tent, forcing together great stones, and bearing sand and limbs and every thing before it, lacking but little of undermining our tent. A tree-top broke off and fell across the fire. The contents brought from the hill nearly filled up our little harbor. The water of the Lake all the rest of the way was turbid, from mixture of red sand and clay. We struck our tent at six o'clock, in the midst of a heavy fall of rain. Lake calm till eleven o'clock, A. M.; but we became, as the Indians say, *ah-pi-che, sah-bah-we*, that is, *drenched.* Now wind sprung up from the north-east. We ran into the River Brule—made a sail of an Indian blanket—took some refreshment and put out to sea. Before we were out long we had all the wind we desired for our little craft. For a time the dense fog almost hid the shore, but it gradually disappeared. We made fine weather and gained the entrance of the St. Louis river before sundown, and camped about eight miles up from its mouth.

June 19th we left our camp at four o'clock, A. M.

We found the river very high, and the lowland completely overflown. It was extremely difficult to tell where and which was the main channel. We were hemmed in with a dense fog, all around, and the men were puzzled to find the way. All the way the current was very rapid. One of the men went ashore and ascended a little hill, and saw, at a distance, some Indians taking up a net. We went to them and obtained directions. We had been on our course. The fog gradually scattered, and, with hard tugging, we reached the Fond du Lac mission at half-past nine o'clock, A. M., in good order for our breakfast. We passed several canoes with Indians fishing, who called to us, "*ba-kah che-bah-qua*," that is, stop and cook your breakfast. They seemed to feel a deep and special interest in the matter. We found brother Holt and wife well, and we were glad to meet each other again, even on a heathen shore. The native missionary, who was a member of the annual conference, and his wife, had sadly fallen and left the place, doing irreparable injury to our mission. It is justice to them to say that they were led astray under the strongest and most exciting provocations. But we must be excused from entering into the unedifying details.

FOND DU LAC MISSION.

There was here, during the winter, a prospect of a good revival. Things looked more than encouraging; but the circumstance just mentioned cast a gloom over the prospect, and tended to dampen the efforts of the missionary. A school was taught, numbering twenty-eight scholars, and a Sabbath school consisting of about thirty scholars. Owing to the late freshet, things about the mission looked like desolation. The river had not been known to be so high in a long time. Where the wigwams of the Indians had stood, they passed with canoes, and they were forced to remove their lodges to the upland. The mission-garden and several other gardens had been submerged, several houses were surrounded with water, and nearly the whole looked like a great mortar-bed. With the exception of a few, the Indians here had made but little advancement from heathenism. But even here there had been good fruit, as a result of missionary toil. In some respects this was a point of importance; but without a speedy change for the better, we had our serious doubts as to the propriety of continuing our efforts here.

INDIAN COUNCIL.

While here I met the Indians in council, to hear what they had to say about matters in general. The head chief, Shingobe, distinguished for nothing but his chiefship, was present, and *Nah-gah-nup*, a subordinate chief, but *the man* of the band, and rather a marked character. Doctor Norwood thought him to be the most talented man in the Chippeway nation. He evidently thought himself to be a great man. He came to see me in the morning previous to the council, dressed in a military coat highly ornamented—a gift from some one—with a cane in his hand, and with airs so lofty that he might have been mistaken for the lord of the land. Quite an assembly met, most of whom were miserably clad; some with their faces painted, others were blackened, and nearly all grotesquely ornamented according to Indian custom.

I told the Indians that I had come as a stranger among them, was glad to see them, and, at their request, had met with them to hear what they had to say about matters connected with the mission. Spoke to them respecting the object of missions; told them I was anxious to learn what good the labors of the missionaries had done among them, and that their friends below often inquired after their welfare, and their progress in religion and civilization. I then gave way for a reply. After a little consultation, *Nah-gah-nup* blew upon his hands, rolled up his shirt sleeves to his elbows, spoke a few words sitting, then came up and gave me his hand, and said in substance:

"My friend, you are from a rich country, where every thing is fine and flourishing. You heard about us a number of years ago, and thought you would come and teach us, and preach the Gospel. As you came this way you found things look poorer and poorer. Very great difference when you came here. You found us very poor people, living in the woods. You always speak to us about the name of God. Now God is a charitable being. His disciples ought also to be charitable. Now I do n't see this charity. Indians are very poor and hungry, but the missionary does not feed them. And now I want to know who pays the money to support the mission? Do the white people below, or does it come from the Indian annuity? And as for the school-teacher, he does not do his work right. When men are hired to work they go at it early in the morning, and work all day. The missionary waits till the sun is up high, just as the farmer. If his boss were here perhaps he would do differently. But the teacher does not teach longer than one can smoke a pipe.* The Indian is like the wild fox in the woods. When we want to catch him we put bait in the trap. But you do not put on the bait; therefore, you do not succeed with the Indians. And now I will say no more, and when you have spoken I will reply."

I answered his speech briefly, reminding him that, for several years, missionaries were sent to them at the expense of the Missionary Society, and that, since the treaty, they had drawn a small portion from the Indian annuity, but that still the Missionary Society bore most of the expense. As to our charity, I told him that we endeavored to do what we were sent to do—that we were not sent to feed them, but to preach the Gospel to them, to teach their children, and point out the way for them to be happy—that if they would only abandon their heathenism and go

* The missionary thought this a pretty good eulogium on his services, as some of them could smoke a pipe nearly all the time.

to work as the white people do, they would not be hungry and go begging about for some one to feed them. I pointed them, for example, to the Indians at Kewawenon, and at Saut Ste. Marie, under the care of our missions. As to what he said about the teacher, I was not fully informed as to the facts in the case, but had reason to believe that, on a little more reflection, he would be disposed to alter his speech. Told him what was customary below about teaching—that it would not be for the children's good to be kept in all day. And more than this, that the teacher was often compelled to desist from teaching for want of children; that Indians often suffer their children to run about and play instead of going to school. Sometimes a goodly number came, and sometimes very few. And finally, that the bait we put into the trap to catch the fox, was to present that before him which would improve him every way in body and in mind, and raise him up to the same station that the white people occupied—that this was the best bait we had to present.

He arose again, and said: "If we employ a man to work he expects something to eat, and we feed him. If you want the Indians to do something you must feed them." He seemed to imply, in what he said, that the Indians were conferring a remarkable favor on the missionaries to send their children to school, and to attend the meetings, and that they ought, at least, to be fed, if not well paid for such meritorious acts.

The head chief, a Catholic, made a few remarks, the principal of which were, that "they did not want our missionaries there any more; and that the right to cut grass on a piece of wild meadow, for which brother Day, a previous missionary, had given him a coat, could not be granted any longer—that he would return the coat again [after having worn it about a year] to the mission." Of course we declined his generous offer. I told them plainly, in conclusion, that if they judged themselves unworthy of the Gospel, after having made sufficient trial, we should turn to others.*

Here I became nearly discouraged respecting the prospect of going to Sandy Lake. An old and experienced voyager told me that I could go, but should need the best kind of men; that we must carry canoe and all around all the rapids, which, he said, would take us seven days, only to ascend. Nearly all the Indians spoke very discouragingly. They said, "If you go you will drink water." They meant we would be drowned. The men who accompanied me from La Pointe became frightened, and were for going no farther. But I was favored with an interview with Dr. Norwood, employed in the geological survey

---

* In regard to the kindness of our missionaries in feeding the Indians, the sick of some of those very persons, who uttered such loud complaints, were visited, almost daily, by brother Holt and his amiable wife, and food carried to them. Their hospitality, to the poor around, had a limit, that was *their means*. The other complaints, as I learned from reliable sources, were not founded in truth, but in extreme ignorance and selfishness.

on the north shore of Lake Superior, and well acquainted with that entire portion of the country, which fully satisfied me that the difficulties and dangers, though not inconsiderable, were magnified. In this view I was confirmed by conversation with *Nah-gah-nup*. I employed an additional man, well acquainted with the rivers. We took a Frenchman from Dr. Norwood's party, who desired to work his passage through to the Mississippi. Brother Holt concluded to accompany us. With a force of six we were prepared to oppose a pretty stiff current. But by adding to our strength we also increased our burden. Thursday, 21st of June, we were ready to start at eight o'clock, A. M.

OUR ROUTE.

About three miles from Fond du Lac, up the St. Louis river, commences what is called the Grand Portage. The distance across is called nine miles. Here is a succession of rapids, impracticable either to ascend or descend. Every thing must be carried by land; not in wagons, or on horses, but on men's backs. We were favored in being able to leave one canoe on this side, and get one of the North Fur Company's on the other side. Part of the way walking was good; but, in places, quite muddy from recent powerful rains. We reached the end of this Portage at two o'clock, P. M. Here we stopped to gum our canoe, but were soon under way, stemming the rapid current. After some exertion, moving at a slow rate, we reached Knife Portage. Distance across is three and a half miles. The fullness of the river enabled us to shorten the portage a mile and a half. Here we landed safely, after having ascended one of the most dangerous places. We soon had all over the portage, and were camped for the night.

Friday, 22*d*. We had a succession of rapids till we crossed Grand Rapids, at one o'clock, P. M. Some of these we had much difficulty in ascending. Poles were used when the water was not too deep. At times we succeeded by getting hold of bushes and limbs of trees, and thus pulling ourselves along. Sometimes when our paddles were insufficient we found it necessary to *cordell;* that is, to use a rope. But this could seldom be done, except for a short distance, on account of trees, etc. Occasionally large trees were found lying in the rapids, which it was difficult to get around. We avoided some difficult rapids by following channels which the river had forced among the trees; but in one of these places we came very near breaking our canoe. Even here the water was very rapid. Having ascended the Grand Rapids, we were over the worst, although the current of the St. Louis is very strong all the way. We traveled till eight o'clock, P. M., and camped; were much annoyed by musketoes. During the night we had a heavy thunder-shower; lightning struck near us.

Saturday, 23*d*. At half-past four o'clock we left our camp. At two o'clock, P. M., we had reached the mouth of East Savan river. This river was spread over all its bottoms; but we found smooth water, and current light, compared with what we had passed over. We now made good headway. Between five and six o'clock a dark cloud arose before us, and distant thunder warned us of an approaching storm. As soon as we could find a convenient spot, we went ashore, and erected our tent. But this was scarcely done before a deafening peal of thunder fell near us, and the lurid lightning flashed in our faces, and, quick as thought, a hurricane swept by us, breaking off a large number of trees as if they were rushes. We all forsook the tent, and stood and took the driving storm, securing a position on the shore where we had no trees in range of the storm. We received a fine wetting, but no farther injury. The storm was fierce, but soon subsided, and we went on again. Just before sundown we reached the head of the river, and camped down on the wet grass, with water all around us, scarcely affording a place suitable for our tent. I thought I had often seen musketoes, but will not attempt to describe the salutations we here met. Supper was prepared, but our situation was so uncomfortable that we could scarcely eat. Another heavy thunder-shower now poured down on us.

Sabbath, 24*th*. We had now some twelve miles of land portage, and about four miles across Sandy Lake, to reach the mission. Had we been below, with an appointment thus near, we should have felt it our duty to go to it. Here we could only meet with our brethren once a year, and make a short stay at best, and besides were not situated for a quiet observance of the Sabbath. Accordingly, obeying the convictions of duty, we went into the mission in the early part of the day, and spent the afternoon with brother and sister Spates, our missionaries, in religious exercises, finding it rest and pleasure both to soul and body, to be out of a dismal swamp, and at the end of a fatiguing and perilous voyage. At four o'clock preached to the little company which assembled. God was with us of a truth. We all felt it good to wait on the Lord. For want of wine we did not administer the sacrament of the Lord's supper either here or at Fond du Lac. It had been administered at both stations during the winter by brother Spates.

Monday, 25th, was a very busy day with us. We had the temporal business of the mission to arrange; many things to talk about respecting the present condition and the future operations of the mission, and various calls to which attention must be given.

FEATS OF A CONJURER.

In the afternoon we were invited to go to the lodge of one of the chiefs, whose son was very sick. It was announced that an Indian medicine man would swallow some bones. The wigwam was spread around with blankets, leaving a square in the center for the fire. The invalid lay on one side, his father seated near him. On the other side were two plates of sugar, and spoons in them. Another plate contained water or broth. In this was a piece of horn cut off at each end so as to leave it hollow. It was about four inches long and perhaps three-quarters of an inch in thickness. Beside this was a bear's claw, with two brass nails in the large end, and several small pieces of bone, two to three inches long, and a fourth to a half an inch in thickness. The plate was covered with a rattle, made similar to their drum, with hieroglyphics painted on each side. It was about eight inches in diameter. The conjurer came and took his seat by the head of the sick man. Another came in with a drum. The performer took a little pail of water and washed his hands—they certainly needed it—and then rinsed out his mouth. Now he offered a kind of prayer to the Great Spirit. He stated that "it was made known to him when a little child that he should swallow bones; that his mother charged him not to make a show of this, and that it was not for the purpose of making a show that we had been invited to see the performance." He spoke very rapidly, and appeared to be in a kind of agony. During this the invalid showed signs of great distress, groaning and pressing upon his abdomen with his hands, and changing his position. The prayer ended, he took his rattle and began to shake it, occasionally beating himself with it on one shoulder, then on the other, then on his back and breast in rapid succession, bending forward toward the plate, and drawing in his breath as if he would take in the bones without touching them. The man with the drum meanwhile kept up a constant drumming and jingling of little bells. Now he put his mouth to the plate, took one of the bones, and made a dreadful struggle as if attempting to swallow it, beating his back and shoulders with the rattle. Then he would spit it out, and take another, and thus he continued till he got them all in—bones, bear's claw, horn, and all—and, for aught any one could tell, had actually swallowed them. Though I watched his throat very narrowly, and could not perceive that he swallowed, still they had disappeared, and they went into his mouth. Then he vomited them all out again, during which his face was all contortions, and he writhed and sweat as if he had been in the agonies of death. Now he would take one of the bones in his mouth, and press it upon the body of the invalid, during which he appeared tranquil and serene. It acted on him like a charm.

Query: Wherein does this differ essentially from modern spiritualism? Is not Satan at the bottom of the conjurer's art, and equally so as it respects modern necromancy? We felt, at least, as if we were in the very precincts of his majesty's darkest domain.

After this the Indians met in council to deliberate on matters concerning the mission. They spoke very highly of their missionary, called him their father, and said they loved him much. But they had some fault to find with him—he did not feed them quite enough. They would be glad also if he would give them more clothing; and they were especially desirous that he should keep a good supply of medicine on hand to doctor their sick. They complained of their inability to make their children go to school as they desired. They had much to say which amounted to but little; and, to close the whole, one of the chiefs remarked, "Our father is here, and does not give us any thing; if our mother were here, we know she would give us something." We left them with such instruction as we thought adapted to their case.

Accompanied by the other missionaries, I went to see the Mississippi, distant only a half mile, where we bathed in the outlet of Sandy Lake, and returned again to the mission. Here we closed the day with a family prayer meeting. It is worth all the world to be in such a praying circle in a heathen land. I shall not soon forget that sweet, refreshing season.

SANDY LAKE MISSION.

I was happily disappointed when I came to see this spot. Here was the most complete contrast I ever beheld between paganism and Christianity, barbarism and civilization. On the one hand were rude lodges, with inmates rolling in filth, and steeped in the moral pollution of heathenism. In the midst of scenes the most revolting stood the Methodist mission, a plain but comfortable log building. Brother S. had paled in a little door-yard, with shrubbery and plants tastefully growing within. He had inclosed his garden with high pickets, and had a small field adjoining, planted mostly in potatoes, which looked very well for the time. Every thing without looked thrifty and prosperous. The gardens of most of the Indians had shared the same fate as at Fond du Lac; they were buried under the freshet. A time of suffering was anticipated among the Indians as a consequence, in the destruction of the rice crop. The mission had not been without a degree of prosperity, though small. There were but six members, and one on probation. The school had been better attended than any previous year. It numbered, for the year, twenty-three male scholars and nineteen female. The children had made some advancement in learning, but, as they were situated, we could not hope for rapid progress. In this survey we felt that our zeal should not rise and fall in proportion as our reports were full or destitute of glowing statistics, but in proportion to the value of *one soul truly enlightened and saved.*

Tuesday, 26th, we parted with our friends at Sandy Lake, at eight o'clock, A. M. At five o'clock, P. M., the next day, we were at Fond du Lac. The distance between these stations is nearly one hundred miles. We passed with great rapidity over the frightful rapids, which caused us so much toil on our way up. Here we spent the night, and preached the next morning to the little society. We left the mission at two o'clock, P. M., and by traveling all night Friday night we arrived at La Pointe on Saturday, before noon. Spent the Sabbath here, entertained, as usual, at the mission of the American Board. I preached once to Rev. Mr. Hall's congregation. Monday we were wind-bound. Tuesday we left for Kewawenon, where, after hard toiling, we arrived on Friday at ten o'clock at night. We met with a happy greeting from brother Barnum's family, whose repose we were under the necessity of disturbing. Found sister B. in a declining state of health, and doubt entertained respecting her recovery. She regretted to be destitute of the counsel and aid of a good physician, but was waiting, resignedly, the will of God.

THE KEWAWENON MISSION.

It was gratifying to witness the degree of prosperity that had attended this mission. The Indians were in a high degree of improvement compared with those before named. Their crops this year were larger than any previous year. They were adding to the comforts of their dwellings, and increasing their stock of cattle. The Church numbered forty-three members, and nine on trial. The school numbered twenty males and thirteen females, which also composed mostly the Sabbath school. The Indians were all busy on Saturday in making a road. I improved this time to transact business matters with the missionaries. In the evening we had a meeting of the Indians to attend to the business of the Church. Sabbath morning, at nine o'clock, we met for love-feast. It was truly a time of God's power. An invitation was given for persons to unite with the

Church, while we should sing. Several old backsliders came and gave us their hand; one young man, also, who had lately renounced heathenism. The hymn was named, and all tried to sing, but the singing was so interrupted with sobs and cries that we could scarcely proceed. At eleven o'clock the house was well filled, and I had the privilege of preaching to them, while they listened with deep and fixed attention to the word spoken. I trust the effort was not in vain.

In the afternoon we baptized the young man who had renounced heathenism, and three infants, after which we administered the sacrament of the Lord's supper. In the evening I endeavored to preach, plainly and pointedly, to the white people, on the new birth. During the three years I had resided at this mission, I enjoyed many precious seasons with my Indian brethren, but none more so than this last. Nearly all the forenoon Monday was spent in conference with them, and I had literally to force myself away to leave for Eagle river at two o'clock, P. M., July 9th. Nearly all, from the least to the greatest, were on the dock to shake hands, and say *bushoo*, as we launched our canoe, bade them farewell, and departed.

We arrived at Eagle river the next evening, where I took leave of my two *voyageurs* and the canoe which had accompanied me for nearly seven hundred miles. The men proved themselves to be trusty and faithful. Thev returned to La Pointe.

EAGLE RIVER MISSION.

Rev. E. H. Day was the missionary at this station. He taught school all the year, and preached two or three times on the Sabbath. There was here a class of thirteen members, and two Sunday schools, numbering about forty scholars. The missionary was indefatigable in his efforts to promote the cause of Christ, but counter influences were at work here which served to hedge up his way, and impede the work of religion. This was especially true of the prevailing intemperance. At a public meeting, which was numerously attended, an individual offered the following resolution, that "temperance, on Lake Superior, is all a humbug." By taking the business of president into his own hands, and putting the question to the crowd, it was carried with a hurra! Several, who before had felt themselves pledged to abstain from the accursed thing, were found returning to their cups. Whisky does most of the mischief at the mines.

Brother Barnum came across from Kewawenon, and spent Saturday and Sabbath with us. The meetings of both Saturday evening and Sabbath were seasons of refreshing from God's presence. Sunday evening brother B. preached on the subject of missions, and we took up a collection to aid the cause.

I was compelled to remain in the vicinity of the Cliff Mine a week before I could obtain a passage to the Saut. On the 18th of July I went aboard the Napoleon, and arrived at home on the 20th, after an absence of six weeks. I had increasing cause of gratitude to an ever-watchful Providence for his kind care over myself and family during this period.

CHAPTER XIV.

SAUT DE STE. MARIE MISSION.

Little Rapids was still the rallying point for this mission, so far as the Indians were concerned. Here were the farm, the mission-house, chapel, and other buildings and conveniences. Missionary operations could have been prosecuted here with increasing advantage, but for the fact that our location was on a Government Reserve, and the Indians were anxious to locate somewhere, in which there was a prospect of making a permanent home that they could call their own. They could not be persuaded that the Government would allow them to do this at Little Rapids. Their desire was to buy land and hold it in *fee simple*, without molestation.

At this station we had a small class, regular preaching, and other religious exercises, a Sabbath school and a day school, numbering twenty-four scholars, taught by Rev. P. O. Johnson, assisted by brother Marksman. Seven children were living in the mission family, and were rapidly improving in every respect. Such was the state of things during the winter.

In the early part of the following summer all the Indian families left Little Rapids and went to White

Fish Point, Lake Superior, to fish, and remained during the summer. Some would have returned sooner but for fear of the cholera, which had broken out at the Saut. With my advice brother Marksman followed the Indians, took lodging in a wigwam, and built a shelter, under which he taught school during the week, and preached on the Sabbath. His school-list showed fifty-two scholars, thirty-five of whom were boys. Owing to their fishing, the attendance was not always regular. The average was sixteen and a fraction.

The work of religion seemed to be gradually advancing despite the many obstacles which the scattered state of the Indians cast in the way. In the spring considerable repairs were made about the mission farm, and the crop yielded well except the grass, which was much injured by drought. Our principal drawback here was the removal of several families to Na-om-i-kong, which made it evident that we must follow them to that locality or give up our efforts to evangelize them. The Indians desired us to establish a school at the place just named. But here was the commencement of new labors and increasing responsibilities.

When the business of the district did not call the superintendent to other parts of the work, he kept up regular religious services among the white citizens of the village of Ste. Marie.

In the interval of the previous conference Rev. J. D. Bingham, son of the resident Baptist missionary, came to the Saut with the intention of ministering to the white population of that place, providing there should be a suitable opening. He resided in his father's family during the winter, and preached every Sabbath afternoon in the same house in which our meetings were held. We had the privilege usually of attending each other's services. Those public meetings were always agreeable and harmonious, and, we trust, beneficial to the community. Mr. B.'s wife is a daughter of Elder Knapp, the revivalist, and a well-educated and refined Christian lady. In the early part of the following summer he took leave of the Saut, and went below to find a field of greater promise.

At the commencement of the year our congregations were small. But we were encouraged, as the year advanced, to have them gradually and constantly enlarge, and they were generally characterized by seriousness and thoughtful attention to the word preached, and occasionally we were favored with seasons of melting mercy to the little few who bore the Christian name.

The winter was a very severe one. About the middle of February the thermometer fell as low as 35° and 40° below zero, and the snow was five feet deep on a level. But the river opened about the first of May, so that on the 9th we had two arrivals, the steamers Tecumseh and Franklin. All was now suddenly changed to a whirl of business. A company of troops was sent up to occupy the fort, and we were obliged to give up our quarters and take up our abode in a log-cabin in the outskirts of the village, the best we could find, and we were glad to obtain that.

During my absence to visit the upper missions, Rev. P. O. Johnson ministered to the people of the village.

August 3d was the day appointed by the President of the United States, to be observed as a day of fasting and prayer to almighty God, to arrest the ravages of that desolating scourge, the cholera. To this the attention of the people was called. We met at six o'clock, A. M., and held a prayer meeting. At half-past ten o'clock I endeavored to preach to the people. Rev. Mr. Bingham, the Baptist missionary, preached at two o'clock, P. M. The day was rainy and the meetings were thinly attended. We felt as though the people did not realize, as they should have done, the loud call for humiliation before God.

Is it not a little singular that the very next day the fell destroyer appeared in our midst, in the sudden death of Mr. Stevens, the proprietor of the Ste. Marie's Hotel? On Sabbath I was called to attend his funeral. The next day we had four corpses in town, three Indians and a Frenchman.

Wednesday there was one death. Thursday two were taken in the morning and died before night. One was Captain Daniel Hicks, of Adrian; the other was a Frenchman, who had lived an abandoned life, and died in most excruciating agony. This was pronounced the most melancholy day that had ever been witnessed at the Saut. Three men lay sick in the fort, two of whom were in the hospital. During the prevalence of the scourge our time was much taken up in visiting the sick and dying, attending funerals, etc.

Alarming as were those instances of mortality, the epidemic was mercifully restrained in its ravages. Many felt symptoms of the disease who were enabled to counteract them. Through God's goodness all our missionaries, and the Indians connected with us, were preserved.

The conference year was now closing. August 24th, accompanied by my family, we took steamer for Detroit, where we spent the next Sabbath. Thence we hastened to Adrian, the seat of the conference, the home of several relatives and numerous old and tried friends. Here I spent the Sabbath previous to the conference, and preached in the morning to a large and attentive congregation, and saw many familiar faces, but some had gone to the spirit-land. Brother Hicky gave us, in the afternoon, one of his warm Holy Ghost sermons. The late lamented Hinman thrilled the evening assembly with an eloquent and elaborate discourse on "the connection of knowledge and virtue." The conference began and passed along very harmoniously; but the Sabbath it embraced was a season of interest never to be forgotten. We met at the Methodist Church at eight o'clock, A. M. The Lord's supper was administered, immediately after the ordination of the deacons, by Bishop Hamline. Then followed the relation of Christian experience. What a heaven below was here realized! In immediate connection with this, the Bishop, in his own peculiarly-impressive way, baptized our infant, Henry Eugene. The religious services which followed were all signalized by the presence of the great Head of the Church. To us it was a most memorable conference, but thus much must suffice.

By the 23d of September we found ourselves at our post again at Saut Ste. Marie, and enjoying a blessed Sabbath with the missionaries and others, bound for Lake Superior. There were with us Rev. E. H. Day, of Eagle river, Rev. R. C. Crane, on his way to Kewawenon, Rev. P. O. Johnson and Rev. P. Marksman, of the Saut; also, brother Pulsifer and wife, going as teachers to La Pointe, under the direction of the American Board. Brother P. was detained with us eight weeks before he could take passage to La Pointe.

At our communion season held at Little Rapids, at this time, it was most pleasing to see Mr. Babcock, of Detroit, the Indian Agent, and his clerk, Mr. Smith, kneeling at the same bench with some of our Indian brethren, and partaking with them of the holy communion. How completely does the love of Christ annihilate every principle and feeling of caste, and enable all of God's children to meet as brethren! Our religious meetings, both at the village and at Little Rapids, were seasons of spiritual good.

CHAPTER XV.

TRAVELS AND EFFORTS AMONG THE INDIANS DURING THE FALL AND WINTER—EFFORTS AMONG THE WHITE POPULATION.

OUR missionary brethren, after some detention at the Saut, were at their posts doing battle, valiantly, for the cause of Christ. With the sanction and encouragement of our Missionary Board, it was thought best to build a mission-house at Naomikong. This place had been noted as a great fishery, and hence the desire of the Indians to concentrate here. Soon after our return from conference I employed two carpenters to put up the body of a plain hewed-log-house, one story and a half high. Brother Marksman and myself, accompanied, as far as the saw-mill, by another person, went to Naomikong in a large batteau. The first day we encountered adverse winds, and just as we neared Point Iroquois, one of those whirlwinds, common in that region, swept by us, making a terrible roaring, and might have capsized us, but brother M.'s instinctive perception of such dangers enabled him to take the warning before it reached us. By a desperate effort we got out of its track in time. It passed us with great force, and was over in a moment's time. We had been toiling long—indeed, it was three o'clock at night before we had landed on the little island near the point, and were ready to rest our weary limbs after our protracted toils.

The next day we reached Naomikong, about four o'clock, P. M. Our carpenters arrived the same day. The next morning, 26th of October, we selected a site for the mission in a beautiful pine grove, on the shore of a little cove, or bay. Aided by the chiefs we soon cleared a spot for the building, and the carpenters had commenced to get out the timber. After night, a fine moonlight night, we manned a large batteau with six Indians, went to the saw-mill and got a load of lumber, and returned just before midnight. Rest, even in a tent, was sweet after such exertion. Saturday we went and got another boatload of lumber. This work ended, we were glad to lay aside our secular employment and prepare for the Sabbath.

On the Lord's day we had several religious services. One thing gave us great pleasure—the Sabbath was quietly observed by all the Indians. Although it was in the hight of the fishing season, not one was seen to go to his nets. Monday and Tuesday we worked on the mission premises. Wednesday we left for home. After reaching Point Iroquois we had head wind, and toiled hard till one o'clock at night before we camped. Thursday morning, by eight o'clock, we had arrived safely, thankful to our heavenly Father for his preserving mercy.

SECOND TRIP.

November 13th we left again for Naomikong. Had, as usual, great perplexity in getting men, and every thing in trim for the journey. We had calm most of the way. Thursday and Friday, aided by J. M., nailed the shingles on our mission-house. Two hard days' work, but, by beginning at daylight and working till dark, it was accomplished. We should have returned the next day, but were held by adverse wind. Sabbath we had religious services, among which was the administration of the Lord's supper. We were blessed in waiting upon God, but nothing unusual characterized the meetings. Monday, by eight o'clock at night, we had reached home.

THIRD TRIP.

January 3, 1850, Rev. P. O. Johnson and myself went to visit this station. We rode the first six miles, and stopped over night, and held meeting with several families residing there. Next day, after a snow-shoe walk of twenty-two miles, we arrived at the saw-mill. At night we held meeting with the Waishkee Indians residing here. Saturday we followed a rough trail leading through the woods, most of the way, to reach the mission—distance some eight miles. On our arrival found brother and sister Marksman hard at work making preparations for the Sabbath. Our new mission-house looked very neat and comfortable. We were glad to find such a home in the wilderness, and to share, for a time, in the results of much perplexity and hard toil. We spent the day in visiting among the Indians. Brother Johnson preached at night. To those present it was a time of spiritual good.

Sabbath morning we had a memorable love-feast. The Indians are apt to speak too long in the class meeting or the love-feast. But not so here. Twenty-two spoke in less than an hour. Besides, a full proportion of the time was occupied in singing. Immediately after love-feast we administered the Lord's supper. Twenty-eight communed. Both rooms of the mission-house were filled, and the stairs crowded with children. At an invitation thirteen came forward to unite with the Church. One had been a Roman Catholic—three were children. It was a time of God's power in the congregation; so much so that we felt constrained to dispense with the usual sermon at that hour, and turn it into a prayer meeting. And such was the engagedness of the members and seekers that the meeting lasted till one o'clock, P. M. Like Peter, on the mount of vision, we felt to say, "it is good to be here."

Just now old mother Waishkee arrived, having walked all the way from the saw-mill. Finding that she was too late she turned about for home, to get there, if possible, to attend the meeting at night, at her son's. After getting some refreshment we started for the saw-mill, accompanied by brother Marksman. Just before our arrival we passed the old lady, who was trudging along, evidently very weary. Now we met her youngest son, a youth of some eighteen years, going to meet his mother, bearing in his hand some *shah-gah-mit-ta.* "Well," say you, "what was that?" It was nothing less than some tea, which he brought in the *nee-bish-ah-kick*, or *teapot.* An act this of great kindness to his aged and infirm mother. What a striking evidence of filial affection! But such a mother ought to have loving and dutiful children.*

We met at seven o'clock, P. M., at the chief's. There were about twenty present, mostly Indians. After preaching I administered the Lord's supper to six persons, besides the preachers. The power of God was strikingly manifest. Old sister W. was wonderfully blessed. It was some time before she could sufficiently restrain her sobs and cries to receive

---

*Crœsus, the Lydian king, once inquired of Solon "which of mankind, in all his travels, he had found the most truly happy. 'One Tellus,' replied Solon, 'a citizen of Athens, a very honest and good man, who lived all his days without indigence, had always seen his country in a flourishing condition,' etc. As he flattered himself of being ranked in the second degree of happiness, he asked him, 'who of all those he had seen was next in felicity to Tellus?' Solon answered, 'Cleobis and Biton, of Argos, two brothers, who had left behind them a perfect pattern of fraternal affection, and of respect due from children to their parents. Upon a solemn festival, when their mother, a priestess of Juno, was to go to the temple, the oxen that were to draw her not being ready, the two sons put themselves to the yoke, and drew their mother's chariot thither, which was above five miles distant. All the mothers of the place, filled with admiration, congratulated the priestess on the piety of her sons,'" etc. (Rollin's History, vol. i, pp. 301, 302.) See the account above where this old lady was drawn on a hand-train, about six miles, to meeting by her daughters-in-law.

the cup of blessing. She doubtless felt well paid for having walked sixteen miles to worship the Great Spirit. Monday, after a walk of about thirty miles, as our trail led us, we reached home. Some places passed over ice so rough as to render it extremely severe and difficult crossing. Brother J. bruised his toes badly. But we were safely home, and had much cause for thankfulness.

FOURTH TRIP.

March 29th brother Johnson and myself went again to visit the station at N. What till then was a novelty, we took a sled and two horses. Indeed, it is but rarely that the ice on Lake Superior will admit of this. Some places it was heavy going for the team, on account of a late fall of snow; but before nine o'clock at night we were at Naomikong. We found sister Marksman in poor health.

Saturday was spent in visiting the Indians. They were considerably scattered; had just commenced sugar-making—a late beginning—evidence of the backwardness of the season. We met at night for divine worship. On Sabbath we had love-feast, preaching, and the sacrament of the Lord's supper. The meetings were not so deeply interesting as those before mentioned. We had reason to fear that the enemy had been at work sowing tares among the people. We went over to the saw-mill, and held meeting at night. Returned to the Saut the next day.

RELIGIOUS SERVICES AT THE VILLAGE.

The moral soil here appeared as cold and sterile as the physical. Still we endeavored in the discharge of duty to hope against hope. In pleasant weather, when there was no arrival of mails or steamboats, our meetings were well attended, and were often seasons of interest and profit. But it frequently seemed that the seed sown fell by the wayside, and was devoured by the fowls of the air. Balls, pleasure parties, business, any and every thing else, save the concerns of the soul, attracted the attention and occupied the time of the great mass of the community. As the season advanced our congregations enlarged. During my long absence in the summer the meetings were kept up by brother Johnson. Ministers from abroad often preached to our people during the traveling season.

Sabbath, July 21st, I preached to a very attentive congregation on occasion of the death of Zachary Taylor, late President of the United States, which had occurred on the 9th inst., from the words, "*The fashion of this world passeth away.*"

In connection with other duties, I had charge when at home of an interesting Bible class. In our religious meetings we were favored with mercy drops and gently-distilling grace, if not copious showers. With all our discouragements, we had reason to believe that we were employed in our Master's business, and that our labor was "not in vain in the Lord."

CHAPTER XVI.

TRIP TO SANDY LAKE—SCENES AND INCIDENTS

THURSDAY, May 16th, I took passage on board the propeller Independence to visit the Lake Superior missions. I had as my traveling associate Mr. Sawyer, who was on his way to Bad river as a school-teacher, under the direction of the American Board. Our boat had been altered from a passenger into a freight craft, and was not very comfortable or agreeable for passengers. The mate's room was assigned to us, though in the worst part of the boat to feel the motion. We had, as was too common, annoyances aboard, arising chiefly from drinking and profanity. After we passed *Pointe au Pin* a stiff head wind gave us a very rough and chopped-up sea, and made me quite seasick. We ran into Waishkees Bay, and found shelter. Saturday, 18th, we passed White Fish Point. At four o'clock, P. M., Michipicoton Island was in sight to the north-west, and the Pictured Rocks to the south-west.

Sabbath, 19th. It commenced blowing from the north-west about four o'clock, A. M. At eight o'clock it blew very hard, and got up a very rough sea. I became very sick. Our ship was badly trimmed—too much lading forward. She ran her bows too much under the seas. The captain had designed to make for Grand Island or Presque Isle; but the stern was so much out of water that the boat would not mind her helm. At nine o'clock the storm was increasing, and we were taking in considerable water. Our boat rolled like a log. Stoves, tables, barrels, boxes, trunks, etc., were thrown about in utter confusion. I left my berth, wrapped up in a large quilt, and lay on the floor. In this manner I avoided farther seasickness. At one o'clock, P. M., the boat labored hard and made bad weather. I heard the captain say, in a low tone, "She is running under as fast as she can;" four feet of water in the hold forward. Five horses and four oxen in the bows had a serious time. The horses got loose, and were made fast again with much trouble and risk. The mate was washed under them two or three times. Only one of the oxen survived; the three to leeward actually drowned; and a more pitiable sight I had seldom seen than those three oxen lying dead, side by side. And there they still remained to weigh us down; they could not be removed. More than five tuns of hay were on the upper deck, considerable of which was now thrown overboard. But for this the captain thought we must have gone to the bottom. The pump was worked briskly, and several were kept bailing near the engine. The water had nearly reached the fire. By four o'clock, P. M., the wind began to die away; still we had a heavy sea. We were soon measurably relieved, being sheltered by Manito Island and Point Kewenaw. Before sundown we took supper, or rather breakfast, as it was our first meal for the day; at the same time doubled Point Kewenaw. Evening was delightfully clear, but cold. The storm had passed, and all was stillness and calm. The land of the Point loomed up to our left in grandeur and majesty. The sun bathed his golden plumes in the pure blue element, and disappeared. The light-house from Manito Island shed a soft, clear light, which we saw for miles, till it seemed to sink in the Lake. Meanwhile light from the Copper Harbor light-house was now clearly seen, and now it disappeared, alternately, till we came abreast.

By the erection of those light-houses a great benefit has been conferred on mariners and the traveling public generally. We had once before entered this harbor in the night—a dark night too—when our only beacon was a globe lamp, sent out in a yawl, and placed upon a lone rock in the channel. Such had been the march of improvement in the brief space of a few years, prior to which the cheerful light of the camp fire had served as a beacon to the Indian in his bark canoe, to give him notice of impending danger.

By ten o'clock at night we were all safe within harbor. The holy Sabbath had passed without affording an opportunity for public worship. But seldom had I felt a greater calm within than during this stormy day. How good is it at such times to be able, as the "untutored Indian," only more intelligently,

> "To see God in clouds,
> And hear him in the wind;"

and to feel, at all times, that "underneath are the everlasting arms."

Monday visited Fort Wilkins. Every thing still looked neat and tasteful, but it was nearly deserted. So was also Copper Harbor. Snow was still visible along the shore. We ran into Agate Harbor, and were detained nearly a whole day to take on wood. In the night ran up opposite Eagle river, and at one o'clock, A. M., were aground on the reef. We did not get loose till nearly ten. Stopped some nine hours at the Ontonagon. On the 23d we reached La Pointe in time to dine at the mission of the American Board.

During the afternoon we made arrangements for our coasting voyage. The N. F. Company furnished me with two men and a boat. Mr. Carlton, the blacksmith, from Fond du Lac, was to accompany us as far as his home.

May 24th left La Pointe at six o'clock, A. M., a delightful day, and made a pretty good run. We reached Cranberry river, some forty-six miles from La Pointe, and camped at eight o'clock, P. M.

Saturday, 25th, we arose between three and four o'clock and commenced our journey, hoping to reach Fond du Lac before Sabbath; a long pull, some sixty miles, before us. It rained part of the forenoon.

Had wind from nearly all quarters through the day, and a heavy rolling sea. But by a vigorous effort we had landed at Fond du Lac by half-past twelve o'clock at night, and were under the mission roof. We were much favored in making so quick a trip. Brother Holt and his family were out *nine days* on the same route the fall previous.

Sabbath preached twice to the Indians that came out, few in number, and fewer that seemed to interest themselves in the message of the Gospel. Monday transacted the business connected with the mission, and met the Indians again in council. They appeared much more mellow in their feelings, less haughty and dictatorial than the previous year. Still they had much fault to find about matters so trifling as not to be worth naming.

Tuesday, 28th, was waked very early by the singing of a whippowil. Arose before four o'clock, and left Fond du Lac by half-past six. At seven commenced crossing Grand Portage. My men went ahead on Monday, and carried the things over the Portage. John Street, interpreter at Fond du Lac, accompanied us. By half-past ten we were over the Grand Portage. At twelve we had crossed Knife Portage. Here we dined, gummed our canoe, and left at half-past two, P. M. At seven, P. M., we had ascended the Grand Rapids, and were camped on a beautiful green, near the delightful pine grove which overlooked the Rapids.

At the end of Knife Portage we overtook Mrs. Hughs, daughter of Mr. Oaks, of La Pointe, on her way to the Mississippi. She had lost her husband about a year before, and was moving with her two little fatherless children. She had a fine large canoe, and two excellent *voyageurs*. We had traveled in company for the afternoon, and now our tents stood close together, and a bright blazing fire between, answering for us all. There noted in my journal: "I feel great peace within in waiting on God, and great confidence in his blessing on the work of my hands. Have the assurance that God is with me, and what more can I desire? Only a greater manifestation of his presence. O for grace to love and serve him more!"

Wednesday, 29th, we were up at four o'clock, breakfasted, and were ready to leave before six. Made a fine run for the day. The two canoes kept in company, and in the evening we camped together, a short distance up the East Savan river. Our men had worked hard, and we pitched our tents in good season to be rested for the morrow. It had been a cold, windy day, and was followed by a clear, frosty night. But all was cheerfulness about our bright camp fire. Just at nightfall a little bird was singing most sweetly near us. The frogs were making the air vocal with their homely song. The stars began to light up the heavens—and how rich those countless globes of light in the transparency of a northern sky! All we saw and heard conspired to declare "the glory of God," and to show forth "his handy-work."

Thursday, 30th, we were ready to leave our resting-place by five o'clock, A. M. A delightful day. We proceeded steadily, but slowly, up the *Savan*, the most serpentine river I ever saw. Now we would go to the right, then to the left; now the direction we had come, and then the contrary, going a long distance to gain a little. But by noon we had reached the head of the Savan river, and were crossing the Savan Portage. By three o'clock, P. M., we were at Sandy Lake, found a canoe, and by making a sail out of a quilt, we sailed over, and at four o'clock we were happy to meet our missionaries once more, and find all well. They were taken by surprise at our getting along so early.

During the evening a goodly number of the Indians came out to see me. Among these was an old woman, who had renounced heathenism the winter before and embraced Christianity. She said that she was very glad that *No-she-sha*, that is, her grandson, as she called me, had come to see her. She went by the name of *No-ko*, that is, grandmother. It is an abbreviation of *No-ko-mis.*

Friday we observed as a day of fasting and prayer. In the morning visited a poor sick Indian, who was near death's door. He could say but little. The Indian medicine man had performed over him for some time, but brother Spates had told him plainly of the wickedness of these heathen rites, and he had turned him off. Made a few visits in the afternoon. At four o'clock, P. M., we called the people together for worship. Quite a congregation assembled, to whom I preached.

WAR-DANCE.

Previous to our meeting a large company had collected in another place, and were engaged in a war-dance. They were almost naked, and were painted most grotesquely. Their heads were dressed with painted feathers and trinkets. One danced in a buffalo skin with horns on his head. Four or five were drumming while the others danced. Those gymnastics were vulgar and most revoltingly unseemly. They danced around a grave in the open air. Occasionally they would yell like savages; then they would sit down and smoke, and at intervals one would make a speech. Before our meeting had progressed far several of those wild painted creatures came in to hear the word of the Lord.

This war-dance was gotten up by some of the Indians who seemed determined to go to war with the *Sioux*, who a short time previous had murdered some fourteen of the Chippeways at Stillwater, and one near Sauk Rapids. This massacre was committed under the influence of intoxication. Since this horrible affair three or four of the Chippeways had killed a Sioux in the vicinity of Fort Snelling.

Saturday I preached again in the forenoon. The congregation was not large. I notified them that I would meet with them in the afternoon to hear from them about matters and things which concerned them.

Before the meeting brothers S. and J. were down among the lodges. A company of Indians, wrapped in their dirty blankets and with their long pipes, passed by. They were about to smoke over some important subject upon which a decision must be made. We soon found out what was to pay, as a result of the subject discussed. Now several Indians were driving the Government oxen; many others were standing and looking on. There was one running with a gun. He fired and the ox dropped. They gathered around like a drove of hungry wolves; took large stones and beat the ox in the head till they had killed him. In a very short time he was cut into pieces and in process of cooking. The ox-killing business kept the Indians back from the meeting till late. But at length we had a pretty good turn-out, and an interview of considerable interest.

The old chief was not present, although he had promised the day before to attend. He was a weak, fickle-minded creature, and of but little account, unless it was to discuss the merit of something to be appropriated to the stomach from the race of bipeds or quadrupeds.

The position taken by *I-ah-be-twa-we-dung*, the speaker, and who, in point of talent, stood at the head of the band, produced a good effect, and is worthy of record. He first addressed himself to the Indians, substantially as follows: "I want to be civilized. Who knows how soon we are going to be removed away from this place? Perhaps I will be in one place, and my wife in another, and my children in another. Some of us go to listen to the missionaries, and when we go home we say, who are these men who come to talk to us? I do not care whether you laugh at me or not, I am determined to pursue a different course."

Martin Luther made a short speech, addressed to me, in which he expressed his thanks that I had been preserved to meet with them once more. He said that "he was poor, but he was not going to do as the Indians at Fond du Lac—want the missionary to pay him for coming to meeting." He said, "Our missionary has too much to do to be left alone; he ought to have more help. I hope you will send somebody to assist him." Martin was one of our Christian Indians, and a worthy man. On one occasion I felt myself rebuked by his piety. He had assisted in carrying our things across the portage. We had dined together, and were about to separate. Martin proposed that we should pray first, which would not have been done had he not been thus mindful. Truly religion is the same wherever found. Those that love God love the atmosphere of prayer.

After he sat down *I-ah-be-twa-we-dung* arose, and made a speech that displayed considerable eloquence. But to realize its power the man must be seen and heard. He had nothing on but his moccasins, and an old dirty blanket drawn around his body, with his arms and shoulders bare. He advanced with a firm step, and gave me his hand. He commenced:

"My friend, I want to say a few words. I am going to speak very plainly. What I say does not come out of the mouth of a chief. I look behind my back, and see what I have done. I am going to turn over a new leaf. I am very poor. I have no shirt but the black shirt. I shall not ask those who have no shirts to go with me.* I am determined to go with them that have shirts, [the missionaries and other Christians.] I shall look to that stove, [pointing to the stove, as one of the fruits of civilization.] If the Great Spirit is willing, he will receive me; if not, he will not. I agree with my brother that has just spoken, that our missionary has not had sufficient help. I hope that the time will come when some of my children will be able to write such a letter as you read from my cousin, [Peter Ringing Sky, who was then attending school at the Albion Seminary, Michigan.] This is all I have to say. You may depend on my word."

After the meeting *I-ah-be-twa-we-dung* came into the mission-house. I gave him a shirt. I told him I gave him that to cover his body, and I hoped that he would pray to the Lord Jesus that he would grant him the robe of righteousness to cover his soul. I conversed with him also with reference to his being baptized and married in a Christian manner.

Sabbath, June 2. Early in the morning had an

---

* The idea here intended is, probably, that he should not select such for his associates.

interview with I. and his wife. She was willing to be married, but wanted to wait and listen awhile to the missionary before she was fully prepared to renounce heathenism. She thought that she should soon follow her husband; was willing that he and the children should be baptized. She had been a great heathen—a medicine woman, and one who initiated others into those heathen rites. The concessions she here made, and the steps she took, were quite an advance for her. About 10 o'clock we got the Indians out for love-feast—it was an unusually interesting time. God's power was displayed in our midst. The little company of witnesses for the Savior spoke very feelingly.

It was after noon before we met for public worship. At the commencement I married *I-ah-be-twa-we-dung*, and baptized him and his children. Named him Benjamin F. Tefft. His children, the three present, which were baptized, we named Julia, Abby, and Caroline, the last two after my wife and daughter. Then read the ten commandments. In the evening we met for the sacrament of the Lord's supper. No formal sermon was preached in connection with any of these services, but the explanations and remarks interspersed through the whole amounted to about the same thing. This last season was a very precious one to all who knew any thing about experimental religion. The services were closed and the benediction pronounced, but no one made any motion to leave the house. They remained, as if waiting for something more. We sung a hymn or two, during which time B., one who had been reclaimed from a backslidden state, seemed overpowered with the presence of God, cried aloud, and got down on his knees to weep and pray. We then had a season of prayer together, and it was a time of melting mercy. When the Indians commenced to leave the house the Christian ones came and gave the missionaries their hand. The expression was repeated to each other, *Ong-wam-e-ze*, that is, *be courageous.* I.'s wife brought the little children I had baptized to shake hands with me, the eldest first, and so on. She took the infant's hand and put it into my hand, as a token that it now belonged to us. She did not offer her own hand because she had not yet been baptized, and she seemed to think she was either unworthy, or had no right to do so.

Martin Luther went and took her by the hand, and exhorted her not to let her husband and children leave her behind. Then he took I-ah-be-twa-we-dung by the hand, and gave him a most affectionate exhortation to steadfastness.

During all the exercises of the day a number of wild Indians crowded into the house, and looked on with astonishment. It began to appear to us as if the Lord had commenced a very gracious work, and was about to open a great door of usefulness in that wilderness after so long sowing the seed.

Just before our last meeting a company of young men, stripped, painted, and decorated with feathers, bells, etc., about their heads and arms, were playing ball.* Such are the strange contrasts constantly meeting the missionary. How ignorant, how depraved and wretched are those poor creatures without the Gospel! Their only hope, their only salvation, is in this. As they are, they are literally "without Christ and without hope in the world."

Before taking leave of Sandy Lake it may be well to name the deep afflictions through which the Indians had passed the previous winter. It was anticipated the year before that the very high waters would destroy the rice crop, and, if so, many of the Indians must starve. This had now become matter of affecting history. In fact, FAMINE, with its terrible disclosures, was upon them. Brother and sister Spates both wrote us touching accounts of this calamity. In view of this fate as approaching, the missionary had ordered a larger supply of provisions than usual. He had been blessed the previous season with a fine potato crop. By this means multitudes were fed, and, doubtless, kept from starving. Brother S. wrote me that "from ten to fifty a day came to them to get something to keep soul and body together." He said that "the people came to them for food as the Egyptians did to Joseph." Many Indians from the far north came to Sandy Lake—some unable to reach there without help. The sights which daily met the eyes of the missionaries were deeply affecting. What

* The game called *baggattaway;* that which was so artfully played at Mackinaw when the British were massacred.

a record would it make if the sufferings of this poor neglected race were only told! As an evidence of their distress, some of those farther in the interior were driven to *cannibalism*, in its most shocking forms, to satisfy the cravings of nature.

Rev. J. P. Bardwell, Agent of the A. M. A., writing from Oberlin, Ohio, November 6, 1852, to the Commissioner of Indian Affairs, Washington, D. C., mentions a most startling fact as having occurred west of Cass Lake, the winter to which we refer. See Annual Report of the Commissioner of Indian Affairs, 1852, p. 51. He says: "An Indian, with his wife, two daughters, and a son-in-law, killed and ate fifteen persons, and most of them were their own children and grandchildren. Many of the principal men among them begin to realize that they must change their habits or perish, and are disposed to do what they can to improve their condition."

CHAPTER XVII.

RETURN VOYAGE, AND THE MISSIONS EN ROUTE.

JUNE 3d, Monday, parted with the missionaries and Indians at Sandy Lake, and were retracing our steps across the portage. It had rained Sabbath evening, and we found the bushes along the trail very wet. But after a wet and tiresome walk, we were over the portage, where we had concealed our canoe among the bushes, and by one o'clock, P. M., were ready to get aboard. We glided, or rather paddled, down the river and entered the St. Louis long before night, and camped several miles below.

Tuesday we were up by half-past three o'clock, and started. By adding our strength to the force of the swift current, we made great speed. We breakfasted near *La Rivier Acluta*, so named from a Frenchman of this name, who, it is said, once broke his canoe here. This is a considerable stream, and for some distance before it enters the St. Louis dashes and foams madly among the rocks, over extended rapids. Soon after breakfast it became very foggy, commenced to rain hard and continued till in the afternoon. The men were drenched, and our things, except such as I could shelter with my India rubber cloak. But the rain did not stop us. We reached the Grand Portage, where we dined, and then addressed ourselves to the arduous task of *packing* the rest of the way. Instead of having a canoe or boat, at the end of the portage, as we usually did, we were forced to clamber over a succession of high hills, some of them so steep and muddy withal, that, but for the aid of shrubs and bushes, we could hardly have ascended or descended them. But, rain, and mud, and hills in the opposition, by four o'clock, P. M., we were at Fond du Lac.

At the previous annual conference the Mission Committee determined that, unless "the signs of the times" were decidedly more encouraging at Fond du Lac, we must pull up stakes there, with a view to extending the work to *Mille Lac.* The Indians, from that point, were calling loudly on us for help. A good report was brought from that band, showing their anxious desire to be Christianized. This place is distant about one hundred miles from Sandy Lake, and must be reached thence by a chain of lakes. In view of this opening, and the favorable indications at Sandy Lake, we thought best to have brother Holt remove to Sandy Lake, to be associated with brother Spates, and, in connection with the work there, if possible, to visit and explore the ground at Mille Lac. The necessary arrangements were now made, and brother Holt and family were to leave soon.

Wednesday, 5th, afternoon, parted with our friends at F. Although the river, to the Entry, is very rapid, most of the way, a stiff wind blowing from the east caused a heavy sea to set back into the river, and we had to pull hard to get down stream. We found a fine place to camp near the Entry, sheltered by trees and elevated ground—from the wind—a large log to build our fire against, and so situated as not to smoke us in the tent. Were quite comfortable on that lone and desolate shore. The following night a drenching rain poured upon us, but we kept most of our things dry by means of our tent.

Thursday, 6th, we were wind-bound, and no telling for how long a time. Hard wind blowing from the eastward, having the rake of the whole Lake. It may be imagined how the mighty waves spent their fury against our shore.

REFLECTIONS PENNED ON THIS WIND-BOUND COAST.

"The rain has ceased and the weather is clearing up. The air is cool, but we are not troubled with flies and musketoes, and with a good fire we can be very comfortable. I have read several chapters in my Bible this morning, and have read through Hedding on the Discipline. Find enough to do when camped, to fill up, profitably, all my time in reading, writing, etc.; so that I am enabled, at such seasons, to advance in knowledge, and, I trust, in grace, and a preparation for usefulness in public. I often enjoy such seasons of seclusion from the world, in which I can commune with God and my own soul.

"I was thinking this morning that a person wind-bound on a desolate coast resembles a person bound for heaven, while navigating the dangerous sea of life. How often does he meet with opposing winds, when he can do nothing but 'stand still and see the salvation of God.' In the midst of a vile world, which is no friend to grace, he often finds himself standing almost alone and forsaken, with wind and tide against him. But his trust is in God. Like the skillful voyager, he holds himself *ready to make the best of every hinderance.* He keeps every inch of ground he has gained. In the calm, or when wind and waves are not too strong, he plies his oars, and when the breeze is fair spreads his sails, rides over the proudest billows, and bids the world adieu. When we are resting in camp we are acquiring strength for more arduous labor. And often when the child of God seems, to himself, to be accomplishing little or nothing for the world, he is, in reality, doing the most important work. The *trial of faith* is as necessary as any thing else to the Christian. While thus situated I often think of my dear companion and the little ones God has given us. But they give me no uneasy concern. I confidently leave them in the hands of God, believing that he will do that which is best, both for them and me. Here then is my rock, my strength."

By six o'clock, the same evening, we were enabled to proceed on our journey, and by twelve o'clock at night had reached the River Brule. Had sailing most of the way, but clouds were dark and threatening—thundered to the north and sprinkled, but the storm went round us. Here we found three tents. One, the Indian Agent, on his way to the Mississippi, to aid the Governor of Minnesota territory in locating the new agency. One tent was Dr. Norwood's, of whom mention has before been made. The other tent belonged to Rev. Messrs. Hall and Wheeler, of the American Board. They were on an exploring tour, to look up a site for a new mission, in view of the anticipated removal of the Lake Superior Indians.

Friday morning my veteran *voyageur*, *Souvra*, called us up about three o'clock. In a few minutes we parted with our friends, and were on our way for La Pointe. A very hot day. Wind followed us most of the day, and bore us along, so that we rowed but little. We arrived at the mission at La Pointe just before dark, having coasted sixty-nine miles. We did not anticipate reaching here before the next day noon. When I got out of the boat I staggered like a drunken man, and was quite dizzy, having been confined to our small craft from the time we breakfasted. I then noted, "In being so remarkably blessed I can but own the good hand of my heavenly Father, who has made this to me, thus far, one of the most prosperous coasting trips I have ever experienced."

Spent the Sabbath here, and was permitted to preach twice to Rev. Mr. Hall's congregation.

Two Indians had just brought Mr. Oaks from the Ontonagon in a bark canoe. Through Mr. Oaks I engaged a passage with them when they should return. They were to leave early the following Monday morning; but, when the time came, they baffled and disappointed me, and it was quite late before I could stir them out of their lodges. At length they came with the canoe to the mission dock. I saw that we were to be burdened with company in no way desirable. An old dirty woman was in the bow of our canoe. Another small canoe was in company, with an Indian, his wife and child. This woman was a daughter of the elderly woman. It was useless to remonstrate. I had paid Mr. O. for my passage, and he had settled with the Indians. I was a mere passenger—had been detained too long already—it was "neck or naught." So I took my place in the center of the canoe, determined to make the best of it. These Indians were related to my men, and were bound for Iron river. The sun was scorching hot. It was two o'clock when we arrived at Bad river, where we took a cold lunch. Here we found that our company had no sign of any thing in the provision line. Along this fine sand beach our young man towed the canoe. When it came to rowing he seemed so intolerably lazy that he could scarcely move. Meanwhile our hero of the other canoe was trying his luck at fishing for trout. He caught three. We took supper at the Montreal river. The Lake was calm—scarcely a ripple on the surface. We traveled all night, and made pretty good headway. I tried to sleep part of the night, but my position was so uncomfortable that I could only doze a little.

Tuesday, 11th, early in the morning, we passed

Black river. About daybreak wind sprung up in our favor. We breakfasted at Presque Isle, gummed our canoe, and were just ready to start, when a canoe with Indians came ashore. They had been to Ontonagon, and were returning to Bad river, freighted, as we soon found out, with whisky. I did not perceive this till I saw the company into which I had fallen drinking. They concealed the bottles under their blankets. All I could do, without using violence, was to remonstrate with them. This had the good effect, at least, to keep my two men from drinking much; and even the man in the other canoe made out to steer his canoe when not attached to ours. Part of the day we had pretty good sailing, and, as his canoe was small and he had no sail, he must be kept along by being lashed to ours. But they kept the old woman in the bow of our canoe drunk all day. At times she waxed eloquent, and talked to her children; then she would sing according to heathen custom. Every little while she must have something more to drink. I pleaded with them not to give it to her; but her son said, "*Kit-e-mah-ge-ze*"—"*Poor*—a poor old woman." I told him that would make her poorer still. To this he replied, "*Mah-no;*" that is, never mind. Then his wife, who sat in reach of her, in the bow of the other canoe, and had the bottle in her keeping, would pour out some in a tin-pan—sometimes in a small wooden bowl—and hand it to her. Lest she should not get every drop, she would turn it up the second time. Then she would say, "*Me sah ewe, me sah ewe, me sah ewe*"—"That is enough, that is enough, that is enough." Poor drunken heathen, she did not realize but that every want was supplied. At one time she sung a kind of song over and over in the following strain. I can not give a literal translation; it was simply an expression of her joyful emotions under the inspiration of the fire-water.

> "*Me-sah neen-ga-to-yaun,*
> *Me-sah neen mah-mo-yaun.*"

I felt much concerned lest all the Indians in the company should get drunk, and then, if we should even escape danger on the Lake, I would be at their mercy on the land. I had no fear of their injuring me personally; but they might prevent me from going on. As we rounded the Porcupine Mountains, and were making for Iron river, our Indian of the other canoe became very merry and remarkably garrulous. He kept up an incessant talking, and singing, and drumming on an empty tin-pan.

At one o'clock, P. M., we landed at Iron river. But I was far from feeling easy. I knew there was whisky here. Here was the home of my men and their friends. They had been out all the previous night, and would gladly have remained here during the night. But I would not hear to it for a moment. I insisted that we should be off immediately. They promised me to go soon. It was two hours before I could get them started. Had we gone immediately, we might have sailed with a good wind to Ontonagon;

but the wind had died down, and now we must row and tow. But we were now rid of our troublesome company, and, what was better, we had no whisky aboard. Went a few miles and camped. I have, probably, never suffered in my feelings more in any one day of my life, than during this most trying time. Let me be any where else than out at sea, in a frail bark canoe, with drunken Indians. This danger will be more apparent a little farther on. We are not done yet with the results of this whisky drinking.

We arrived at Ontonagon early the next morning. Called at Mr. Beezer's, and what was my surprise to learn that the wife of Mr. C. C. Douglas was a corpse in the house! She was taken sick several miles back in the woods—was brought on a bier to the mouth of the river by hand. But no help could be obtained; the summons was imperative, and she must go. She left her husband and an infant to feel the deep pangs of human sorrow. I found Mr. L. Hanna's family here, and spent part of the time with them. But for them the place would not have seemed like home. Preached at night, on the subject of the cross of Christ, to a pretty good assembly. The people listened attentively.

On account of the crowd of visiting friends at Mr. H.'s I was obliged to find lodging at a public house. But such a night! Several rough fellows were drinking, swearing, dancing, and singing, all in perfect tumult. My bedroom was in close proximity to all this disorder and wickedness. In the house adjoining was the deceased wife of Mr. D. What evidences here of the most confirmed depravity! And what but the intoxicating agent could render men so lost to every sense of shame, not to say principle and feeling of virtue!

Thursday, 13th, I was waiting the arrival of a boat to go to Eagle river. Spent most of my leisure in writing.

THE FATAL CUP.

The same morning a small boat and two Indians arrived from La Pointe. They were out on the Lake the same day on which we came in contact with the Indians having whisky. They also fell in with them, and, as might be expected, were induced to drink. One of their number, whose name was Green, became so intoxicated that his companions could not keep him still in the boat. He upset the boat and was drowned. They were about half a mile from shore, near Black river. The two surviving men got on the boat and floated ashore with it bottom upward. As we afterward learned, young Green had affectionate parents and friends at La Pointe, whose hearts must have been wrung with anguish by this painful intelligence. Some one at Ontonagon let those Indians have this liquor, and took their money. A judgment day will tell the whole story.

About nine o'clock at night the Napoleon came in, and in two hours and a half I left the Ontonagon for Eagle river. The next day, Friday, arrived before breakfast. Walked to the Cliff afterward, and found brother Day quite unwell, scarcely able to walk about. Things about the Mine appeared to be in rather a confused state. Several persons had left, and some were about leaving. Spent most of the afternoon at the North American. Accompanied Mr. Kelsey to witness the removal of the remains of his recently-deceased wife. They were now exhumed and sent below on the Independence.

Saturday made a few visits—spent the day at the Cliff, and preached in the evening. Sabbath preached and administered the sacrament in the new chapel built by the Company. Had a class meeting in the afternoon, and a missionary meeting at night. The meetings were well attended, and we trust profitable. Though things here looked unpromising, there was the germ of something good to come. Some of our best members had left.

On Saturday two men arrived from Kewawenon. This was providential for me. I prevailed on them to wait and accompany me, as they had a boat at the head of Torch Lake. Monday morning we left, and walked sixteen miles to Torch Lake. The sun shone very hot, and the musketoes were very annoying. We had reached the Lake by half-past one o'clock, P. M., much fatigued. The boat had lain on the dry sand beach, and leaked badly when put into the water. It kept me bailing considerable of the time. About sundown we reached the mouth of Portage river; stopped at Mr. Sheldon's long enough to eat a bowl of bread and milk—a great treat, and the most I had eaten for the day. Again we were in the boat making our way for the Methodist mission. It was two o'clock at night before we arrived. Found all as well as could be expected, but the deeply-devoted and amiable sister Barnum was still wasting away with lingering consumption. Brother Crane had buried his youthful companion soon after his arrival at the mission. Our missionaries were called to drain the cup of sorrow, but a good work had been going on in the Church, and thus was their cup again filled with gladness.

Wednesday, 19th, we met at 11 o'clock, A. M., in our new church, which had recently been completed. The brethren had delayed occupying it till my arrival. We now had the pleasure of dedicating it to the worship of the living God. It was a refreshing time to our souls. Our new house was neat, commodious, for the place, and an honor to our mission. It was worth about $550.

At three o'clock, P. M., we met the Indians to consult about their temporal matters. The principal topic was in relation to turning over to them the lands bought by the Missionary Society. This I was authorized to do if it should be thought best. But there were circumstances that served to render it unadvisable to do so at this time. I advised them to let the Missionary Society still retain the title, as the safest course for them for the present—told them that it would make no difference as to their occupying or using them. To this they all readily agreed. John Southwind said:

"I am getting old and may die suddenly, and my son is young, and it may be, that, if my land was in my own hands, it might be lost. I am thankful for what the Missionary Society has done for us in purchasing the land."

After several had spoken briefly, David King, the chief, said, in substance:

"I wish to say a few words. I have very little mind, and know but little. The Indians are just like little children; they know but little till they are instructed. I may be told what is for my good, and may see differently. It may be after the Indians are well trained they will understand better. If the Indians only knew what you have done for them, they would be very thankful. The missionaries came among us when we were heathens, and have been teaching us how to live. And now we are just beginning to live. But the Indians are very poor. To give you an example—if a little child cries and is hungry, we give it something to eat. Now, the good people, the Missionary Society, have bought us some land, which they allow us to keep and replace the money when we get able. We have not the money to do this now, but we hope the time will come when we can replace it all. I am very thankful for what has been done for us."

Not a word of fault or complaint was uttered about the missionaries, or any thing else, save a little misunderstanding between them and two persons who had married into the band, and wanted to secure claims among them.

At seven o'clock, P. M., we met again for religious worship. The people were out as if it had been the Sabbath. I preached to them with much freedom. The whole congregation praised God aloud in singing, and yet there did not seem to be a discordant note. Several were deeply affected during the meeting.

Thursday morning we had love-feast and the sacrament of the Lord's supper. It was a most melting and precious time. We closed by singing a parting hymn, when the people all passed before the altar, and shook hands with the missionaries, and with each other. Seldom have I witnessed a more affecting scene.

Afternoon parted with the brethren and friends at K., never expecting to see them all again in this world. Accompanied by brother R. C. Crane and William Bass, crossed over to the mouth of the Portage river. We were kindly entertained by the family of Mr. Sheldon. The musketoes were almost insufferable. Friday we reached the head of Torch Lake about noon, and, after a fatiguing walk over the trail, and a well-fought battle with our mortal insect enemies, we were at the Cliff Mine, at six o'clock, P. M. Saturday went to the Lake and dined with Mr. Write's family. Afternoon, *via* Eagle Harbor, walked to the North-West Mine, distant from the Cliff seventeen miles. Found here my old friend D. D. Brockway and family, from Copper Harbor. Mr. B. was now Agent of the Mine. Here spent the Sabbath, and preached twice to a very respectable congregation. In the evening returned to Eagle Harbor, about five miles, and stopped for the night at Mr. Boden's.

Before we were up, Monday morning, the Napoleon came into the Harbor, on her way to the Saut. I was thankful to get aboard, with my face once more turned toward home. On our way down we touched at Carp river—now Marquette—ran into Grand Island Harbor to wood, and on Wednesday, the 26th June, before twelve o'clock, was permitted, through much mercy, to meet my family and find all well.

CHAPTER XVIII.

BRIEF STATEMENT OF THE CONDITION OF THE MISSIONS IN THE DISTRICT—REMINISCENCES PLEASING AND SAD.

THE Indian Mission district enjoyed a year of prosperity after deducting all our losses from various causes beyond the control of the missionaries. At the extreme posts of Fond du Lac and Sandy Lake, we had never been able to count much on members. Fond du Lac returned six Indian members, four less than at the previous conference. Sandy Lake numbered, the year before, sixteen, now returned but five—nine out of the sixteen were on trial. To any one acquainted with those stations and the adverse influences which had been at work, these fluctuations will not appear surprising.

At Kewawenon a good revival had been in progress during the winter. Fifteen, as a result, were added to the society; but by deaths, removals, and the necessary exercise of Discipline, the number returned to conference was fifty-six, the same as the year before.

It was intended that the brethren at Kewawenon should visit the miners in the vicinity of Ontonagon, and also at Carp river. In the extreme ill health of sister Barnum, this part of the work, for the winter months, was committed to brother Crane. He traveled on foot during the winter nearly seven hundred miles; visited the Ontonagon twice, and spent some time at the various locations; went once to the Cliff Mine and twice to Carp river. At his first visit to this last place, things looked very dark and unpromising. He received three persons into society on trial, as a result of his efforts. The next time a most gracious work broke out, resulting in the happy conversion of about twenty-five or more, and the formation of a flourishing class. At the time brother C. wrote me a detailed account of his efforts and the success attending them. I give here an extract or two as evincing the character of this work, and also the deep sorrows of the missionary, to which allusion has been made before:

"O what a work the Lord has wrought here! This wilderness, brother, doth bloom. Our class now numbers twenty-three, and the most of them are bold to tell what a dear Savior they have found. O, they are happy in God's pardoning love; and others are seeking the Savior! Very different the atmosphere now to what it was four weeks ago. Difficulties have been settled that could not have been otherwise.

"You see, brother, from what I have written, that the Lord is with us. And, indeed, if he were not my stay and staff, O, how could I endure the *deep, deep, heart-rending* afflictions through which I have been called to pass, in being bereft of my dear wife, who was permitted to stay with me so short a time! O my brother, my feelings are indescribable! I could not tell them were I to attempt. But you appreciate them in a measure, and I have your prayers and sympathy. My dear Minerva was with me only three weeks after we reached *L'Anse;* then the Savior called her. She bade me farewell, and the angels quickly flew with her thrice happy spirit to a happier and more congenial clime. I think I can see in the removal of my wife the workings of my heavenly Father's hand. Perhaps it was the only means of the salvation of many souls at *L'Anse*, and, for aught I know, at this place too. My Lord is a God of providence, and I have always endeavored to trust him as such."

For the reader to appreciate those labors and sufferings, he must follow the missionary through a wintery wilderness, and for five or six successive nights camp down with him in his lone and comfortless resting-place. In years yet to come those primitive toils to plant the Gospel on that wild and desolate shore will be duly appreciated. The time draweth nigh.

At Eagle river but twelve members were returned—two less than the previous year, owing to removals. The mining population was very floating.

At the Saut Ste. Marie mission, with all the disadvantages arising from the removal of the Indians to Naomikong, and other causes, the number returned was fifty-six, an increase of four members. The Minutes show for the district a decrease in the Indian membership of eleven, and an increase in the white membership of twenty-six.

The district contributed, during the year, $148.85 for the missionary cause—an average of more than ninety-one cents per member, counting the Indians. But it must be remembered that they were not called on for any of this. Divided among *forty-eight* paying members, it averages $3.10 each. Besides the district raised $31.80 for Sunday schools. It numbered 5 Sunday schools, 141 scholars, 490 volumes in library, 2 Bible classes—took 12 Sunday School Advocates. These facts go to show a healthy state of our societies, and that the missionaries endeavored to care for all the interests of religion and Methodism.

"*Be not forgetful to entertain strangers, for thereby some have entertained angels unawares.*" While living on this great thoroughfare we often realized what it meant to comply with the apostle's precept, whether we were always so favored as to find our guests *angels* or not. In one instance we had a striking illustration of the text at the head of this. Brother John Peterson, of Ninth and Arch streets, Philadelphia, on his way to visit Lake Superior, had arrived at the Saut, and put up at a public house. He had invited a special friend, an experienced Methodist minister of the same city, Rev. A. Atwood, to accompany him at his expense. Mr. Atwood had left home in poor health, and crossing the lakes had aggravated his complaint, which he feared, if not soon checked, would terminate in cholera. We opened our house, and took him in, and would gladly have kept brother Peterson also, but he refused our invitation. He left brother Atwood in our care, and proceeded to Lake Superior. We did the best we could with such accommodations as our little domicile could furnish—homely at best. Brother Atwood could hardly find terms sufficiently expressive of his gratitude; thought he should have died had he been left at the tavern. The simple means used were blessed, and he began gradually to improve. After an absence of about a week brother Peterson returned, and was much rejoiced at the evident improvement of his friend and companion. Before taking leave of the Saut he sent us *ten dollars* by the hand of brother Atwood. After this he came and took tea with us. While seated in the parlor he took out some loose bills from his pocket, and remarked, "I think I have a little more loose change than I shall need for traveling expenses," and passed them over to me, requesting me to accept them. On opening them I found them to amount to *twenty-five dollars*. Such generosity was embarrassing; but it was shown with such earnest good will as seemed to say that it must be so. He stepped into the dining-room, and, on bidding my wife farewell, left a *five dollar* gold piece in her hand. He had previously presented me with a very handsome pocket map of the United States. He gave Carrie a gold dollar and little Henry a half dollar. So far as our experience is concerned, this instance of generosity is unique. Our liberal donor afforded us help in a time of need. If it be more blessed to give than to receive, he received the greater blessing. Our most fervent prayer was that God would abundantly reward the cheerful giver. Should this incident come under the notice of those to whom it relates, they will please pardon the liberty I have taken with their names.

August 16th found me on board the steamer London, *en route* to attend the annual conference. We had a rough time in crossing Lake Huron. We lay at anchor most of the day, Sunday, under an island in the vicinity of Thunder Bay. The Sabbath passed away quietly. I preached once to those aboard, and Rev. Peter Jacobs, the Indian preacher, who had spent the last thirteen years at Hudson's Bay, and was just returning to Canada, closed the services with a very interesting account of his conversion, life, and labors.

We arrived at Detroit on Monday, about nine o'clock at night. Tuesday we spent in attending to business in the city. The same evening we took boat for Sandusky City, Ohio; thence by railroad went to Tiffin City, and thence to visit an aged mother in Crawford county, now pressed down with a weight of infirmities. Here I preached several times, and met with many old friends and acquaintances. I preached once in the elegant new church in Tiffin City, which had supplanted the old brick, in which some of my most notable boyhood hours had been spent. Every thing here had changed. Twenty-one years had passed and gone since mother, with her six children, had been ferried across the Sandusky river in a log canoe, to take up their residence in Tiffin, after the recent death of a dear father, which had occurred in Licking county. Then Tiffin was a small county town, much of it situated among the stumps and logs, and much of the surrounding country a dense wilderness; now a city—a teěming population, and all the evidences of thrift and progress. But many of the old familiar faces were not to be seen. A brother H., under whose roof I had spent more than five years, was of that number. Death had aimed at them his unerring darts, and they had fallen. I should exceed the limit within which these stray leaves should fall, if I were to pen here the vivid boyhood scenes that rushed before me, and were uneffaceably daguerreotyped upon my mind. Thus much by the way.

From Tiffin I proceeded to Adrian, Michigan, and spent a Sabbath with old friends there; thence repaired to Albion, the seat of the conference, which commenced the next Wednesday, September 5th, and closed on the 10th. The session was one of much interest to me, as such seasons have almost invariably been.

From the seat of the conference we went to Detroit, where we procured our winter supplies for the missions, and were again accompanied by several of the missionaries on our way to the Saut.

September 20th landed on M'Knight's wharf, at the Saut, and was instantly hailed by Carrie, whose first expression was that her little brother was very sick. This was to me the first announcement, and found its way like an arrow to my heart. I was soon by his couch—but what a change! The evidences were too apparent to be mistaken—death was doing his mysterious work. About the time of my arrival he became unconscious; he did not know me. Four days and nights of nearly sleepless anxiety had passed, and some heavenly messenger came and kissed away his infant breath, and on golden pinions bore his unsinning spirit up to the bosom of its God. Could it be that our sweet Henry had been snatched so suddenly away? We could hardly realize it, and yet we knew it was a stern reality. We had lost friends before—the dearest friends—but no more tender cords had ever been entwined about our hearts than those which bound us to this dear boy. Carrie's heart was nearly broken, and her eyes were turned into channels of grief and sorrow. But while the stroke fell so heavily upon us, we could but realize that the chastening rod was in a Father's hand. Our soul submissively responded, "The Lord gave, and the Lord hath taken away, and blessed be the name of the Lord."

During those trying hours we had with us brother and sister Barnum and brother Stacey, bound for Kewawenon; and brother and sister Benson, on their way to the Eagle River mission. Brother Barnum preached the funeral, and wrote a note addressed to Dr. Durbin, which was published in the Missionary Advocate. The following is an extract, with the editor's—Dr. Durbin's, I suppose—note of kind symathy with us in our affliction:

"'*Ye know not what shall be on the morrow.*'—Brother Pitezel very unexpectedly found his little son, an interesting child, a little less than two years old, sick. Disease, congestion of the brain. All efforts of physicians, and fond parents, and kind friends proved unavailing; and on the 24th, at half-past eight o'clock, P. M., he left us, and took his exit to the world of spirits. The parents feel their affliction deeply, as little Henry Eugene was an only son; but they have grace in their affliction to say, 'The Lord gave, and the Lord hath taken away, and blessed be the name of the Lord.'*

"Brother Steele and family have just arrived.

"Yours, in the Gospel,

"NELSON BARNUM.

*"We are afflicted with our dear brother Pitezel, having traveled the same road four different times. Next to the precious word of God, we commend to him and his bereaved companion the perusal of the 637th and 639th hymns in our New Collection.—EDITOR."

Brother Salmon Steele, who had just arrived with his family, had been passing through the furnace of affliction. Death had made a sure aim at one of his own dear friends. Himself and several of his family looked like walking shadows when they landed. They had come to take charge of the station at Naomikong, and were with us about a week before going to their new home. In the midst of our afflictions so many active duties constantly pressed upon us, that we had little time to indulge in gloomy apprehensions, had we even been tempted to do so. I made this note on the 1st of November:

"For two months I have made no record in my journal. They have been eventful months, but filled with active duties. To-day I preached the funeral of a little boy—Mr. Godfrey's—that died with scrofula. Thus are our blooming prospects of life cut off by death."

CHAPTER XIX.

SAUT DE STE. MARIE MISSION—PASSING EVENTS.

After the missionaries had left us for their appropriate fields we found, as usual, much to do preparatory to the approaching winter.

Besides the necessary business and care connected with a general oversight of the missions in the district, the mission farm at Little Rapids required no small attention. Up to this time one of the mission families lived there. The place was now leased, and thus lessened very much our care and perplexity.

On the 22d of November I went to Naomikong to hold our first quarterly meeting. The ground was covered with snow. It was cold and wintery, but we were favored with a good wind to sail, and arrived before night. Found brother Steele on the schoolhouse, in true mason-like style, topping out the chimney. He and his family had recovered their health, and were in "labors more abundant." We had a good quarterly meeting, but nothing extraordinary. I was chained here till Thursday afternoon following, by contrary wind. The snow was several inches deep, and I concluded that I should have to walk home—a hard undertaking at that season. I took leave of the mission and walked to the mill, some eight miles, by the coast. Part of the way I walked in snow water, by which means I took a severe cold, and it laid the foundation of a pretty serious illness soon afterward. At the saw-mill we remained all night. Friday morning the wind sprung up in our favor. Our boat was sent to us from Naomikong, as I had ordered if the wind should become favorable, and before night we had reached home.

IMPROVEMENTS.

At Naomikong we had purchased rising of sixty acres of land for the mission. The Indians had bought all around us, and were building considerably. We had built since conference a comfortable school-house, and made an addition to the mission-house. Had also fitted up a comfortable dwelling for the interpreter. The school was opened on the 27th of November, numbering twenty-four Indian children, most of whom could read in the Testament; nine were writing, five studying arithmetic, and two geography.

"*Religious Prospects.*—Brother Steele says, 'Our religious prospects are of decided improvement.' Meetings of all kinds well attended, and interesting. Brother Marksman says, in a letter received the same time, 'the Lord is now troubling the careless and hard-hearted sinners here. Last evening after the exhortation of brother Isaac, brother Steele told me that I might speak also, and immediately I lifted my cries to God in prayer: 'O Lord, thou hast permitted thy poor servant to see sinners converted to thee in former times! O let us see sinners coming to thee this evening!' In the name of God I got up and exhorted sinners to come to Jesus and be saved. Four persons came forward to the mourner's bench. We labored till nearly ten o'clock—had a most excellent meeting. They all prayed till the tears rolled down their cheeks; every soul in the house was in prayer. One of brother Steele's boys prayed with all his might." (Missionary Report.)

The state of religion was very encouraging most of the winter. Early in March I visited Naomikong again. It was then fine going on the ice. Went in a two-horse sled, accompanied by my wife and daughter. This jaunt was pleasantly executed, as it took us only one day each way, and is the more worthy of note as it was very seldom that we could travel so comfortably. We had a good meeting with the missionaries and the Indians that were at home—several were off hunting. The conveniences for boarding native children were limited at our new station. Still four or five children were supported under the mission roof. One of the greatest disadvantages here was the isolated position of our missionaries, and the difficulty of transporting supplies from the Saut mostly in small boats. It required no small degree of self-sacrifice to live in so secluded a spot, shut out from the world mostly, and deprived of the endearments of such society as the missionaries had been wont to gather around them. Still this was a more desirable residence than several of the remoter stations.

Soon after the visit to Naomikong mentioned above, my health was, for a time, much impaired by that most painful and debilitating disease—piles. At no time during my connection with the missions was I so completely prostrated. But I soon obtained relief, and gradually recovered my strength through the good providence of God.

During this winter I added to my other duties the charge of a school. I did this in compliance with an urgent request of some of the leading citizens, who had failed to secure the services of a teacher from below before the close of navigation prevented them.

We still continued preaching at the village, with variable signs of prosperity. During most of the winter and spring we had excellent congregations, and often deep and serious attention to the word preached. We were visited by brother Steele occasionally, who preached several very excellent sermons to the people. Our sacramental seasons were generally seasons of heart-felt interest. The hearts of the few, representatives of several different Churches, were blended as the members of a common family. But there were times when the general neglect of divine things led me almost to adopt the words of the sorrowing Psalmist: "Woe is me that I sojourn in Mesech, and dwell in the tents of Kedar."

TEMPERANCE.

In a place like this any thing that could conduce to roll back the tide of intemperance, and avert its untold evils, was to be hailed as the harbinger of good. In the fall of 1849 the Sons of Temperance organized a Division—"Algic Chippeway Division, No. 107." This Division soon increased in numbers, and was steadily gaining in the confidence of the people. Several persons, who had been far gone in intemperance, were by this means reclaimed. In the spring of 1850 I entered heartily into this reform, and lectured soon after to very crowded audiences. The meetings in the hall were very orderly and business-like seasons, exerting a most wholesome influence over several of the soldiers, who were members, and were thus kept away from drinking and gambling saloons. The public lectures were invariably well attended, and many home-darts were there thrown, not at random, among the mixed multitude. It is with pleasure that I call to mind my association with this Division of the Sons of Temperance. Its members are now scattered; some have gone to their long home. There are several that I have hope of meeting on a better shore, which the fell destroyer, intemperance, will never approach.

SICKNESS AND DEATH AMONG THE INHABITANTS.

In the spring we had a number of very sudden deaths. There seemed to be something mysterious in the manner of several of these deaths. Persons would be taken sick, but not considered dangerous, and yet the next word would, perhaps, be that they were no more. These cases did not all originate in the same disease, evidently, though there was prevailing at the time a kind of influenza, which was, no doubt, the exciting cause in most cases. Myself and family were attacked, and I did not fully recover till I reached Sandy Lake the following summer. There was some interest attached to some of these occurrences, as noted in my journal, a brief mention of which may not be amiss. They were interwoven with our missionary life. The following was penned on the 23d of March:

"This afternoon I preached a funeral discourse on occasion of the sudden death of one of the members of the Division of the Sons of Temperance. The members were all in attendance, and such a crowd flocked out as I have never seen in this place to a Protestant meeting. The house was filled, and the doors were crowded with persons standing, and a number went away that could not be accommodated. I was blessed with more than usual freedom in speaking from 2 Samuel xiv, 14. There was fixed attention, and many wept under the word preached.

"Mr. D. had lived in sin, and died, it was to be feared, without hope in Christ. He was taken last Thursday evening and died yesterday—Saturday—morning, about four o'clock. I knew nothing of his being sick till requested to attend his funeral. After he was taken sick his wife asked him if she should send for me to come and talk with him. He replied, that '*people would think it a whim.*' She told me that these were the last words he uttered. How terrible for death to come and find any one thus unprepared! I endeavored faithfully to warn the people of the absolute necessity of a preparation for death."

On the 20th of April another of the members of the Division died, a Mr. W. He had been one of the best mechanics that ever had been at the Saut. But he was enticed and led away by strong drink, till he brought upon himself that horrible disease of *mania a potu.* At that time he could scarcely have drawn a sober breath. By this destructive poison his constitution became shattered, and he was dragging out a living death. He had, some time before, united with the Sons, and totally abandoned his cups. As a result an entire change came over him for the better.

I visited him daily for several days, conversed with him about his spiritual state, gave him a Bible and some tracts, read the holy Scriptures and prayed with him. He told me, on Thursday before his death, that "he was resolved, from that time onward, to serve God; that he had endeavored to be religious in days gone by, but had strayed far off; that he believed in the dear Redeemer, and that in him was his only hope and consolation." He had been baptized in infancy, and brought up under the influence of the Presbyterian Church. At his request, that evening

I administered the sacrament of the Lord's supper to him, to his evident comfort. Friday he appeared much better—spoke of the sweet rest he had enjoyed the night before. Saturday he did not appear so well, but neither he nor myself thought his end to be so nigh. After reading and prayer with him I urged him to cast all his care on the Lord. Thus I left him, and before midnight his spirit had left the clay tenement. On Monday, 21st, I preached his funeral from "*Then shall the dust return to the earth as it was, and the spirit unto God who gave it.*" The people could not all get into the body of the house. The Division of Sons attended in a body. Several were present not accustomed to listen to Protestant preaching.

We had a number of similarly-crowded funerals, some of which occurred in the summer. But I have given the two above as a little out of the ordinary course, and they must suffice. According to an old proverb, "straws show which way the wind blows;" these seemingly-unimportant events tend to throw some light on the influence at work among us. Their voice to the living is that of warning.

The last day of July, about midnight, a sad casualty occurred on Lake Superior, near White Fish Point. The Monticello ran into the Manhattan on her larboard quarter. She began to sink, and, it was said, in five minutes was under water to her guards on the upper deck. By the dexterity, self-possession, and heroism of Captain Wilson and several others, on board the Monticello, all the passengers and others were taken from the sinking vessel, and every life saved. We were told that the passengers on the Monticello had just been dancing, a thing of common occurrence on the Lake Superior boats, and, at the time of the collision, were partaking of an oyster supper. Thus are people often, in the hight of conviviality, intoxicated by trifling amusements and sinful diversions; as thoughtless about their souls as though they had none, and indifferent about the retributions of eternity as if such things were idle dreams, when "there is but a step between them and death."

CHAPTER XX.

ANNUAL TOUR AMONG THE MISSIONS.

WITH all our increased facilities for travel on Lake Superior, by the increased number of boats, we were often subject to great detention. I had expected to leave the Saut by the 21st of May, to visit the missions, but was detained till the 29th, when I left on the propeller Manhattan. I was accompanied by my wife and daughter as far as Eagle river, where I left them to visit old acquaintances and friends, and proceeded on my journey. After various detentions at Copper Harbor, Eagle Harbor, Eagle river, and the Ontonagon, we landed at La Pointe early in the morning of June 4th, having been on the way nearly a week. The day was spent in making arrangements for the coasting voyage ahead.

Thursday, 5th, accompanied by three voyagers, I left La Pointe at eight o'clock, A. M. A little before eight o'clock, P. M., we pitched our tent by a small river emptying into Siskowet Bay.

Friday, 6th, after a comfortable night's rest, I was awakened between three and four o'clock by the sweet music of some little birds. We left our camp at five o'clock; Lake delightfully calm. At twelve o'clock we had a fine sailing breeze, which continued to blow steadily from the north-east till we entered the St. Louis river. As we drew near the entrance, the Lake presented the most angry and terrific appearance, owing to the meeting of opposing currents. The water for miles was very turbid, as if torn up from the bottom, and resembled the boiling of a vast caldron. To ride in over the foaming breakers, to all appearance, looked hazardous; but we succeeded in making the entrance, and before night had camped on a point to our left. While seated in the boat, and looking out upon the angry waters, I wrote with pencil the following lines, which are here inserted, not as a specimen of poetry—we pretend to no intimacy with the Muses—but simply as expressive of our feelings at the time:

"Great Maker of the earth and sea,
Preserver of all things that be,
Where shall a worm, an heir of dust,
In aught but thee repose his trust?
While toss'd upon the turbid wave,
Thine arm, we know, is strong to save;
Keep then, 'and bring us safe to land,'
Held 'in the hollow of thy hand.'"

Saturday morning we had occasional showers. We arrived at Fond du Lac a little after noon; stopped with Mr. Carlton, the Government blacksmith. We missed our missionaries very much, and were inclined to wish, in view of the shape of things, that we again had a missionary on the ground.

On Sunday the people were called together at the mission-house for religious worship. Just as we were on our way a large boat from La Pointe arrived with Indian provisions, and, of course, became the center of attraction for some time. But few were at meeting on this account. Baptized an infant of Stephen Bungo, a colored interpreter. It was quite rainy during the afternoon. In the evening I preached to a few Indians—S. B. interpreted.

Monday morning, in pretty good season, we were *en route* for Sandy Lake. At half-past six o'clock, P. M., we were over Knife Portage, and had camped. Our canoe had been badly broken, and must now be mended. Another canoe full of Indians was in company, some looking quite respectable, but one, a Sandy Lake Indian, was grease and dirt from top to toe—a perfect specimen of a lazy, worthless fellow. When my men were getting our dinner he said he would eat with us, and drew up near to us. But he received no encouragement, and so crept back and messed with his comrades.

I had suffered considerably all the way from influenza, which attacked me at the Saut—was slowly recovering. The river was at a good stage, neither too high nor too low.

Just below our tent the water of the St. Louis falls about ten feet nearly perpendicular, and, for a long distance, dashes and foams among the rocks. Tuesday, 10th, we contended successfully against the long succession of rapids, and camped at night, some distance above the Grand Rapids, near a place called by the Indians *Che-ba-gah-me-goons*, or little grave.

Here a Mr. Aitken, brother to the Sub-Agent at the Saut, once lost a little child as he was passing over this route. The lone grave is pointed out by some cedar pickets which inclose it.

Wednesday, at half-past ten o'clock, we were at the mouth of the East Savan river. In following the devious windings of this stream our way was often obstructed by trees, which had fallen across, and by flood wood, which must be removed. By eight o'clock, P. M., we were at the head of the river and camped for the night.

Thursday we arrived at the Sandy Lake mission a little after noon. Found sister Spates in poor health; the rest of the missionaries were well. Found things about the mission in a better condition than I had anticipated, in view of the troubles through which the missionaries and Indians had passed, a particular account of which will be found farther on Our great lack here, at this time, was a good interpreter. There was no person that we could rely on to attend to this duty. I was, therefore, compelled, during this visit, to conduct our meetings among the Indians in my own broken style of speaking Ojibwa, without any interpreter.

Friday was spent in the transaction of business. Saturday afternoon we had public worship. Sabbath, at half-past nine o'clock, we had prayer meeting. At the close of this I related to the Indians, as well as I could, something of my religious experience, and gave them an exhortation. I succeeded much better than I could have anticipated. At eleven o'clock the house was well filled with whites and Indians. We sung in Indian. Then I read appropriate prayers in Ojibwa, including the Lord's prayer. After this, a part of the second chapter to the Hebrews was read. I then read my text in Ojibwa, and offered, in broken Indian, some remarks on man's original purity as God made him; how he sinned and brought upon himself guilt, pain, and death; how God loved man in his fallen state, and sent his Son to die on the cross, and by this means procured a great salvation for us; that if we embraced Christ and his Gospel it would make us happier every way in our condition here, and make us happy forever in heaven; but that if we rejected this Gospel we must perish forever. I exhorted them to cast aside their heathenism and embrace the truth. The Indians were very attentive, and I thought the most of them understood what I endeavored to say to them. Afterward read my text in English—Hebrews ii, 3—and spoke with more than common point and freedom to the whites present. In the afternoon commemorated the dying sorrows of our Lord. It was a deeply-solemn and interesting time to the small company who partook. At night we had a refreshing prayer meeting with the missionaries. We never all expected to meet again on earth. But we felt as if we could antedate a better meeting in the skies. We could but think, at the time, that if the Church could only witness the holy fervor which seemed to characterize our missionaries in this heathen land, they would not despair though they should be compelled to labor long without apparent fruit.

In the month of the March previous one of the heathen Indians had killed an ox, belonging to the mission, under the eyes of the missionaries, and in a most aggravating manner. Brother Spates was absent at the time. The Agent was called upon to interpose his authority. He came and forbade the Indian to take any of the meat. Brother Holt got the ox into the stable, closed the door, and was about dressing it when the Indian broke open the door with an ax, and was determined to have the meat. Brother Holt again went to call the Agent, and while gone the Indian cut off the head and one of the fore-quarters, and took them away. Brother H. returned and put the rest on a hand-train to get it into the house. The Indian took hold of it, and determined that the missionary should not have it. The missionary persisted, and took it away, to the great chagrin of the savage, who brandished his butcher-knife in brother H.'s face. The Agent had threatened to take this Indian into custody and have him punished for this outrage, but nothing had yet been done.

Monday morning, before I left Sandy Lake, the Indians must have an interview with me to know what was to be done with the transgressor. They were anxious to have the matter settled on the spot. But I told them that this was the business of the Agent, and that they must wait till payment time to have it adjusted. Told them that I hoped the Government would punish this man as his crime deserved. During this same season our mission lost a fine horse, valued at one hundred and fifty dollars. It was suspected that a half-breed from Fond du Lac had killed and eaten him. Thus was our best mission property exposed to the depredations of lawless savages, and even the lives of the missionaries were often in jeopardy.

We left the mission before ten o'clock, A. M., and got pretty well down the East Savan river before night. My influenza had now left me, and my health was every way greatly improved. We camped the next night at Knife Portage. It rained nearly all night, accompanied with loud thunder. Wednesday we were at Fond du Lac early in the afternoon. Stopped here an hour or so, and were again on our way. As it was quite rainy we camped about four o'clock, P. M. Thursday we coasted about forty miles, and camped early at the Brule river, much fatigued. Three large batteaux arrived here from La Pointe, on their way to Fond du Lac, with Indian provisions, in the employ of the Fur Company—a merry company of men, about thirty in number. Friday we had a rough sea and a pretty hard day's toil, and were forced to camp in a very close and uncomfortable spot, near the water's edge. Saturday we were chained to our camp till four o'clock, P. M. Rainy and uncomfortable weather; wind ahead and a very rough sea. We then removed our camp and traveled till near midnight, and camped not far from Raspberry river. Sunday morning my men called me up very early. A stiff breeze was blowing in the direction of La Pointe. We hoisted sail, and before nine o'clock were at the Fur Company's establishment; breakfasted at Mr. Oaks's, and had the privilege once more of uniting with the missionaries of the American Board in the worship of God.

Monday 23*d*. The morning was spent in transacting business. In the afternoon, accompanied by Rev. Mr. Hall and wife went to Bad river to visit the station there, under the supervision of Rev. L. H. Wheeler. The Indians had made very considerable improvements here in clearing land, building, etc. A school and religious meetings were kept, and much had been done, by the self-sacrificing missionaries, to better the condition of the natives, and with apparent evidences of success. Tuesday morning, after a pleasant night spent with our friends at the mission, returned with brother Hall to the mouth of the river, where my men and boat from La Pointe were waiting. Camped that night five or six miles west of Black river.

Wednesday, 25th, about half-past two o'clock were aroused by swarms of musketoes and gnats. We got ready, started immediately, and found good sailing. Breakfasted at Presque Isle, and were soon on our way with a fresh wind from the south-west, and were sailing very fast. Wind had increased considerably by nine o'clock—sea became quite rough—wind rather flawy—had to lessen sail. We had a good Mackinaw boat, a fine sailer, or we should have been in a bad fix. We seemed to pass the land like a streak. As we rounded the points of the Porcupine Mountains, we had a very rough sea. We paid little attention to the deep bays on our route; generally made a straight wake across them. By noon we were opposite Iron river. Here we laid our course direct for the Ontonagon. By two o'clock, P. M., we were there, having sailed about fifty miles from the time we left camp. Such sailing, in open boat, is of rare occurrence. I had never before sailed so far in the same time; twice had nearly equaled it in a bark canoe, sailing faster, perhaps, but not so far at a time. Here I expected to have met with my family, but they had waited for the next boat. Every house and hovel in the place was crowded, and scarcely any thing like appropriate or comfortable accommodations could be found. Every boat that arrived was crowded with passengers. Houses could not be built to supply the demand for want of lumber.

Friday the Manhattan arrived, having on board Rev. W. Benson and wife, from Eagle river, and my family. The captain ran into the river—quite an era in the history of Ontonagon—the first steam craft that had ever made the experiment. The citizens expressed their gratification on the occasion, by crowding upon the dock, and by loud and enthusiastic cheering. After discharging freight, the captain ran some distance up the river, but, getting aground, was forced to retreat. The Ontonagon river might have been navigated for several miles, but for obstructions lodged in places on the bottom. I could get no promise of entertainment for my family, on shore, and we were compelled to find lodgings on board the Manhattan for the night.

Saturday, 28th, we all went ashore. My wife and daughter and sister Benson remained at the mouth of the river with sister Day, while brother Day, brother Benson, and myself, went to the Minnesota Mine to spend the Sabbath. The trail was now exceedingly muddy—much of the way we waded nearly knee-deep in mud and water—distance, fourteen miles. We arrived about three o'clock, P. M., and were kindly received by Mr. Roberts, the Agent.

Sabbath morning I preached in the upper part of the *whim house*, to a respectable congregation of men—but one female. Brother Benson preached in the afternoon, after which we administered the Lord's supper to six or seven persons; and at night I preached again to a good congregation of men—not a woman present. A good influence pervaded these seasons of worship; but this was as yet the day of small things, religiously, for the Minnesota location.

Monday we returned to the mouth of the river, where Mr. T. Hanna kindly entertained me and my family. Wednesday morning the Monticello came into the river, on which boat we left the Ontonagon the same evening. Thursday morning we arrived at Eagle river before day. Here I parted with my family at nine o'clock, A. M.; they bound for Copper Harbor, to await my return from the Kewawenon mission. The day I spent in the vicinity of the Cliff Mine, and the night with brother Benson at the Phœnix Mine.

INDEPENDENCE.

Every true American must hail with patriotic delight the birthday of the independence of the United States. This must be so, whether surrounded by the pomp and glitter of a regular celebration, or, like an exile, shut out from such exciting scenes, and left a lone wanderer in the wilderness. Friday morning, July 4th, I started for Kewawenon. Two men were to meet me at the Cliff, or at the North American, to accompany me. I called at each place, and was detained in waiting an hour and a half; then went some eight miles to the Forsythe Mine, and waited again four hours. My disappointment being now confirmed, I shouldered my sachel and started, resolved to make the best of it alone. Eight miles over a hilly trail brought me out of the woods, to the head of Torch Lake. A Dutchman was living here in an old, dilapidated storehouse, which more resembled a filthy stable than a human habitation. I took a lunch to stay my stomach. There was nothing here peculiarly interesting for a Fourth of July entertainment. At half-past six o'clock, P. M., I left in a small log canoe.

The Lake fortunately was calm. Soon after I had

crossed Torch Lake night shut in around me. I fol lowed the meanderings of Torch river till it led intc Portage Lake, and still kept on my course till aftei midnight, having paddled some fifteen miles. It now became very dark, and the clouds were threatening. For some distance the shore was fringed with tangled bushes, logs, and grassy bogs. Several times I ran the canoe into these obstructions, and had to back out, and feel my way along as well as I could. I was near an Indian cabin, but could not tell where was the landing, which was in a little cove. I called out several times, and as often heard a voice distinctly from the opposite shore of Portage Lake—the echo doubtless of my own. Now the dogs barked, by which means I found the landing. On going to the cabin I found it locked, and no person about. I had perspired freely from such severe exercise. My clothes were quite wet from the water splashing over my little dug-out, and, from my cramped position for more than six hours, my limbs were sore, and I felt exhausted. Without bed or blanket, and with the dogs for companions, I kindled a fire, took the soft side of a piece of puncheon, which I had placed before the fire, occasionally changing sides to dry my wet clothes and relieve my aching limbs. I rested some, but did not sleep. At day dawn it seemed as if I should be devoured by the sanguinary swarms of insect tribes, which gathered around for a morning repast. I arose and prepared my breakfast. My store was a little hard bread, some tea and sugar.

I had a little tin-cup, which sister Benson thoughtfully had put into my sachel to drink out of. How I made it answer for tea-kettle, tea-pot, cup, saucer, and all, the reader must guess. Braced up for the toils of the day with such a repast, I was again in the canoe, headed for the Entry, or mouth of the Portage, some five miles farther. On my arrival I found the Indian and his son at whose cabin I had sought shelter. In the afternoon they took a boat and conveyed me over to the Kewawenon mission. For want of sleep I could scarcely keep my eyes open sufficiently to steer our boat. We arrived at the mission just before sundown. But I felt rather worse for the wear, owing to my *independent* way of spending "*the glorious Fourth.*"

The Sabbath spent at the mission was, as usual, a time of interest and profit. Sister Barnum was still lingering on the shores of time, ripening for heaven. When I left the mission each of the two preceding seasons, I did not expect to see her again in time; but God had kindly prolonged her stay.

I will not detain the reader with particulars of our consultation with the Indians on Monday, except to give a brief speech made by *Kog-wa-on*, a very sensible and, in many respects, exemplary man, though not a professed Christian: "I wish to say a few words, and I do not wish you to throw them out of doors. I wish that my grandfather had embraced the Gospel. If the Gospel had come among us first, then we would not have had the fire-water; but the fire-water came among us before the Gospel, and we received it, and it was the strongest and overcame us. I do not blame the Indians for drinking the fire-water. If the white people did not make it and bring it to us, we should not have it."

I replied that "it was not good white men who made and brought them the fire-water; that this was done by bad men; that all good white men hated this business, and would be glad to put it down if they could; and that the only way for the Indians was not to touch the accursed poison—they could let it alone if they would. If you put your hand into the fire, it will burn you; and if you drink this fire-water, it will burn and consume your souls."

Tuesday, on account of head wind, I did not get away from the mission till three o'clock, P. M.; reached the Phœnix Mine, at Eagle river, Thursday morning, in time to breakfast with the family of brother Benson. I spent the rest of the day and the day following in the vicinity of Eagle river. Saturday afternoon we attended to the business of the quarterly conference; preached in the evening. Sabbath morning some twenty-six were in attendance at the love-feast. God was in the midst to bless. I preached to a respectable congregation at half-past ten o'clock, and baptized two children. I preached again at half-past two, P. M., and administered the sacrament of the Lord's supper. Afterward I went to the North American, and baptized Captain Paul's little daughter. At night I preached again at the

Cliff; the house was well filled with attentive hearers. I took up a collection of $10.81 for the support of the Gospel. After the meeting had closed I walked with brother Benson and his wife some three miles, to their residence at the Phœnix Mine. After a day so filled up with active duties, rest was most welcome.

Monday walked to Eagle river; here got an Indian to take me in his canoe, some eight miles, to Agate Harbor. Thence I endeavored to follow the old trail to Copper Harbor, which, since I had traveled it last, had grown up with grass, and was obstructed by fallen timber and bushes, so that in one place I missed my way, and traveled a considerable distance before I got into the trail again. When I reached the Harbor I was wet, *cap-a-pie*, from the dripping bushes and grass. Here I was rejoiced to unite once more with my family. Wednesday we took passage on the Monticello for the Saut. We were out only nineteen hours till we were at M'Knight's wharf at the Saut—probably the quickest trip ever before made from Copper Harbor. After the vicissitudes of a tour of seven weeks, lacking a few hours, it was grateful to our feelings to set foot again in our unpretending home.

CHAPTER XXI.

CONDITION AND PROSPECTS OF THE MISSIONS

WITH the exception of some slight amendments, the following statement of the condition and prospects of the missions in the Indian Mission district was penned near the close of the summer of 1851:

I. INDIAN MISSIONS.—Impediments have been thrown in the way of our efforts to evangelize the Indians in the western part of this district, by the efforts of the Government to effect their removal. The Indians have already suffered much. They have felt, in consequence, chafed in their minds, and, to a considerable extent, they are jealous of their best friends, because of the wrongs they have suffered. To give a brief detail of facts.

Removal of the Payment to Sandy Lake.—Since the treaty the payment had been made at La Pointe. This place was quite central, so far as the Indians connected with our missions were concerned, and easy of access. But with a view to effecting the removal of the Indians west the payment was removed to Sandy Lake, and a refusal to go there to receive it amounted to a forfeiture. The Indians about Kewawenon did not go, and, as a result, got nothing. A large band of Indians at *Lake Vieux Desert* also suffered the loss of their payment before they would consent to go to Sandy Lake. If I was correctly informed none of them went. Many, however, from different points did convene at the call of the Agent.

Troubles after their arrival at Sandy Lake.—They were in a most destitute situation. As their route led across land portages, some of them miles in extent, they could not take with them bark to construct lodges. Nor could any thing be obtained at Sandy Lake to afford even a tolerable shelter for several hundred Indians from the pelting rain and snows of autumn. Their clothing was scarcely a circumstance. The wood they burned, as the missionaries informed me, they carried on their backs the distance of a mile to a mile and a half. Nor were they any better off for food. They waited a long time for the arrival of the Agent—threatened to force open the provision store and help themselves, and would have done so but for the resolute manner in which it had been guarded. Their provisions they must and did get, which were nearly or quite consumed while waiting for their pay. Another aggravating circumstance was connected with their provisions. The contractors had stored a large quantity of the flour near the Mississippi. The river rose, and, for some time, the flour was submerged, and consequently badly damaged. But, such as it was, it was fed out to the hungry Indians. Almost incited to insurrection by past grievances, they were measurably quieted in hope of being paid off on the arrival of the Agent. After waiting about two months, what must have been their disappointment to be met with the cold comfort that their *Great Father* (?) was not yet ready to pay them; they must wait another year for their money!

Sickness and Death.—Meanwhile disease had been making terrible ravages among them. It assumed the form of dysentery; some thought it to be a modification of cholera. Simultaneously the measles was prevailing. As a result of the malignant diseases abroad, there were about two hundred deaths. Frequently seven or eight died in a day. So alarming was the mortality that the Indians complained that they could not bury their dead. Coffins could not be procured, and often the body of the deceased was wrapped up in a piece of bark and buried slightly under ground. At times a hole was dug and several corpses together thrown in and covered up. Often when one died in a wigwam, the surviving friends would dig a grave in the center, bury their dead, and remove their lodge. All over the cleared land graves were to be seen in every direction, for miles distant, from Sandy Lake; they were to be found in the woods. Some, it is not known how many, were interred by their friends on their way home. I was credibly informed that there were instances in which the sick were unable to accompany their relatives, and were left alone to perish in the wilderness. One man, it is said, importuned his wife to remain with him and not to suffer him to die alone. She replied that if she should remain she must die too, and thus left him. On my way to Sandy Lake I saw a number of those recent graves, and, in some places, there were remaining racks or frames constructed for the support of the sick. The evidences of a terrible calamity every-where met the eye.

Destruction of Canoes.—The Indians who went to payment *via* the St. Louis river, left their canoes at the confluence of the East Savan and the St. Louis, thinking that it would not be safe to take them to the head of the Savan, as that might be frozen over before they returned. But they did not dream of being detained till the large and rapid St. Louis should be frozen over. Such, however, was the fact. Finding the rivers closed on their return, and all a snowy wilderness around, some were so enraged that they broke their canoes in pieces for fuel, others were purposely broken to prevent them from being stolen; many more were simply left in the snow, and, on the opening of spring, some were stolen, many were carried down the St. Louis and lodged among the flood-wood, or against the banks. I saw quite a number in this situation. A few were still remaining, when I passed, where they had been left. The number of the canoes thus sacrificed is not known. The Indians said a hundred or more. They were worth from eight to twenty dollars each, which shows a heavy destruction of property, besides the inconvenience and hardship to which the Indians were subjected in being compelled to walk home, and carry their effects on their backs.

With this chain of distressing evils, the cause of which the Indians charge upon the Government, it is not to be wondered at that many should have been driven almost to desperation. And, as it is difficult for the Indians to distinguish between friends and enemies; as they can not be expected to make due allowance for the unavoidable failures of the Government, it is no great wonder that they should feel jealous even of the missionaries; rank them with others as enemies and treat them accordingly. This may account for the treatment received by our missionaries at Sandy Lake the past winter. It must, however, be set down to the credit of the Indians that the ill treatment suffered by the missionaries is to be charged, not to the Indians *en masse*, but to a few of the most abandoned.

My report, which was forwarded to the Corresponding Secretary of the Missionary Society some time near the close of the summer, and published in the Missionary Advocate, will give a succinct view of the condition and prospects of our missions. It is here given entire, with Dr. Durbin's brief notice at the head:

INDIAN MISSIONS.

MICHIGAN CONFERENCE.—The following is the report of the Rev. J. H. Pitezel, Superintendent of the Indian Missionary District, dated August 25th. It is made up of sunshine and clouds, yet we discern in it the promise of blessed fruit. The reader at home will not read without reflecting on the toils and dangers of the missionaries and their families:

"SAUT STE. MARIE MISSION—*J. H. Pitezel, S. Steele, and P. Marksman, Missionaries.*—This mission embraces two places where religious services are kept up regularly on the Sabbath; and occasionally we have meetings at two other places, at each of which are a few Indians.

"SAUT STE. MARIE VILLAGE.—Here our labors are confined to the white population. In the summer this is the great thoroughfare to Lake Superior, and persons of all ranks pass through, from most parts of the world. Many of these travelers, from time to time, attend upon the worship of God with us, and obtain, we trust, a passing benefit. It is in this respect, more than in view of any very permanent religious society, that this place is important, and continues to be occupied by us. Even here we are not without tokens of Divine favor, and feel that we are doing something at least to extend the kingdom of our Master.

"NAOMIKONG.—This has been the residence of brothers Steele and Marksman, and most of our Indians live here. These Indians, as a body, are sober and respectable. Intemperance is only occasional among them, though they are brought into frequent contact with the destructive fire-water. Now owners of good land, and in the vicinity of a saw-mill, they are building houses and cultivating the soil as fast as their means will allow. They are gradually, but certainly, improving in the arts of civilized life. A day school has been kept up most of the time, numbering twenty-one boys and seven girls. Five children have been boarded in the mission family. Most of the children were quite regular in their attendance; some not so. They are reported as having made good proficiency in the common English branches.

"The Church has been decidedly prospered and blessed this year. It numbers—white members, five; Indians, fifty-eight; and probationers among the Indians, ten. We have an increase of twenty-eight members over last year. This is a large increase among a small Indian community. A meeting was commenced the 13th inst., and closed last Sabbath evening. I was present the first two days. While there we were blessed in waiting upon the Lord together. Brother Steele informed me that the meeting increased in interest to the close; they had the best of the wine at the close of the feast. On Sabbath the school-house would not hold all the people. When built we supposed it would hold all the people in the settlement; but others are gathering in around us, and if we are only suffered quietly to pursue our work, we have reason to believe that much good will yet be accomplished.

"At SHAW'S place, six miles above this, we have meetings occasionally.

"WAISHKEES BAY is the name of the other place occasionally visited by the missionaries.

"KEWAWENON MISSION—*N. Barnum and Ira Stacy, Missionaries; Joseph Bushay, Interpreter.*—At this station we number forty-four Indian members and one probationer; two whites. This shows a decrease of seven during the year. We are not surprised at this. The small-pox and other diseases broke out last winter, and operated much against the public meetings. And then the unsettled state of Indian affairs generally—the fear of having to remove, more than any thing else—operated against the religious prosperity of these Indians. The school has been small, numbering only eighteen scholars. The children belonging to the band are not numerous. Brother I. Stacy has taught the school. The children in general have learned well. The temporal condition of the mission was never as good as now. We have a good church, and every convenience to prosecute our labors successfully; more so than at any other point in this district. Will the Government force us to pull up stakes here?

"CARP RIVER.—This place is situated on the south shore of Lake Superior, about forty miles west of Grand Island, the *depot* of the *iron mines.* Some three or four companies are working in the vicinity. The settlers are mostly Americans, intelligent and enterprising. It is destined to be one of the most important points on the Lake; it has opened already a large trade. Brother Barnum recently visited the people, and spent some time among them. He was very kindly received, and they insist on having a

Methodist preacher next year. They must have one, if one is to be had. We have, in the vicinity, twenty-eight members. Union meetings and a union Sabbath school are kept up by the representatives of different Churches in the absence of a preacher.

"SANDY LAKE AND MILL LAC MISSIONS—*S. Spates and J. W. Holt, Missionaries.*—No flattering report can be made of this mission for the past year. It has been a year unparalleled in its history for deep and sore trials among the missionaries, and scarcely ever have such calamities befallen the Indians. To them it has been a year of mourning and woe. They carry this in their countenances and upon their blackened skins. The infrequency of their accustomed *mittas*, the few dances they celebrate, and the comparative silence and gloom that has seemed to settle down upon them, are proofs of this. We have among them only four members and two whites, but even in these we see the effects of the power of the Gospel. They stand as a beacon to others. In the midst of the sorest trials, the little few have experienced the greatest Divine support.

"The school, taught by brother Holt, has numbered thirty scholars. Their attendance has not been very regular, nor have they made as much progress as the children at other stations. There is a cause for this: they are just emerging from the dense darkness of heathenism, and with a succession of calamities, they have been ill prepared to learn.

"The afflictions the missionaries were called to

endure, and the hostile demonstrations of some of the Indians, prevented the former from visiting Mill Lac. They still call to us for help; and, if possible, a missionary should be appointed among them. Brother Spates is inclined to go there next fall if it is in accordance with the will of the appointing power.

"FOND DU LAC has been unoccupied the last year; but there are important reasons why this station should be reoccupied. About four hundred Indians are now there, and their number will, doubtless, be much increased soon, if the Government succeeds in coaxing the Indians that way. We have a tolerable mission-house and garden well inclosed, and a log-house, which with small expense could be finished off. This would be comfortable for school and meetings.

"EAGLE RIVER MISSION—*Wm. Benson, Missionary.*—The work here is among the copper mines, and has been prospered the past year. From twelve, the membership has increased to forty-two. The appropriation from the Missionary Society was one hundred dollars. The brethren and friends there have sent you back *sixty dollars*, missionary collection, and nobly sustained their missionary and his family. A flourishing Sabbath school is kept up at the Cliff Mine. A church has been built, which we use; but it is owned by the Pittsburg and Boston Company. The work here is greatly enlarging, and will need next year two missionaries. Thus the people *who were not a people*, have become the people of God. Our quarterly meeting at the Cliff, a short time since, was a most blessed season. Seldom have I witnessed a more deeply-impressive meeting, especially the love-feast. Our hearts were strangely warmed while we listened to the heart-felt experience of our brethren from across the Atlantic. Five joined us on the occasion.

"ONTONAGON MISSION—*E. H. Day, Missionary.*—This is one of the most prominent points on the Lake It has about twenty mines, which make the mouth of the river of this name their *depot.* Other mines will be constantly opening. This section is superior to almost all others about the Lake for fine agricultural land. From its natural resources it is capable of supporting a dense population. It must and will be occupied. It forms already a large and laborious circuit. The missionary has traveled afoot round a circuit of one hundred and sixty or one hundred and seventy miles, once in four weeks—in winter on snow-shoes, and in summer over trails, wading often in water knee-deep, annoyed by flies and musketoes, enduring all the fatigues of the most severe physical labor. It was an experiment to send a man there last fall, not knowing where he was to take shelter, or whether he would be sustained; but, with one hundred dollars' appropriation from the Missionary Society, the people have generously given him his support. There is now work in this field ample for two men, if they could be sustained. We have twelve members. I might say many more things about the station among the miners, but it would extend my report to an undue length. I will simply say that *Eagle River mission* is the *first branch* from the *Kewawenon mission; Ontonagon* is the *second branch* from the same stem; *Carp River*, among the iron mines, will, we hope, next year constitute its third branch. Thus it will be seen that Providence has been accomplishing an important work by means of our *Indian* mission at Kewawenon. The Lord's name have all the praise!"

Several scattering mines in the vicinity of Portage Lake had recommenced work with flattering prospects of success. An additional field was here opening, inviting the missionary to new toils and successes.

As evidences of the general prosperity of the work in the district the following statistics will speak for themselves: We numbered 6 Sunday schools, 32 officers and teachers, 170 scholars, 560 volumes in library, 2 Bible classes; raised $26.38 to defray expenses of schools, and $15 for benevolent purposes. Seventeen Sunday School Advocates were taken. One conversion connected with this department. For the missionary cause there was raised $106.81, a falling off here of $42.04 from the previous year.

The Indian membership returned to conference was one hundred and seventeen—two less than the previous year, owing to falling off at Fond du Lac, Sandy Lake, and Kewawenon. Among the white population there was an increase of forty-eight, and one local preacher over the previous year. Total white members, ninety-two.

With all the mutations above stated we think the reader will perceive unmistakable evidences of prosperity as connected with the missions of Lake Superior. If there were fluctuations in the Church, the same may be said of the state of society outside of the Church; the one is sufficient to account for the other. "The wilderness and the solitary place" was gladdening, and "the desert" was beginning "to blossom as the rose." Toward the close of the summer of 1851 our missionaries at Sandy Lake were again sorely afflicted. The following account is taken from one of my reports published in the Missionary Advocate:

"*Sandy Lake and Mill Lac.*—In the latter part of the summer the scarlet fever broke out here, and among the victims of its rage were the children of the Rev. S. Spates, the missionary. Brother Spates writes, that, for a time, it was doubtful whether they would live or die. 'But,' he says, 'God had mercy on us, lest we should have sorrow upon sorrow.' This letter was dated July 29th. He writes again, August 9th: 'Our health has greatly improved since my last: still the little girl, Imogen, is not well; her neck is much swollen. I was quite sick for about two weeks with sore throat.' It seems that nearly all the white people were similarly affected. Let it be remembered that while those missionaries are thus attacked with the most fatal diseases, *they are more than two hundred miles distant from the aid of a physician!* The few deaths that have occurred among the missionaries about Lake Superior, during the last sixteen years, either from disease or accident, is striking evidence of Divine interposition."

CHAPTER XXII.

TRAVELS AND MISSIONARY EFFORTS IN THE WINTER OF 1851-2.

THE Michigan annual conference had once more been in session, and the preachers had repaired to their various fields of labor and responsibility. Once more, in company with several other missionaries, we were on our way to the Saut. As we were borne along on the bosom of the deep the following note was penned:

"We are just about to enter upon our work for another year. There is much in the past to humble us—our want of devotedness to God—our want of usefulness. O for a fresh baptism from heaven for the work! 'Not by might nor by power, but by my Spirit, saith the Lord of hosts.'

'Give us thy strength, thou God of power,
Then let winds blow or thunders roar.'

All will be well if God be with us."

After our arrival, the missionaries bound for Lake Superior were, for some time, detained with us till they could leave for their respective fields. Some of the time we had ten besides our own family under our roof. After a lapse of more than two weeks, all had left except brother Marksman and family, whose appointment was to the Fond du Lac mission.

Word just now reached us of the wreck of the Monticello, on the rocky coast between Eagle river and the Ontonagon; providentially, no lives were lost. But this disaster tended greatly to derange business about the Lake. Owing to this, brother Marksman was detained for the winter, which he spent at Naomikong. This was, in the end, providential, as the interpreter for this station, whose residence was near Saginaw, did not arrive. To have been left in this condition our mission must have suffered greatly. I may as well add here, that circumstances did not justify brother M.'s leaving in the spring for Fond du Lac; that post was, consequently, not reoccupied.

About the middle of October I accompanied brother Marksman and his family to Naomikong. A day was spent in procuring lumber to add to our mission improvements. Sabbath day was filled up with religious exercises. Monday, assisted by only one man, I sailed home in the large batteau in which we had boated up supplies to the mission. We arrived before three o'clock, P. M., highly favored with such a fine run.

The Episcopal missionary, Rev. Mr. Anderson, who had been stationed at Garden river, Canada West, had left. The Wesleyan Methodist Missionary Society sent a very active and devoted man, Rev. Mr. M'Dougall, to this place, taking into his field the Bruce Mine. Brother M'D. was not an ordained preacher, and had solicited my aid in administering the ordinances to his people, which was cheerfully rendered, and for which, in return, we received valuable help from him. It was exceedingly gratifying to have such a neighbor in the mission field.

On the 31st of December I went, with my family, to Garden river, to aid brother M'D. in holding a watch meeting. It was a season of interest and profit. During its progress I had the privilege of baptizing an infant of the missionaries, and administering the sacrament of the Lord's supper to the Indian membership and others. Sugar Island here forms the American shore of the Ste. Marie's river. Some two miles below, on this island, is the residence of Mr. S. P. Church, who, with his excellent lady, belonged to the Congregational Church at Detroit. Mr. Church is making a fortune here at *farming* and making raspberry jamb, out of this delicious fruit, which grows so abundantly in all that region. While at Garden river we had a delightful visit with this Christian family, who accompanied us on the 2d of January to Rev. Mr. M'Dougall's, where I administered the sacrament of the Lord's supper to a little group of eight persons—all white but one. In those delightful services we had proof not only of the unity of Methodism, but of the essential unity of Christians of every name.

Early in January I visited again the station at Naomikong. I employed a cutter to carry me to Waishkees Bay; thence walked to the saw-mill. It was a fatiguing walk of four hours and a half. On the way I lamed one of my knees badly, and became much exhausted. I was kindly entertained at Mrs. P.'s. But when I sat down to the supper table, I became so faint that I had to go out in the open air. I finally took some refreshment, and, after a good night's rest, was all right, except the lameness.

Friday, 9th, my brother J., who was then at the mill, accompanied me to the mission. We had meeting at night—a good religious feeling seemed to prevail. The ice had but recently formed, and most of the Indians were engaged in fishing on Saturday. At night we had preaching again. The word was heard attentively. Our meetings on Sabbath were well attended, and generally spiritual. On Monday, accompanied by J. O., I walked to Waishkees Bay, *via* the saw-mill. By this time my lame knee was quite stiff. I took a short rest here and some refreshment; walked on about an hour more, and met W. J., who had come after me with horse and cutter. It was six o'clock, P. M., when we reached home. Having no overcoat with me, I became much chilled from riding in the cold.

TRIP TO THE BRUCE MINE.

Thursday, February 19th, I left the Saut to accompany brother M'Dougall to the Bruce Mine, Canada. The day was fine. After about four hours walking we reached Garden river. Here I preached at night, and administered the sacrament of the Lord's supper.

After the meeting I went with brother Church to his residence on Sugar Island, and spent the night with his kind family.

Friday, 20th, about eight o'clock, A. M., brother M'Dougall came along with an Indian pony and cutter. We had another fine day, but the going was hard. The upper crust was not sufficient to bear, which made it slow and fatiguing work for the pony. We went about ten miles, and stopped at an Indian shanty to feed and take a lunch. We then traveled about eight miles farther, and put up for the night with *Belonzha*, a Frenchman. We should have rested comfortably but for two things—our bedstead was too short and the covering light. Saturday, about half-past one o'clock, P. M., we had reached the Bruce Mine, after a cold ride of eighteen miles—wind strong in our faces all the time. We were cordially welcomed, and every attention bestowed upon us to render us comfortable.

At night we had an interesting and profitable temperance meeting, well attended. Brother M'Dougall offered the following resolution, to which he spoke at some length and with good effect:

"*Resolved*, That the temperance cause is the cause of humanity, and deserves the support of every philanthropist, and especially of every Christian."

I seconded the resolution, and spoke at some length and with much freedom. Twenty-two signed the pledge of total abstinence, and several others promised to do the same. Great attention was paid throughout the meeting to what was said. No opposition was offered to any thing except by a Scotchman, the pedagogue of the village. On being asked to sign the pledge, he replied, "I am not going to do any thing to hurt my ——," *alias*, *stomach*.

Sunday, 22d, was a gracious day to the people of Bruce Mine. The small class, consisting of seven members, met together before preaching; and a melting time it was to those present. At half-past ten o'clock I had the privilege of preaching to a very attentive congregation. I felt that the word of God was not bound. At two o'clock, P. M., we met again. I baptized five children. The congregation was larger than in the morning, to whom brother M'Dougall preached a good sermon from Matthew xvi, 26. Preaching was followed by the love-feast—another time of heavenly influence. One female confessed her sins and cried aloud to God for mercy. A backslider who had fallen, through strong drink, and who had signed the pledge the evening before, confessed his wanderings, and was resolved to return to God. I saw some weeping who did not speak. At night the congregation was larger than it had been before, and was deeply solemn and attentive while I strove again to proclaim the truth of God. Afterward we partook of the eucharist together, during which we felt that the Lord of the feast was present to sup with us. There appeared among the little few much of the revival spirit, and we saw no reason why a good revival would not be the result of a little extra effort. I hope ever to retain in my remem brance the seasons of heavenly communion I enjoyed with our English brethren at the Bruce Mine.

Monday afternoon we left the Bruce Mine—wind in our face. We reached the Frenchman's, where we spent the night. Tuesday was a snowy and stormy day. The wind blew hard, and snow fell so thick as at times to darken our prospect. We returned by the way of Hay Lake—a route different from the one we went—and reached Little Rapids by one o'clock, P. M., where we fed our horse and got something to eat. At three o'clock, P. M., we had reached home in safety. In the evening brother M. left us for his home at Garden river. The following night was exceedingly stormy. The next morning our door-yard was nearly filled with the drifting snow, and the storm still increasing. It was reason for thankfulness that we were not exposed to the pelting storm.

Thursday, March 11th, Rev. Mr. M'Dougall and his interpreter arrived at our place, to accompany me to Naomikong. He preached to our people at night. Friday we took a horse and cutter, and set out on our journey. The snow and water on the ice rendered it very bad going, and we were forced to walk much of the way. At ten o'clock at night we reached the saw-mill, twenty-eight miles. Mr. P.'s family were in bed, but arose and got us some refreshment, and kindly entertained us. Saturday we walked the rest of the way; had very wet feet from constantly breaking through the upper crust. Most of the day was spent in visiting the Indians. At night brother Blaker—brother M'Dougall's interpreter—preached to the Indians. The meeting was well attended, and all seemed interested. Sabbath morning we had a precious love-feast, at the close of which four united with the society on trial. Brother M'Dougall preached afterward from Isaiah xlv, 22. His sermon was listened to by the Indians with marked attention. This was followed by the sacrament of the Lord's supper. Brother M'D. preached again at night; after which seekers of religion were invited forward for prayers. Nine came, and among them three of the mission boys. Two or three professed to have received comfort. One Catholic Indian came, and said that he was now convinced of his error. One young man in the congregation was much affected, but did not venture forward. He kneeled down and prayed where he was.

Monday we left the mission, and walked to the mill. Here we got some refreshments and dried our wet moccasins. We now left the mill, and rode about two miles, when it commenced to storm terribly—fortunately it was on our backs. The horse got along so tardily that we left it with brother B., and brother M'D. and myself went on foot, till we reached Waishkees Bay, a little before night. Our moccasins and pants, from the knees down, were thickly crusted over with ice, from constant wading, and became quite cumbersome. But we had a good meeting here with the

Indians at night, and were comfortably entertained. Tuesday the ice bore up the horse well, and we rode most of the way to the Saut, which we reached about noon. While those missionary exchanges were most agreeable to all concerned, they exerted a quickening influence on our mission stations on both sides of the line which divided the two governments.

CHAPTER XXIII.

REVIVAL AT THE SAUT—THE INEBRIATE—MELANCHOLY CASUALTY.

DURING the fall and early part of the winter the prospect at the Saut de Ste. Marie seemed dark and unpromising. The sacredness of the holy Sabbath was often violated by the arrival and departure of boats, and the tumult and business which ensued. As a specimen, on the 9th of November three steamers left for the lower ports, two American and one British. Sometimes those arrivals and departures were just about the hour of public worship, and made our congregations fluctuating. But "the sound of the church-going bell" faithfully warned the people of the hour of prayer, and a constant use of the stated public means of grace was as a beacon-light amid the surrounding darkness.

Our winter commenced quite early. By the 16th of November snow was several inches deep, and sleighing good. November 27th was the day set apart for thanksgiving by the Governor of the state. It was arranged to have a sermon on the occasion. One of our steamers advertised to leave at twelve o'clock, M., which, as in many other instances, made our attendance at Church small.

Our last mail for the fall arrived the same day on the steamer London.

As the winter progressed things became more settled, our congregations increased, and a religious interest began to be manifest among the people. The hand of Providence was clearly traceable in this movement, and a somewhat particular account may not be unacceptable to the reader.

In 1832 a very gracious revival of religion broke out here, under the labors of Rev. Mr. Porter, of the Congregational Church, and Rev. A. Bingham, the resident Baptist missionary. This was confined mostly to Fort Brady. Two years after a very precious work again broke out in the Fort, under the labors of Rev. John Clark, of precious memory. See the account given in Hall's Life of Rev. John Clark, pp. 110, 111. But, from numerous changes in the army, if from no other cause, no fruit of those revivals was to be found at the Saut.

On our arrival at the Saut we found no class among the whites. How long before this was the case I can not say. We need not wonder at this when we reflect that the masses are Roman Catholic; that the few of the nominally-Protestant population have been fluctuating, differing much every season; and that the place has been noted for intemperance and kindred vices. It has only been by spells that half a dozen praying persons of different persuasions could be convened for prayer.

On returning from conference in the fall we resolved to make one more trial in the strength of the Lord, and, if no change could be effected, to recommend a discontinuance of effort here. Notice was given that a prayer meeting would be conducted at our house every Thursday evening, whether any one should meet with us or not. If we could do no better we could make it a family prayer meeting. These meetings were, accordingly, strictly kept up, and, with the exception of an evening or two, for a long time, there was but one person besides myself and wife to take part in them. In the month of December Mrs. M., wife of one of the sergeants of the Fort, became powerfully convicted under the preaching of the word. She came to the prayer meeting, but did not make known her feelings. Her convictions became deeper, and the sense of her condition more alarming the more she heard the Gospel preached. After attending two or three of the prayer meetings her exercise of mind became so great that she thought she could attend them no more. When preaching one day from 2 Peter i, 5–7, she said that her mind was greatly enlightened. She referred to this as the time when her burden was removed. She desired to converse with some one, but dared not to open her mind to any person previous to her happy release. Now she felt an indescribable inward peace and happiness.

At length she made known her feelings to a pious lady in the place, and expressed a wish to converse with me on the subject. This lady proposed to mention it to me, but Mrs. M. wished her not to do so. The cross appeared too great for her to make an open profession.

At this time I was at Naomikong. Measurably conquering her fears, she came and told Mrs. Pitezel the state of her mind. On my return I went to see her, and found her in the happy frame of mind before described. She said, "I am very weak, but I hang upon Jesus, from whom I derive continual support." She read the word of God much, which was to her very precious. She immediately erected the family altar. I found her husband very serious as a result of his wife's conversion. What she had already experienced she said she would not exchange for all the world. She wanted to tell to every one what the Lord had done for her. While speaking of God's goodness her eyes were suffused with tears, and a heavenly joy seemed to light up her countenance. After a truly-edifying conversation with her and her husband I read a portion of Scripture, and in prayer commended them to God.

An incident connected with this conversion should serve as a lesson to all who preach the Gospel. We are too apt to judge of the good effect of preaching by our own feelings; that we accomplish most when we have most liberty. In my journal for that occasion I noted: "Did not preach with even my usual freedom." Yet God approved, and this woman was released from the burden of her sins. To him be the glory!

One evening I called to see the sergeant's family in the Fort. I found them and two other soldiers surrounding a cheerful fire, one of the number reading Bunyan's Pilgrim's Progress—a book Mrs. P. had loaned them—and the rest listening with deep interest. Mr. M. told me that "he had frequently formed vows to serve God, and had broken them; that he had fallen into bad habits, which had strengthened with his years; that, in particular, he was passionate, and often used profane language. He was now striving to leave off all these. He could not muster courage to attempt to pray in public; but he sought God in secret prayer." I conversed with the other two soldiers, who spoke seriously and rationally on the subject, and seemed desirous to be partakers of this great salvation. They spoke of the difficulty of being Christians in the army—said that "it was the school of vice." I endeavored to show them that religion does not unfit us for any necessary duty in the station in which our lot is cast; that, on the contrary, it enabled us to perform it the better. This interview was closed by reading a chapter from the Holy Scriptures, accompanied by prayer. The following was recorded at the time in my journal:

"Mr. M. accompanied me when I left to the gate of the Fort, speaking all the way about his situation. Just as we left the house he exclaimed, 'There is a great change in *that* woman,' meaning his wife. What a blessed change has this one conversion made in this family! O for a shower of grace to transform this wicked village!

"*Thursday night, 22d.* We have just closed the best prayer meeting I have ever attended at the Saut. Several were present besides our own family, and all were induced to pray. Mr. M., husband of the converted lady, prayed with humility and fervency. He has experienced a degree of comfort. Mr. R., a soldier, confessed the downward course he had been pursuing, and prayed for strength to live a new life. A woman prayed for God to change her wicked heart, to give her a new heart, and make her clean in the blood of Christ.

"*Sabbath, 25th.* Our meetings during the day were pretty well attended. This evening our prayer meeting was a blessed season. One backslider has, I trust, been reclaimed. He testified that he had once indulged a hope in Christ, but never came out and united with any Church. He prayed in public to-night for the first time, and prayed and spoke very feelingly. Mrs. R. testified that for a long time she had read her Bible and prayed, but that she never had felt as she did last Thursday night at the prayer meeting. After she went home and had retired to rest, the words of the hymn came into her mind,

'Come hither, soul, I am the way.'

She felt a change in her mind from that time."

The same evening I organized a class of ten members.

" *Thursday*, *29th.* We had another blessed season with the little flock God has recently raised up among us. I read the General Rules of our societies. Then we prayed round, and spoke with each other respecting God's dealings with our souls, mingling our exercises with the songs of Zion. Some time ago we had none among us to sing; now the Lord hath put a new song into the mouth of several. Two joined us— one of these, a soldier, has been noted for Sabbath-breaking. He mentioned one instance. I give this as an illustration of the proverb that '*the way of the transgressor is hard.*'

" 'Last spring early, while it was yet cold, I took my gun and went out to hunt ducks. I went to Mr. B., the Baptist missionary, and asked him for his boat to go down to Little Rapids, two miles below. Mr. B. replied, "I am astonished; this is the Sabbath." He endeavored to dissuade me from my purpose. I went away much ashamed, but did not follow his advice. With my comrade, I succeeded in getting another boat. We glided down the river very nicely to Little Rapids. There we picked up a duck which I shot the other day, but could not get for want of a boat. We then went among the islands in front of the mission. Here I got thrown out of the boat into the water, which was exceedingly cold. I got into the boat again, and crossed over to an island, where I made a fire, and had to strip off and dry my clothes. I had on a pair of new boots which had cost me four dollars. While drying my clothes

I burned one of the boots, and spoiled it. With considerable difficulty, as well as suffering from the cold, we worked our way up stream, and returned home. This was the last of my Sabbath-hunting.'

"Now, for the first time, he met with us. He confessed what a miserable sinner he had been, and prayed earnestly to God to have mercy on him. He stated that he was much relieved before he left. Thus, of late, at every meeting the Lord gives us some fresh token of his favor.

"*Sabbath, February* 1. One of the most delightful days we have had this winter. But, from the severe storm of the two previous days, the snow was much drifted, and the road, in places, filled. But for all this, our congregation was much larger than usual, both in the forenoon and afternoon. In the morning I preached with an unction I have seldom felt on the "Immutability of Christ," from Hebrews xiii, 8. In the afternoon my subject was "God's Poor," from James ii, 5. I was amazingly blessed in trying to proclaim the truth. Throughout the day there was deep emotion evident in the congregation.

"Before going to the house of worship, my soul was much drawn out in prayer for that faith by which I might preach with success. I felt an uncommon struggle in prayer, and an assurance that I was heard and owned of God.

"At night our room was comfortably filled for class meeting; and a gracious season it was. We had several prayers. All spoke, and in nearly every case a great change appears evident. Two more united with us. The Lord's name be glorified for his boundless goodness! How truly may it be said, that '*the people who were not a people are become the people of God.*"

Thus had the Lord wrought a very gracious work among us, and a class of some fourteen was formed. It was confined mostly to the Fort. The sergeant's quarters became a house of prayer. Here the other soldiers who were seriously inclined were accustomed to meet every morning before breakfast for prayer. Five of the persons thus brought in were of the native or mixed population. It was not for us to predict how far this might tend to a permanent establishment of religious society in the place. At all events we felt to say that, "as long as souls are converted and saved we rejoice, yea, and will rejoice!"

THE INEBRIATE.

Toward the close of February we had extreme cold weather, frequent hard wind, and driving snow-storms. The night of the 28th had been of this character. About three o'clock of the same night we were awakened by a rapping at the door. It was a Garden River Indian, who had become intoxicated, and the only wonder was that he had not perished in the cold. He had lost his cap, was covered with snow, and was much chilled. I took him into the kitchen, built a good fire, gave him a blanket, and told him to wrap up and go to sleep. I left a light burning and retired to rest again, but I had scarcely gotten in bed before he began to knock at the door separating our apartments, and calling out, Nee-je, nee-je, that is, *friend, friend.* I told him he must lie down and be quiet, or I could not keep him. He laid him down again, and, for some time, sung as drunken Indians usually do, till at length he fell asleep. In the morning we gave him a warm breakfast and a hat, and sent him off nearly sober, and quite comfortable. He soon came back and returned the hat, having gotten a cap at one of the stores. The day had not passed before I saw him staggering again in the street. He was ten miles from home, and the following was one of the stormiest nights of the winter. We were appre hensive that he would perish, but he reached home without serious injury, except that inflicted by drunkenness itself—injury enough surely. Had we not taken him in the night before he would, in all probability, have perished. Such are the tender mercies of this miserable business! What is human life when offset against the cupidity of the liquor-dealer? A small matter surely.

MELANCHOLY CASUALTY.

Wednesday, 28th of April, a sad event occurred at the head of the Portage, connected with the launching of the steamer Baltimore. Several persons were at work at the capstan, which was placed on the end of one of the docks. The beam by which the capstan was turned, by horse power, broke, and flew back suddenly, instantly killing two men, seriously wounding two others, slightly injuring the fifth; the sixth in the group, when he heard the beam crack, dropped instantly, and it passed over him without harm. The survivors all soon recovered. One of the unfortunate men killed was a Catholic, and was here without relatives. The other left a wife and five children to mourn his loss. He was said to be daringly wicked, and among his last utterances was the heaven-insulting oath. I was requested to preach the funeral of this man the next Sabbath, but this arrangement was soon after changed, and I was called on Friday, a few minutes before the time, and requested to preach immediately. So with scarcely any preparation I went to the school-house, which was soon thronged. I spoke with great plainness, about twenty-five minutes, from the words, "Because there is wrath, beware lest He take thee away with his stroke: and then a great ransom shall not deliver thee." Job xxxvi, 18.

"How shocking must thy summons be, O death,
To him that is at ease in his possessions,
Who, counting on long years of pleasure here,
Is quite unfurnished for the world to come!"

CHAPTER XXIV.

ANNUAL TOŬR.

THE following record was made in my journal, Tuesday, May 25th:

"I have been for some time making preparations to visit our missions above. The Algonquin for about two weeks has been advertised to go to Fond du Lac, and I had concluded to go on her. Saturday evening she took on her last barrel of freight. The captain said that if the wind should be fair, of which he thought there was every appearance, he should leave the next day, Sabbath. I told him that he had better hold on till Monday; but that, if he must go, he need not expect me to accompany him, though it would add some hundreds of miles to my coasting. I told him, however, that I thought he would be here on Monday—that I should pray for head wind if he attempted to go. He said that he would pray for fair wind, and we would see who would be answered.

"Sabbath proved to be a lovely day—calm nearly all day; part of the time a fair breeze, but not enough to spread sails; part of the day quite a breeze ahead, so that the captain did not move from the spot. Monday all day wind blew strong ahead. This morning wind fair, the captain got off, and has no doubt made a good run; but I am not with him. Having been so much longer detained than I anticipated, I can not visit Fond du Lac, Sandy Lake, and all the other places in the round, and get back for our camp meeting. I have, therefore, arranged my business with brother Spates at Sandy Lake by letter communication. There is nothing of sufficient importance to call me to Fond du Lac, as we have no missionary there. I shall, therefore, the Lord willing, visit the missions among the miners, which are assuming prominence and importance, and the Kewawenon mission. In all this I believe I am directed by Providence. It will save the Missionary Society about seventy dollars and myself about five hundred miles of coasting; will give me ample time to spend among the missions about the Lake, and I doubt not more good will be accomplished than if I had gone to Sandy Lake. It is also probable that by this time our General conference has set off Sandy Lake into another conference."

The steamer Baltimore was just about to make her first trip up Lake Superior. On the evening of the 25th I went aboard, bound for Kewawenon. Here we found ourselves very comfortably situated. Our boat had excellent accommodations, and every thing was conducted in a quiet and orderly manner; not crowded with passengers—day delightful—almost a dead calm. I busied myself during this pleasant trip in reading the doings of our General conference, which I had up to the 12th inst., and in perusing Larrabee's Evidences of Natural and Revealed Religion, which work I read with much interest. I could but contrast, thankfully, the agreeableness of this voyage with the rough and perilous one made over the same route on the Fur Trader, in 1846. At four o'clock, P. M., the 26th inst., we were opposite the Pictured Rocks. It was at this time that we had such a sublime view of this great natural curiosity, delineated in another place.

Just after dark we reached Carp river, now Marquette, where we stopped about half an hour. Had just time to go ashore and see our missionary, brother Benson, and wife, whom I found well and in good spirits.

Thursday morning, about six o'clock, we anchored at the mouth of Portage river, where we were detained most of the day. Just before night we reached the Kewawenon mission. Found all in usual health. Sister Barnum still lingered on the shore of time, to the astonishment of every body. For five or six years wasting disease had been feeling after her heart-strings, but her time had not yet come. As the gentle disappearing of the unclouded sun such was to be her exit from this world of conflict and pain.*

Temporally things looked flourishing about the mission—never more so. Spiritually some of the old members had recently proved unfaithful to the

* Since this she and her husband have both left the world in triumph.

trust committed to them; by falling into known and open sin they had brought reproach upon the cause of Christ. The boat also brought trouble among us by furnishing liquor to some Indians, who became intoxicated in a short time. No tongue can tell the evils arising from this one source at our missions. Their name is legion. But that the mission through the year had been blessed with a good degree of religious prosperity is evident from brother Barnum's report, published in the Missionary Advocate, dated January 1, 1852, as follows:

"TO THE CORRESPONDING SECRETARY:

"DEAR BROTHER,—Again would we record the goodness of God for the preservation of our lives through another year with thankfulness. The past quarter, with afflictions—an unusual amount of sickness among the Indians and a few deaths—we have had the Divine blessing, very much to our encouragement. The Indians I mentioned in a former communication, who came among us and had the small-pox last winter, have again come in from the woods, accompanied by some of their relatives and friends. They came this time last fall for the avowed purpose of taking up their abode with us, and becoming Christians. They have been for several weeks listening with marked attention to the word, which has been preached, mainly, with special reference to their case. Now they are members of our Church. Last Sabbath they came—old and young—renounced their heathenism, and then received Christian baptism. I baptized twenty then, which, with two previously baptized, makes twenty-two the last quarter, nineteen of whom were from the woods. Our congregations are good, and our schools, both Sunday and week-day, though small, are larger than they were last year. With our troubles we will not trouble you further—for our blessings you will help us to praise the Giver.

"Yours in the Gospel,

"NELSON BARNUM."

The Indians referred to in brother Barnum's report were from *Lake Vieux Desert*, distant some three or more days' march in the wilderness from Kewawenon. Till quite recently they had adhered to their heathen customs and superstitions; now they were disposed to abandon them for the faith that is in Jesus.

Saturday and Sabbath we held our quarterly meeting here—a season of some interest. Especially on the Sabbath there was great solemnity, and much deep feeling in the congregation. Our sacramental occasion in the afternoon was deeply solemn and impressive. The meetings throughout the day afforded proof that God was still with our people at Kewawenon.

On Monday we had a very tedious council, in which sundry matters, important and unimportant, were considered. But the details I pass over.

Tuesday, June 1st, I was prevented from making an early start for Eagle river by rain. Left about ten o'clock, A. M., accompanied by David King and N., and reached *Wim-e-te-go-zhenses,* or the *Little Frenchman's,* as this name imports, some seventeen miles distant, where we spent the night.

Wednesday we were up at three o'clock, and in half an hour were again on our way. We breakfasted at the head of Torch Lake. Thence we walked nineteen miles to the Phœnix Mine, where we arrived at five o'clock, P. M., and were kindly entertained by the missionary, Rev. S. Steele.

Thursday, 3d, left Eagle river, on the steamer Baltimore, for Ontonagon, where we were anchored at four o'clock on Friday morning. The day was spent in business, making calls, etc.

Saturday, accompanied by the missionary, Rev. E. H. Day, I walked over the trail to the Minnesota Mine, where we arrived about five o'clock, P. M. The trail was not so wet as the year before, but was bad enough at best. Sabbath I preached twice to the people, and administered the sacrament to *two* persons, besides the preachers. The state of religion at the mine was low. There were but five or six professors of religion, and some of them were backward in using the means of grace.

Monday we traveled over a muddy, rugged, and mountainous trail, some fourteen miles, to the Trap Rock Mine. In our way we passed the Forest, the United States, the Cushman, the Plummer, and Norwich mines. Two of these had been abandoned, the others were encouraged by flattering prospects. At the Trap Rock Rev. J. Buzzo, a very intelligent local preacher, was agent. I preached at night to some fifty or sixty men—quite a company for such a wilderness.

Tuesday, 8th, after a fatiguing walk of about eighteen miles, over an intolerably-muddy trail, we were again at the mouth of the Ontonagon. Preached here at night. Wednesday and Thursday I was detained in waiting for a boat.

Friday morning the Baltimore came in before we were up. About ten o'clock I left for Eagle river, where we arrived at half-past five o'clock, P. M. Shared again brother Steele's hospitality.

Saturday went with brother Steele to the Cliff. Met at the chapel and held our quarterly conference. Thence went to the North American, where brother Steele attended to the funeral obsequies of an unfortunate man, who was killed the day before by falling into a shaft of the South Cliff, a depth of some forty feet. The poor man died—without leaving an evidence behind of his conversion—having in England a wife and seven children. The funeral was numerously attended.

In the evening I preached at the Cliff to a pretty good attendance. Sabbath morning I was taken quite ill with diarrhea, and felt indisposed for the labors of the day. A faintness came over me during the love-feast. I was obliged to stop in the midst of the opening prayer before preaching. Brother Steele gave out the hymn. After singing I arose, not knowing whether I should be able to preach. But the Lord strengthened me for the work, and I was enabled to speak with more than usual freedom, on the cross of Christ, Galatians vi, 14. But in proceeding to administer the sacrament I was barely able to conclude the consecratory prayer, and was obliged to call on brother Steele to conclude the service. After meeting I went to the North American, where Dr. Senter gave me an opiate. His kind lady furnished me with a comfortable bed. After two or three hours' rest, and a cup of tea, and a little boiled rice, which I ate at the Doctor's, I felt much refreshed. With the Doctor's family I then repaired to the chapel for our evening meeting. A fine congregation came out, to whom God gave me strength to preach, with at least usual freedom. This quarterly meeting was, on the whole, the best one I had witnessed on Lake Superior. When the meeting had closed I accompanied the family of brother Steele to their residence, at the Phœnix Mine, much fatigued of course. I never felt more fully than during this day, of great bodily weakness, that *Christ was my strength.* The Church was quickened by this quarterly meeting, and the effect did not cease when the meeting closed. Reference is made to this farther on.

Monday felt the effects of the illness of Sabbath; rested most of the day, waiting the return of the Napoleon; left on this boat in the evening for the

Saut; crossed over to Isle Royal, about fifty miles, during the night. Half the day Tuesday was spent at Rock Harbor, discharging freight. Thence went to Siskowit Bay, about eighteen miles west, where we were detained till after night. Returned to Rock Harbor again before morning.

Wednesday, the 16th, we took our leave of Isle Royal, early in the morning, and after being in the fog most of the time for two days, arrived safely at the Saut Thursday evening. What was a little remarkable, we had had no rough sea from the time I left till my return. I was happy to find all well at home.

TRIP TO CARP RIVER.

Friday, the 25th, left the Saut in the evening on the propeller Manhattan, to visit the mission at Marquette. We had a pleasant and quick passage, and arrived Saturday at noon. Spent the afternoon in making calls. Preached in the evening to a pretty good congregation, considering that they were called out without any previous warning.

Sabbath morning our love-feast was a precious season. An intelligent congregation assembled at half-past ten o'clock, A. M., to whom I proclaimed the counsel of God. At two o'clock, P. M., the people came out again—preached again, and administered the sacrament of the Lord's supper. Felt liberty both times in preaching. The congregation were not only very attentive to the word spoken, but several gave evidence of considerable emotion. We realized the presence of God in the breaking of bread. A Presbyterian minister was present who was traveling for the benefit of his health. He communed with us and aided in the services. About thirty communed.

In the evening we had a prayer meeting, in which several prayed with great fervency. God was in the midst to bless. Brother Babb, the minister referred to, offered some very appropriate remarks. Before the meeting closed I spoke with reference to the great change God had wrought about Lake Superior, since I had become acquainted with the country. "Stated that, in the fall of 1844, I had coasted along the shore, near the place where we were worshiping, with my family, on our way to Kewawenon; that, a short distance to the west, we were wind-bound two days and a half; that, at that time, no traces of civilization were to be seen where we now are; and that, from Saut Ste. Marie to La Pointe, there was but one station--Protestant—where God was statedly worshiped, in public, and that one was Kewawenon. I stated, also, that, in January, 1846, I passed on snow-shoes over the ground where we now worshiped, to visit a band of Indians at Grand Island, and that *then* there was no trace of civilization at Carp river. Remarked that I could never forget the day of my arrival at this place. I was excessively fatigued. My feet were badly blistered, and when I had reached the wigwam of *Mah-je-ge-zhik*, I was so rejoiced that tears involuntarily crowded to my eyes.

That I was much refreshed on a repast of small potatoes and fresh venison. Now behold the change! We have several congregations at Ontonagon, who delight to worship God. On Point Kewenaw there are several interesting congregations. Stated that, two weeks before, I had enjoyed a refreshing quarterly meeting at the Cliff Mine, when we were permitted to see about fifty in the love-feast, and a large and respectable congregation in attendance upon preaching. And, with reference to Carp river, we could but say, 'what hath God wrought!' The Yankee had found his way here and begun to level the forest. A village had sprung up as if by magic; and here the banner of the cross had been unfurled, and we had this day sat together in a heavenly place in Christ Jesus."

This train of thought awakened grateful feelings in my own mind, and from the attention of the audience, we judged that they were deeply interested in these buddings of hope and promise. Thus closed the Sabbath and our quarterly meeting, a season owned of God, and which will doubtless be remembered in eternity.

Monday morning, before I was up, the Napoleon came up to the wharf, on her way to the Saut. I was thus remarkably favored, to be able to return so soon. I then noted in my journal: "It has seemed to me this whole season, as if God was leading me along in the way of his peculiar providence. My mind has seemed to be constantly staid by faith on him, and such an abiding sense of his presence—such tranquillity of mind I have seldom felt. He has also made my way smooth across the great deep. Not the first rough sea have I had in all my journeyings this summer. O, how great is his goodness! My soul, praise the Lord!"

Toward evening of this day, the sky became very dark and threatening; clouds flew in different directions; it thundered; the heavens were now in a blaze; then all was dense darkness again, and anon the lightning, in a zigzag track, would part the sky. God "spoke in thunder and breathed in lightning." I stood upon the deck, and gazed as upon the Eternal, revealed in fire—I heard his voice in the thunder. In the dark wave now lit up with the lightning's glare—then nearly shut out from vision by the dense cloud which hung over us; in the vast expanse of waters, scarcely disturbed except by the rotary force of the screw by which we were propelled, leaving behind us a foaming wake; overhead and all around were displayed the wisdom, power, and goodness of God, seeing which I could but adore. It rained through the night; but, farther than this, the dark clouds only threatened. We had calm sea to the Saut, which we reached by four o'clock the next morning.

On the way I read the life of Summerfield, much to my edification. "Wonderful man!" as I then exclaimed. "How meek, how humble, how much like the beloved disciple! How much did he commune

29

with God! What a career of usefulness did he run! But how soon was he taken from the Church! Surely he lived a long life in a few years; gathered many laurels, all of which he hung upon the cross of Christ; and after having suffered, as well as done the will of God, he died in peace, and in hope of a glorious immortality. O for a measure of the flame by which he was consumed!"

The following Sabbath, being the Fourth of July, I had the privilege of delivering a national discourse to a large audience for the place, who heard attentively the word addressed to them, founded on Psalm cxlvii, 20: "*He hath not dealt so with any nation.*" In this I endeavored to delineate some of the striking evidences of the guiding hand of Providence, in the birth and progress of our nation, as clearly traceable in the pages of her history.

CHAPTER XXV.

LAKE SUPERIOR INDIAN CAMP MEETING.

On the 12th of July we had quite an arrival at our place, of Indians and ministerial brethren from Canada, to unite with us in a camp meeting to be held at White Fish Point, about fifty miles distant, on the shore of Lake Superior. Most of the next day was spent in procuring supplies and arranging preliminaries. We arrived at the encampment early on Wednesday morning the 14th, a day in advance of the time, and were happy to find several tents already on the ground, among which were those of Rev. E. Steele and Rev. P. Marksman, from Naomikong, whose families were with them.

The following account of this camp meeting, with slight additions from my journal, was published in the Christian Advocate and Journal, and in the Missionary Advocate. It is dated Saut Ste. Marie, Michigan, 27th July, 1852:

"TO THE CORRESPONDING SECRETARY:

"Rev. and Dear Brother,—In my last I apprised you of our intention to hold a camp meeting at White Fish Point, Lake Superior, to commence on the 15th instant. As this is the first thing of the kind, per haps, ever held north of Lower Michigan, in the vicinity of the Great Lakes, and this is certainly the case so far as Lake Superior is concerned, it may be acceptable to the friends of missions to learn the result.

"It was a union meeting. Rev. Mr. M'Dougall, from Garden river, Canada, united with us, and brought with him forty Indians, from his mission.

"Through his influence we were favored with other very valuable help from Canada, for which we can not in too strong terms express our sense of gratitude. Their labors were greatly blessed to the good of our people. These were—

"*Rev. L. Warner, chairman of the Barrie district, Canada West*, a large and laborious mission district, including eighteen stations. Mr. Warner is a gentleman of a large robust frame, a broad and full English face, the very picture of perfect health. From the cast of his cranium a stranger would award to him a high degree of intellectual prominence. There is in his carriage an air of *hauteur*, but this is only in appearance. If the discourses he preached while among us were a fair specimen, he ranks considerably above mediocrity as a preacher. They were excellent, not as specimens of pulpit oratory in the popular sense, but as clear, full, Scriptural exhibitions of Gospel truth, practically applied to the hearers, and accompanied with the unction and power of the Holy Ghost. Blessed with uncommon strength of lungs and great compass of voice, he made the encampment resound with his thundering appeals to the hearts of sinners. Nor was he any where more at home, or more active, than in the prayer meeting. This last remark is true of all our English brethren who were with us. While in their sermons they cast into the deep the Gospel net, by the fervency of their *prayers* they helped to draw it ashore, and gather up the fishes.

"But much as we prized the services of Mr. Warner, we were, if possible, still more rejoiced to have with us the experienced, venerable, and much-beloved *Indian preacher*, Rev. Peter Jones, whose praise is in all the Churches. His dignified appearance, holy walk and conversation, the sweetness of his spirit, the holy fervor of his soul, and the persuasive eloquence with which he preached Jesus and the resurrection, won the hearts and affections of all on the ground. We esteemed him not only as a brother beloved, but were constantly reminded by his deportment of some of our venerable bishops—an office which, *de facto*, he fills among his Indian brethren, though *untitled* and *not in the line* of the *would-be* succession. Long may he yet live to bless the Church! And may his crown in heaven be filled with stars, as seals of his ministry on earth!

"Next we had with us Rev. Mr. Sallows, lately stationed at the Bruce Mine—a man of a delicate constitution, of fair preaching abilities, and an ardent devotion to the interests of his Master's kingdom. These were our visitors from abroad.

"Rev. Mr. M'Dougall, who is our neighbor, we

'esteem very highly for his work's sake,' as a devoted, untiring, and successful missionary. And his assistant, Rev. brother Blaker, is a good helper.

"As to the preachers on our own side, I will only say, that, 'by the grace of God, we are what we are.'

"We had, in all, nine preachers, and Jesus in the midst. We had throughout the meeting a demonstration that Methodism *is one*, and Methodist preachers *are one*, the world over.

"*Commencement.*—As the missionaries and a goodly number of Indians were on the ground on the 14th inst., we commenced on the afternoon of that day, instead of the next, the time appointed. We had, in all, twenty tents on the ground, two of which were connected with our mission—one for the preachers, and the other, a large tent, occupied by Rev. E. Steele's family from Naomikong, where, in connection with brother M'Dougall's tent, the kind sisters, with much hospitality, ministered to our wants. About two hundred Indians attended the meeting; not as many as we had expected; many were providentially hindered. There were four tents from Kewawenon, a distance of two hundred miles.

"*Divine blessing.*—From first to last we were constrained to own the hand of a kind Providence. We were much blessed in getting to and from the ground. We were remarkably preserved from sickness, though we had no small ground to fear that the small-pox might make its appearance among the Indians, as some had been exposed. Some from Garden river, after having come as far as the *Saut*, returned home again for fear of this. We were favored with excellent weather, and with no disturbance from any source. There was not a dog to move his tongue against us. A more orderly camp meeting was probably never held. The Indians who had been on the ground before us, fishing, caught abundance of fish, and came and threw them on the shore for common use; so that, with the bread we took from home, we had a good supply of the same food to eat on which Christ fed the hungry multitudes. And the best of all is, we were fed spiritually; sinners were powerfully converted, backsliders reclaimed, the Church greatly quickened, and God's name glorified, in the salvation of souls. Under the very first sermon a shower of melting mercy was poured down upon us, while brother Jones, who preached, gave us an account of the work of God among the Indians in Canada, and then related his own Christian experience.

"*The meeting a novelty to the Indians.*—But, though an unction and power attended the word preached, it was with some difficulty that the Indians were led to drink into the camp-meeting spirit. All was new. They had only heard about these meetings. But at last, *en masse*, they threw off the shackles. With the mighty weapon of prayer they besieged the eternal throne. In the hand of omnipotent faith it became the *key* to unlock the door of mercy and salvation, and the healing stream flowed plenteously all around. There was seen the wounded penitent, whose conscience had been transfixed by the arrow from Jehovah's quiver, crying for mercy. There lay prostrate the soul, smitten to earth, under the mighty power of God. There was seen the prodigal returning again to his father's house. Mingled with the cries and groans of penitents were heard the shouts and praises of souls redeemed and saved. Parents were seen bending over their weeping children, to point them to Jesus, and children were seen weeping and praying over unconverted parents; brother interceded in behalf of brother, and sister in behalf of sister. Here was a struggle which, to a thoughtless world, might have appeared like disorder. But it was with each a struggle for salvation, and, in the view of heaven, presented a scene of greater moral sublimity than all the boasted pageantry of earth. 'There is joy in heaven among the angels of God' when sinners repent. We do not know how many were converted; we think at least thirty, besides those reclaimed. And among those converted it was matter of rejoicing to see an old heathen woman, perhaps eighty years old, the mother of David King, chief, from Kewawenon. She, with several others, infants and adults, was baptized in the name of the holy Trinity. About thirty united with the Church, to be enrolled at their respective residences. We think there are others who will unite at their homes.

"*Marriage.*—A wedding took place on Sabbath evening in the altar. The couple were from Garden river. They appeared very young, and the mother held in her arms a sprightly infant. Their missionary held the child in his arms, while brother Jones performed the solemn service, after which the child and its mother were dedicated to God in baptism. One of our clerical friends present, not understanding much Indian, and supposing the whole to be a baptismal ceremony, and noticing that the officiating minister paid almost exclusive attention to this couple, to the neglect of some candidates for baptism standing near, exclaimed, 'Brother Jones, you have forgot *them*,' the persons above alluded to. Who ever witnessed such a scene before!

"*Missionary meeting.*—Saturday afternoon we had a deeply-interesting missionary meeting. An Indian brother—Rev. Mr. Blaker—was called to the chair, and, after a pithy opening speech, presided with much dignity. Short speeches were made by several ministers and Indians, and a very cheering missionary spirit pervaded the meeting. As time had advanced, and much remained to be done preparatory to the holy Sabbath, no collection was taken up on the spot. But this was done privately, by brother Blaker among the Indians from Canada, and by brother Marksman among our own. The result was announced on the Sabbath, which proved good, for our people pledged and paid over forty dollars; all of which we hope to have ready by conference. The Indians from Canada contributed liberally, according to their numbers—over thirteen dollars, I think. On account of the poverty of our Indians, we have made no attempt of this kind before; but we judged that the time had come to inculcate more fully the truth that 'it is more blessed to give than to receive.' An Indian from Kewawenon gave three dollars in money; and a pious widow came into our tent, and said that she had not much to give, but left, as a testimonial of her love to the cause, *fifty-six cents.* The widow's mite will have its reward.

"*The love-feast and sacrament of the Lord's supper.*—We spent the Sabbath till afternoon in these delightful exercises. *Thirty-three* persons spoke of the dealings of God with their souls. While so doing our hearts were strangely warmed with God's love. The day was beautifully clear; the very atmosphere seemed benignant with the smile of heaven. The slight rustling among the forest pines was only indicative of the heavenly zephyrs which were fanning our spirits. The bright sun reminded us how brightly the Sun of righteousness was shining into our hearts. The surrounding stillness seemed to say that the dove of mercy was poised over the congregation, to witness the confession of sinners saved. Angels, with intense interest, were gazing upon the scene. All things conspired to say, 'How dreadful is this place! This is the house of God, and this is the gate of heaven.' Many who would gladly have spoken could not for want of time. At the sacrament, which immediately followed, seventy-nine persons communed. Many will in heaven, we trust, remember this blessed season. At the risk of extending this sketch, I copy the testimony of several of our Indian brethren given in the love-feast. I am enabled to do this through the kindness of Rev. Peter Jones, who interpreted what they said. There are some whose remarks we did not get; and of others, only a part was obtained:

"*Rev. P. Marksman* said: 'I will tell a little what God has done for my soul. I am happy in my heart. I love God and my brethren. I desire my Indian brethren to be converted. The day is clear.* I know that trials are ahead, but I will overcome all through Christ. I hope to receive a crown of glory. It is a high day to us all. May God in Christ bring us all to meet in heaven!'

"*Rev. Mr. Blaker*, from Garden river, said: 'It is seven years since my father died, who exhorted me, on his death-bed, to serve God. *Joseph Skunk* was the means of my conversion, five years ago. I will fight my passage through till death.'

"*Rev. Joseph Taunchey* said: 'The sun shines in my heart. I am in poor health. Am resolved to serve God. I was rejoiced to see some converted to God last night.'

"*Thomas Nah-ben-a-osh* said: 'I am young.† I gave my heart to God while young. I have passed through many trials. Many of my relatives have gone to heaven. I hope to meet all in glory. I desire the prayers of all God's people."

---

* He meant spiritually as well as literally.

† He is, doubtless, over thirty years of age, but he *felt* young.

"*Pi-ah-be-dah-sing*, one of the chiefs from Garden river, said: 'I would be glad if the weather—sun of the Great Spirit—would stop to allow the meeting to continue longer. I am thankful for the labors of brother M'Dougall. I am very happy in my heart. I know that God has changed my heart.'

"*John Ogishta*, once a boarding-scholar at our mission, said: 'Since I heard brother Pitezel I have been trying to serve God. I was converted last spring, in the sugar-bush, under brother Marksman's preaching.'

"*Ah-be-tah-ge-zhik* said: 'I was converted to God, in the sugar-bush, last spring—same time as the one above. I was very happy. I long for the conversion of my relatives. I am very happy now, and ever since I came here.'

"*G. Bedell*, from Kewawenon, said: 'I think I have just come to life. I am very happy. Last night, while praying for sinners, it was like heaven on earth. The singing was heavenly. I feel as if I must go and tell all the Indians how good Jesus is.'

"*Johnson Sky* said: 'I feel that I must give thanks to God. Seven years since I was told that I was a sinner. I felt sick in my heart and prayed. By and by my wife left me, and, on her dying bed, exhorted me to serve God. When I heard last winter that this camp meeting was going to be held, I was glad. I have been greatly blessed since I came here.'

"*Moses O-mon-o-mon-ee* said: 'I have been a stumbling Christian; I rose up, and then fell; I found that I was not soundly converted. But since I came here my soul has been blessed, and now the sun shines very bright and clear.'

"*Mother Waishkee* said: 'I am very happy. One of my sons died, and on his death-bed exhorted me to be faithful. I am glad that I am here. I know that God loves me. I am thankful to see my children turning to God. I hope to meet my brethren and sisters in heaven.'

"*Ruth Nah-ben-a-osh* said: 'I am glad in my heart. I am glad to feast with my brethren. Religion is very good for me. I will try to meet all in heaven.'

"*Sarah Pwaun* said: 'I feel very small in my heart. By faith I see my children in heaven, who exhorted me to be faithful. I often shed tears of joy. I am very happy now, and want the prayers of the brethren.'

"*David King*, chief, from Kewawenon, said: 'It has been ten years since I began to pray. I am very glad to be here to unite with the people of God in this feast. I am thankful that I have heard the words of the Great Spirit which were brought to me from the east.'

"*Adam Ah-nun-goo*, from *Lake Vieux Desert*, converted from heathenism last winter, at Kewawenon, said: 'I feel the good feeling in my heart. As the sun now shines so does the heavenly sun now shine in my heart. I feel as if I could now arise and go to my Father.'

"*Nancy Asher* said that she was happy in the Lord.

"*William Pwaun*, one of the chiefs from Naomikong, said: 'About ten years ago John Kah-beege came here. I then began to pray. I was converted in the woods when alone. I was very happy all the night. I could not sleep, I was so happy. When the morning came I felt as if a host of angels were around me. I looked up to heaven and saw, by faith, the glory of heaven. I went and told my family what God had done for my soul.'

"*Metash*, from Garden river, said: 'I have Jesus for my sun.'

"*Louis Waishkee*, chief, from Waishkees Bay, said: 'I have been taught in all the arts of the old Indian ways; but I have cast them all away. Religion grows better and better.'

"*Henry Kakakoons* said: 'I am well known by my Indian brethren, and what I have been—a great sinner. I am very poor.' This is all I got of what he said, though he was evidently much blessed.

"*Isaac Kakakoons*, who had apparently been a long time waiting for an opportunity to speak, said: "I know that my mind centers on Christ. It goes right to God; for this reason I am very thankful.'

"*Ogishta*, chief, from Garden river, arose and stood upon a bench in the altar, and said: 'I put myself in a conspicuous place, that you may look at a poor Indian who has a very heavy load. I want to tell what is the state of my poor body and heart.

I am almost fifty years old. I have seen a good deal of earthly pleasure. And these things now make me cry. Nothing formerly could make me cry, only when my children were called away from me. I have lost several. My eyes have often wept; I have lost my brothers and sisters; I have seen them die. Now since I have come here I rejoice to hear the words that I have heard, and to see what I have seen. I am glad that brother M'Dougall was determined to bring me along. About twenty years ago I heard about the Great Spirit. Rev. Mr. M'Murray—of the Protestant Episcopal Church—continued with us about six years. I then exhorted the Indians to become Christians. *Metash* joined in with me. But I found that I was only deceiving myself. Now I have found out what the true religion is. My eyes weep and my heart shakes. When I lost my children I felt very sorry. I was very anxious that they should all do well. When I was young I was accustomed to fast, and to blacken my face with charcoal. Some years ago I gave my son John to the mission school—at Saut Ste. Marie. He did not do right when he ran away from the school; but now he is weeping on account of the goodness of God. I wish him to be useful. When I heard of the *fast*,* I set apart the whole day, *that my soul might be fed.* I desir

* *Saturday*, till afternoon, was set apart for fasting and prayer. *Ogishta* did not break his fast till Sunday evening! and then was urged to eat! *Christian*, here learn *self-denial*. The body was unfed for two days, "*that the soul might be fed.*"

to walk with my brethren, and go on with them in the good way, and met them in heaven.'

"*Close.*—The camp meeting—*formally*—closed on Monday afternoon. A sermon was preached by brother Jones, and we then marched around the ground and sung, while each gave to the other the hand in affectionate farewell; but, in truth, though most orderly, it was the driest farewell I ever witnessed. The wind was ahead, and, much as our brethren from abroad wanted to leave the ground that day, the Indians were sagacious enough to know that this was out of the question; they, therefore, rather *smiled* than *wept*, at being so hoaxed.

"Well, camp meeting was now over, but we were all as firmly fixed as ever. Something must be done. The first thing we knew the Indians were collecting about the stand, and we soon discovered that the *rite of Indian christening* was about to be performed.

[In the published account of this meeting I did not give the particulars of this naming process. Its novelty was interesting to us, and may be equally so to the reader, and is, therefore, here briefly described.

The chief, from Garden river, made an opening speech, in which he mentioned "the benefits which the Indians had received from the labors of the ministers, and that they wished to remember them, but they had names that it was difficult for them to speak. He was going to give Mr. Warner a name that any *child* could understand." He then named him so that all could hear—"*Shing-wauk*," the "*Pine*-

Tree," by the way, the name of the aged Garden river chief, O-gish-ta's father. He then said that, "when Shing-wauk should come among them the next year, and should lift up his voice, they must all gather around him as chickens around an old hen;" to which all heartily responded, "*Haiah!*"

They next named the writer through *Wm. Pwaun,* who acted as speaker. The name "*Wa-zah-wah-wa-doong,*" the "*Yellow Beard,*" is an old family name, and was the name of one of the best Indians ever connected with the *Te-quah-me-nah* band, who died a few years since, in the faith of the Christian, lamented by all who knew him. I was then addressed as a *brother* by the acting chief, *Pwaun.*

Rev. E. Steele was next named, "*I-ah-be-wa-dic,*" which signifies "*Male-Elk.*" He was warmly greeted afterward, as were the rest, as a brother now adopted by the Indians.

The other ministerial brethren having had this honor conferred on them before, were now left out of the list. Thus closed this novel performance.]

"At night we had a famous temperance meeting. This, we hope, in its future bearing upon the Indians, will prove as beneficial as any meeting we had. Louis Waishkee, an Indian chief, made us a dignified president. The meeting was addressed by several speakers. Marked attention was paid to all that was said. Meanwhile a pledge of total abstinence was presented, and one hundred and five persons signed—most of the Indians then on the ground.

"Tuesday morning, after breakfast, we left the encampment, in a large batteau, with the Indians from Garden river, and the preachers from Canada, amidst abundant cheers, the firing of guns, etc.

"Now, my dear brother, I have given you a hastily-written account of this *first*, and, to us, interesting, Lake Superior camp meeting. You can only get a glimpse through this imperfect sketch. But I hope that at least it will be seen and felt, that true religion is the same,

'In the void waste as in the city full;'

the same in the heart of a poor northern Indian as in the heart of an Anglo-Saxon; that the name of Jesus is that which charms the fears and soothes the sorrows of the heathen; and that,

'Where He vital breathes there must be joy.'

"That souls have been saved and God glorified, is to us cause of rejoicing; 'yea, and we will rejoice.' Pray for our continued prosperity.

"Affectionately yours, J. H. PITEZEL."

After Rev. Peter Jones returned home, he wrote a very interesting account of his missionary tour to Lakes Huron and Superior, which was published in the Christian Guardian, Toronto, in which our camp meeting was described quite minutely. Mr. Jones's complete acquaintance with the Ojibwa, enabled him to seize upon the peculiar expression of the language, so as to present it with great force. I can not better close this chapter than by giving a brief extract frcm this account. It thus describes our temperance meeting:

"The wind being contrary, we were obliged to tarry on the ground another night. In the evening we held a temperance meeting. Chief Waubojeig Washkee was called to the chair, and made a short speech, after which the following brethren addressed the meeting: Warner, Pitezel, Steele, Gregory, B. Shing-wauk and myself. The usual pledge was then readily signed by one hundred and five Indians. Chief Ogestaih was then requested to proclaim the number who had given their names to the cause of temperance, which he did in a masterly manner, causing his powerful voice to resound through the woods and along the shore of the Lake to a great distance. He rose up and said, 'Hear me, hear me, Ogestaih has been chosen to proclaim the result of this meeting; the number of Indians who now say that they will never again drink the fire-water, is one hundred and five. These one hundred and five Indians now say, that there shall be no more deaths by drowning in the water—no more burning to death—no more quarreling nor fighting—no more bruised eyes—no more dragging the wife by the hair of her head—no more murders—and you who are husbands now say, you will no more be jealous of your wives, and you wives say you will be no more jealous of your husbands—and last of all, Ogestaih says, that he also will no more be jealous of his wife. This is all I have to say.' At the conclusion of each sentence, the usual Indian exclamation of '*Kaih*,'* was shouted from many voices throughout the camp-ground."

---

* This is evidently a misprint—it should be '*Haiah*.'

CHAPTER XXVI.

A GENERAL VIEW OF LAKE SUPERIOR MISSIONS.

A FULL account has before been given of the revival which was in progress at the village of the Ste. Marie, during the winter. Toward the close of the summer we had to record with pain that some, who gave promise of better things, measured their steps back again to the world; but most of the converts went on their way rejoicing. A message was received at the Fort from the War Department, by which the troops were ordered to California. This broke in upon our ranks. Sergeant M. and his family, of whom such particular mention has been made, received an honorable discharge from the army. I gave them certificates of their standing in the Church, which they took with them into Wisconsin, where they located, and again united with the Church. In the fall I had the privilege of seeing the minister at the Wisconsin conference who received them into the Church. After these removals we had left eight members, six of whom were on probation. We continued to have an intelligent and interesting congregation to attend upon the preached word, and had reason to believe that, though much of the seed sown fell upon a floating community, it was not all lost.

Our Sunday school was kept up with a good degree of interest.

Naomikong.—The signs of progress were very encouraging at this Indian station most of the year. A letter from Rev. E. Steele, of December 6th, speaks on this wise: "Our congregations are large considering the population. The house is frequently crowded to overflowing. The Indians are attentive to the preached word. They all, *saint and sinner, male and female, old and young, kneel* in time of prayer. We have had some interesting meetings, in which the presence of Christ was realized among his people."

In the following, which I take from my report, published in the Annual Report of the Missionary Society for 1852, we have the ripe Gospel fruit in death of the seed which was sown in life:

"Since the last report two members have died—one, a young man, whose name was Francis Bangs.* He not only died in great peace, but in the triumphs of faith, praising God, and exhorting all to meet him in heaven. The other was a man somewhat advanced in life. His name was Henry *O-ge-mah-be-nas*, which signifies *king of birds.* He embraced Christianity about two years since, and we trust he now rests in Abraham's bosom. There is now a sister in the last stages of consumption, and, from all appearance, near

*"See a tribute to the memory of this young man, by Rev. S. Steele, in the 'Ladies' Repository for January, 1852,' under '*The Dying Indian.*'"

the spirit-world. She is resigned—willing to die—says Christ is precious, and believes she shall go to heaven." The sister has since died, leaving a family of nine children with her husband to mourn their loss.

Brother Steele, in a letter dated January 30th, 1852, gives an account of a pagan woman who has recently embraced the Gospel. I think it well worthy a place in a missionary report. In a conversation with brother Marksman, she said, "'My husband, who is a pagan, went to Grand Island to live last fall. I told him I would not go, but stay at Naomikong with my daughter, that I might have an opportunity to hear the word of the Lord preached. And now I can understand the preached word better than ever before. The light has broken into my mind gradually. Some time since I was very sick—thought I should die—could not bear the thought of dying and being buried as a heathen, but felt a strong desire to die and be buried in a Christian manner. When I felt unhappy in my heart I went and prayed, and my mind became calm and happy; and for some time past I have felt a desire to unite with this people—Methodists—but last Sabbath evening I became more convinced of my duty than ever before. I now present myself. I am now willing to be baptized.'

"The next Sabbath she was baptized, and received into the Church on probation."

I copy the following from the same letter:

"Sabbath evening, the 25th instant, after a warm exhortation, and an invitation, seven kneeled at the altar of prayer, and cried aloud for mercy. Praise God! O Lord, carry on thy blessed work!

"Tuesday evening, January 27th, we had meeting again, and twelve came forward as seekers of religion, among them three of the mission boys. A young woman spoke. She said, 'The Lord blessed me last Sabbath evening when I came forward for prayers, and I have been happy ever since; and, by the grace of God assisting me, I will live faithful till death.'

"Thursday evening, January 29th, we assembled for our usual prayer meeting, and ten came forward for prayers. One young man was converted. He arose and said, 'While I was wrestling in prayer with God, I felt joy in my heart, and my heart arose up to meet God. And now I know that Jesus is precious to my soul.'

"We hope that what we have seen is but the dropping from the cloud which precedes the sweeping shower. O pray for us, that God may bring all these children of the forest to a knowledge of his salvation."

We have lost and gained some members, so that the statistics are about the same as before reported—sixty-three—of whom four are whites and eighteen on probation. The day school numbers twenty-eight scholars, eight of whom are girls. They are reported as progressing well in their studies. The Sabbath school is also doing well. The children are succeeding well in committing Scripture to memory; seventeen children in six weeks had recited four hundred and seventy-six verses. This seems small to such as are accustomed to the recitations of white children; but let white children commit Scripture to memory in Indian, then compare them with Indian *beginners*. The school is comprised of twenty-one scholars, and four officers and teachers.

Four children board in the mission family; and, since the death of his sister, brother Marksman has taken into his family two of her children.

The property of the station, including land purchased, mission-house, school-house, etc., is estimated at four hundred dollars.

Within one year these Indians had built eight or ten comfortable log-houses. They were gradually laying aside the chase and turning their attention to agriculture and other industrial pursuits. From their proximity to the Lake, and their superior skill as fishermen, fishing must always be one of the pursuits of this people, and one which, if properly followed, may be made lucrative. It must be to them what the farm and the trade is to many others. Our camp meeting was made a great blessing to this station. The Indians spent much of the summer at White Fish Point, engaged in fishing. They remained longer than they would have done on account of the small-pox which broke out at the Saut, and had been conveyed to the saw-mill, within six miles of the mission. Though some of them had been exposed to this dreadful scourge, up to the time of my latest intelligence, none of them had taken it. One woman had the varioloid. We see and own in this the hand of Providence.

Kewawenon.—The following is from my report sent to the Corresponding Secretary, dated Aug. 23, 1852:

"This mission has shared its usual prosperity. During the year, several heathen Indians have become the subjects of converting grace. As an evidence of the genuineness of their faith, they brought their bad medicines, and various instruments of sorcery and idolatry, and delivered them to the missionary, who has them now in his possession. These Indians are continuing to improve in civilization, and we look forward to the time when they shall stand forth—not white men, but *Indians* renovated and saved—elevated far above what they once were physically, intellectually, in their moral and social condition. According to the latest account I have received, the Church numbers fifty-three members, of whom thirteen are on probation.

"The day school has numbered eighteen male and nine female scholars—average attendance, thirteen. The children have been instructed by brother Barnum, and are reported as progressing in their studies.

"There is one Sabbath school, six officers and teachers, thirty-eight scholars, and one hundred volumes in library, a good supply of primers, tracts, question books, hymn-books and Testaments. If suffered to remain, and properly encouraged by the Government, I think these Indians must continue to improve."

Eagle River Mission.—This was a laborious field, embracing work enough for two men. It comprised most of the mining stations on Point Kewenaw, which were visited, as far as possible, by the missionary. Rev. S. Steele was warmly received by the people, and well sustained in his efforts to build up the cause of Christ. This was the most prosperous year since the mission commenced. The following statement from my report of July 7th, including a postscript, will show the condition of this charge:

"*Eagle River.*—The labors of Rev. S. Steele have been blessed in the conversion of souls and the building up of the Church. The people have done nobly in defraying the expenses of the mission. They have raised *seventy-five dollars*, missionary money, for the purpose of commencing a German mission among them. This is a mission evidently demanded. The German population is more numerous than any other, and the labors of a good German missionary would tend greatly to advance the cause of religion about the Lake. I hope the Missionary Society will give us encouragement in this matter, and that the object may be brought about at our next conference. The Church numbers fifty members and fifteen probationers; the Sabbath school, fifteen officers and teachers, sixty-five scholars, and one hundred and fifty volumes in library.

"P. S. I have just received a letter from Rev. S. Steele, at Eagle river, in which he says: 'I am happy to inform you that the work of grace, which has been steadily increasing at the Cliff Mine for months, was quickened by our quarterly meeting exercises. On the following Sabbath evening, under the preaching of the word, there was a general weeping all over the house, and the house was literally jammed to overflowing; several cried aloud for mercy, and one professed conversion at the time. Prayer meetings have been held nearly every night during the week, and several are converted. Last Sabbath I was at the north-west, and there is an unusual manifestation of religious feeling in that location.'

"Let not the friends of missions despair. We shall yet gather a harvest of souls on the shores of the Great Lake. J. H. P."

Ontonagon.—The society connected with this mission is fluctuating. It numbers about twenty-five members. No special outpouring of the Spirit has been witnessed on the mission; and yet the labors of the missionary, Rev. E. H. Day, which have been arduous, have been every-where encouraged by the people. He has been well sustained in his work. The people there will want next year, it is thought, *three* men, instead of one; two, at any rate. Brother Day reports three Sunday schools, six officers and teachers, fifty scholars, and two hundred volumes in library.

Carp River.—This was the first year of sending a missionary to this station. Here are the great *iron* mines of Lake Superior. Rev. William Benson was appointed to this charge, and went directly on with his family. But the failure in getting up supplies had reduced the people to great straits. Several persons left, and went through to Bay de Noquette for fear of starvation. One company sent most of their horses through for want of feed. Brother Benson had been advised to leave, and had about concluded so to do, but determined finally to stay. He says that, "after doing so, one man came and said I need take no thought; he had enough for me." The letter bringing this intelligence was dated November 19th. After that, very late in the season, providentially, abundant supplies were sent to Carp river. Our missionary thought that he found Methodists here of the "old stamp," all of whom seemed disposed to aid in advancing the cause.

Another call.—"Why don't conference send us a minister?" Brother Benson took passage on the Napoleon in moving from Eagle river to Carp river. The boat touched at Isle Royal. Several of the miners situated on this lonely spot met him, and asked the question at the head of this. Comment is needless. Toward the close of the year the society numbered rising of forty members, including fifteen probationers. A very encouraging degree of success had attended the labors of brother Benson. Between the Lake shore and *Bay de Noquette* there were about five hundred lumbermen, whom he had visited twice during the winter. They were calling loudly for help. A missionary was greatly needed among them. Thus it is seen that the work was gradually enlarging on all sides. Carp River reported one Sunday school, eight officers and teachers, thirty scholars, and two hundred and fifty volumes in library.

STATISTICS.

MISSIONS.	Members	Probationers	DAY SCHOOLS.			SUNDAY SCHOOLS.				Expenses of Schools	S. S. Advocates taken	Conversions
			Schools	Male Scholars	Female Scholars	Schools	Officers and Teachers	Scholars	Volumes in Library			
Saut Ste. Marie	60	12	1	19	8	1	4	34	...	.....	..	2
Whites	6	..	..	..	..	1	5	20	175	.....	13	..
Kewawenon	47	11	1	18	9	1	6	45	100	.....	1	..
Whites	3	..	..	..	..	..	..	..	...	.....	..	..
Eagle River—Whites	51	15	..	..	..	2	15	65	150	.....	..	..
Ontonagon—Whites	25	..	..	..	..	3	6	50	200	$17 00	4	..
Carp River—Whites	29	15	..	..	..	1	8	30	250	.....	..	..
Total	221	53	2	37	17	9	44	244	875	$17 00	18	2

P. S. These statistics will be found to differ slightly from the estimate made in the written report. These last have been corrected by the returns from the missionaries, presented at the close of the conference year.

In the above report it will be seen that *Fond du Lac* and *Sandy Lake* are not enumerated. The Sandy Lake mission, by the decision of the General conference which sat in May of this year, fell into the Wisconsin conference. Fond du Lac was unavoidably left unsupplied, and hence no report was made.

STATISTICS

OF THE INDIAN MISSION DISTRICT, EMBRACING THE QUADRENNIAL TERM JUST CLOSING.

Date	Nation.	Members	Local Preachers	Probationers	Sunday Schools. Schools	Officers and Teachers	Scholars	Volumes in Library	Bible Classes	Scholars in Infant Classes	Expenses of Schools	S. S. Advocates taken	Conversions	Missionary Collections
1849	Indians	137	..	18	..	..	...	...	..	..	.....	..	..	......
	Whites	16	..	..	..	..	...	...	..	..	.....	..	..	$50 54
1850	Indians	101	..	15	5	18	141	490	2	..	$31 80	12	..	148 85
	Whites	17	..	28	..	..	...	...	..	..	.....	..	..	......
1851	Indians	106	..	11	..	..	...	...	..	..	.....	..	..	......
	Whites	81	1	10	6	32	170	560	2	10	26 38	17	1	106 81
1852	Indians	107	..	23	..	..	...	...	..	..	.....	..	..	......
	Whites	114	2	30	10	69	305	1,210	5	60	65 00	18	2	157 25

In this statistical account I have followed the printed Minutes of the Michigan conference, except in the membership of Carp River, for 1852. An error was here committed, probably typographical, in printing "9" for "29," as found in the table connected with my report of August 23d, as given above.

In the year 1848 the Indian membership for the district, including probationers, was one hundred and thirty-three. From this it appears that we lost *three* Indian members during the four years. But it must be remembered that thirty-two of these were counted for Fond du Lac and Sandy Lake in 1848. Most of these were on trial and were soon dropped. And from the calamities and fluctuations connected with those outposts they were now left out of the account. The mission at Kewawenon and the Indian station, near the Saut, were favored with several seasons of spiritual growth and prosperity, as the reader has seen in our narrative. That we, at times, suffered losses is no less a fact, though painful to record. I have taken pains to state facts as I find them, leaving the indulgent reader to his own reflections as to their bearing.

Amid all the fluctuations in the mining population, and the obstacles in the way of cultivating this new and wild region, our white membership had increased from *thirteen* to one hundred and forty-four. As it regards other particulars the facts and statistics above given speak for themselves.

CHAPTER XXVII.

JOURNEY TO THE WISCONSIN CONFERENCE—LEAVE OF THE INDIAN MISSION DISTRICT.

I HAD received a communication from the Corresponding Secretary of the Missionary Society, Dr. Durbin, calling me to attend the Wisconsin conference on business connected with the missions. It had reference to the transfer made by the General conference of Fond du Lac and Sandy Lake missions to this conference. Monday, 23d, with my wife and daughter, I took passage on the steamer London for Detroit. We were detained nearly all night at brother Church's, near Garden river, to wood. Rev. Mr. M'Dougall and his wife, missionaries at Garden river, came to see us, and spent two or three hours—a delightful interview, and, perhaps, the last we were to enjoy together in this world, where the fondest ties are often riven. Tuesday, at two o'clock, P. M., we touched at Mackinaw, and were again on our way, with just breeze enough to cool the air a little, which had been uncomfortably warm. The following record was made Wednesday, 25th: "Lake calm all night. We had a comfortable night's rest. Very foggy this morning. We are across Saginaw Bay, ten o'clock, A. M., and the fog is disappearing. We have a fair prospect of getting over Lake Huron without a blow. How wonderfully have I been favored all summer, thus far, in traveling on the Lakes! This seems to call loudly for gratitude, especially at a time when such serious accidents are constantly occurring. We just received word before leaving that the steamer Atlantic was run into by a propeller, and sunk, with a loss of three or four hundred lives. How dreadful such a calamity!

"Another conference year, with its labors and responsibilities, is about closed. I have experienced much of the Divine goodness the past year. No year of my life has been, I think, more serene. The light of God's countenance, in the midst of surrounding darkness, has, in general, shone brightly upon my pathway. While I have cause for devout gratitude, I have reason to mourn over my own unfaithfulness, and want of more extended usefulness. But I feel fully resolved to be God's for time and for eternity. O for a new consecration to the work whereunto God has called me!"

Thursday we reached Detroit, and spent one night in the city. Friday went to Toledo on the steamer John Owen, and stopped at Mrs. Allen's, sister to my wife. The cholera was raging in the place, and some twenty dying daily. It was confined mostly to emigrants, and persons of intemperate habits.

Saturday we reached Adrian. Here found our friends in pretty good health. My family were to remain here till after conference. Rev. J. F. Davidson, pastor of the First Charge, was confined to his bed by a violent attack of bilious colic. Some of the brethren greeted me warmly, and requested me to supply his pulpit on the coming Sabbath, which I did, not very satisfactorily to myself. But the people were attentive, and I trust some good was done. Great changes had taken place here since my first acquaintance with the people, in the fall of 1836. Many of the old inhabitants had either died or gone to other parts. Some who were then children, that I had often dandled upon my knees, were now grown up and married. From a thriving village the place had grown up to a city. The Church had also greatly enlarged her borders. But those early days were *halcyon days* for the Methodist Church in Adrian, the bright traces of which were still left in the memory of several of the older members, and to which they referred with delight. Left Adrian Tuesday morning, August 31st. Passed over the S. M. and N. I. railroad to Chicago. Wednesday morning, September 1st, left Chicago on the steamer Baltic for Sheboygan, where we arrived safely about midnight. Here six of us hired a private express for Fond du Lac, the seat of the conference, where we arrived before eight o'clock, A. M., on Thursday. After breakfast I found my way to the conference, which was in session in the new Methodist church—Bishop Ames presiding. The conference was made up of a hundred or more members—a fine-looking set of men.

Almost without exception they appeared in good health, and carried in their bearing the marks of sterling men for the itinerant work. I soon recognized in the company my old friend and brother from Ohio, Rev. E. Yocum, one of the presiding elders, by whom, before the session closed, I was introduced to the Bishop, who introduced me to the conference. I was glad also to meet here Rev. W. H. Sampson, whose acquaintance I had made in 1838. During my sojourn at Fond du Lac I was very kindly entertained in the pleasant family of Dr. Adams, who had under his roof, among others, Rev. C. Hobert, a leading and influential member of the conference. Brother Hobert was now in the pioneer work in Minnesota.

The time spent at this conference, which was till the next Thursday morning, passed very agreeably, part of which I was permitted to be in the cabinet. The business of the conference, in general, moved on harmoniously. The anniversaries and seasons of public worship were, some of them, seasons of much interest, to detail which is not my business.

Two of the Sabbath meetings were seasons of spiritual profit, not soon to be forgotten. The one was the conference love-feast, remarkable for the number of preachers who bore a clear testimony to the great blessing of perfect love. Methodism has nothing to fear so long as her preachers preach holiness, and exemplify it in their experience and deportment.

The other occasion, which proved so interesting and

profitable to many, was the sermon preached in the morning by Bishop Ames. His text was, "*Have faith in God.*" It was a masterly effort, full of heavenly unction and mighty power. It was a combination of convincing argument and happy illustration from first to last—the most lucid illustration of Christian faith it had ever been my privilege to hear. Infidelity was driven from its retreat back to its native hell, and Christianity stood forth in strength and grandeur, robed in habiliments of loveliness and attraction.

The Catholic priest was making quite a stir here among his deluded followers. He held meeting all day Thursday and Friday after our arrival. He had erected a huge cross, which stood in the center of a platform about eight feet high and five or six feet square. The cross was adorned with ribbons and tassels. From this elevated platform he harangued the people in English and French on the superior claims of the Romish faith, performing all kinds of gyrations and manipulations, and appeared to be as much in earnest as if the destiny of his Church hinged upon this effort. It was a complete Jesuitical maneuver to keep his people—as it seemed to some of the spectators—from under the influence of Methodism, which was evidently annoying to him. A religion which needs such flummery to keep it in countenance, is in striking contrast with the simple and unostentatious religion taught by Christ and his apostles.

I left the seat of the conference in company with brother Cox, acting agent for the New York Book Concern, *via* Chicago. I arrived at Niles, the seat of the Michigan conference, by noon the next Saturday. Here I had a most pleasant home assigned me, in the intelligent and kind Christian family of Mr. Laramour, of the Presbyterian Church. My home was rendered the more agreeable by having Dr. Kidder for room-mate two or three days.

The next day, at the request of my ministerial brethren, I preached in the Congregational, Methodist, and Baptist churches—once in each. I was blessed in bearing the standard of Christ before the people, who seemed to appreciate the blessings of the sanctuary.

Conference opened on the following Wednesday. Bishop Scott presided. It closed on Wednesday evening of the 22d. It was one of the most harmonious and agreeable sessions that we had ever attended. For the Bishop and presiding elders it was a very laborious session. We had to work night and day. Toward the close I began to feel the effects of such incessant toil and want of regular and sufficient sleep. We received our appointment to the Kalamazoo station. I knew but little about the state of things there, except a hint which the presiding elder gave me. He said that he desired me to go there, and "pour oil on the troubled waters." My predecessor had left the Methodist Episcopal Church in the midst of the year, and had been inducted, by the imposition of Episcopal hands, into the *true* (?) *apostolical* (?) succession!

I noted then in my journal: "I feel much relieved in mind to think of being released from so responsible and laborious a district as that of the Indian mission. I have prayed earnestly to God to be qualified for my new charge. O for grace to help!"

The evening on which conference closed I crossed over to the Southern railroad to South Bend, Indiana. I here took the cars at eleven o'clock at night, and reached Adrian by nine o'clock the next morning. It seemed desirable that we should spend the next Sabbath at our new charge. On Friday morning, accompanied by my family, I went by railroad to Jonesville. Here I hired an express to take us across to Albion, where we arrived at five o'clock, P. M., and were hospitably entertained under the roof of my old friend, Rev. W. H. Brockway. Saturday morning I was permitted to visit the seminary, and open the school by prayer. I had the privilege of meeting a number of old acquaintances, whom I had not seen in some years. That afternoon, in the midst of a cold, disagreeable rain, we reached Kalamazoo, and were kindly cared for under the roof of brother T. Paige.

Sabbath I was introduced to my new charge, and preached twice with a good degree of liberty, met the general class, and attended the Sunday school.

Monday, September 27th, at one o'clock, A M., I took leave of my family to go to the *Saut Ste.*

Marie after our things. I was detained in Detroit till Wednesday before I could get a boat. I met here my brother Joshua, on his way to Lake Superior, who was company for me to the *Saut.* We left Detroit on the Northerner, and arrived at the Saut on Friday about noon. We had a rough time in crossing Saginaw Bay. I became seasick, the effects of which I felt more after I landed than while on the water. That afternoon I packed my books, and did what I could to get our things ready for removal. Brother Measures and wife, missionaries on their way to Ontonagon, brother Marksman, my brother, and myself were stopping together in our all but deserted homestead, with coarse living and every thing in a confused and transition state. At night I was quite sick—my appetite gone, and a feeling of faintness.

Sabbath was to us a day of quiet rest. Rev. S. Steele preached to us in the morning, from, "O, taste and see that the Lord is good!" The food was sweet to our taste. I preached my farewell sermon in the afternoon, from Acts xx, 22–24, to an attentive audience. Here closed our efforts in this interesting field. Rev. James Shaw was appointed on the district in our stead.

Monday I had our things all boxed up and down to the warehouse shortly after noon. I now parted with my brother and the missionaries bound up Lake Superior, who left on the Manhattan.

Having emptied the house of our movables, I fell

down upon my knees, and for some time held a season of hallowed communion with God. O, what scenes rushed into my mind! The events of the four years spent on the district all seemed to be present. My own want of faithfulness tended deeply to humble me. The trials through which we had passed—the scenes of the last hours with our dear little Henry, were fresh as of yesterday. But, O, what a heavenly peace, and love, and joy filled my soul! I could realize that "God is love." I felt that my ransomed powers were consecrated to him. Arising from my knees, I took my small trunk and sachel and went to the *Ste. Marie House*, where Mr. N., the landlord, treated me with every attention that could subserve my comfort or convenience.

Thursday made several calls, and took leave of old acquaintances. Went once more to the cemetery, where repose the ashes of our dear Henry. I went there not to repine at that Providence which had bereaved us, but to contemplate the glorious resurrection morning, when the mortal of our dear babe should be clad with immortality, and when our kindred, having died in the Lord, "though sundered far," and scarcely two buried in one graveyard, should be reunited, and be forever with the Lord. Sweet and hallowed were my reflections as I gazed, it may be for the last time, on the tomb of our little innocent.

Before noon we left the Saut on the London. We were favored with delightful weather. Reached Detroit Thursday morning before nine o'clock, just

32

in time to take the cars for Kalamazoo, where I arrived at four o'clock, P. M., grateful to that Providence who had kept me in my recent journeyings, by land and water, of more than two thousand miles.

CHAPTER XXVIII.

WIFE AND CHILDREN OF THE MISSIONARY AMONG THE INDIANS.

Woman has been found generally to bear her equal share of the toils, responsibilities, privations, and dangers connected with the struggles of the nation or of the Church. A work professing to delineate the phases of mission life among our aboriginal tribes, would be defective without at least a chapter on the part which woman, surrounded by her children, is called to act in so noble an undertaking as the evangelization of this interesting portion of the human race.

There is much of romance in the first interviews of a stranger with the Indians. The *Christian lady*—which we must take to be true of the missionary's wife—in taking up her residence at an Indian mission, finds herself environed by sights, and sounds, and influences, to her entirely new and strange. The conversation of the inhabitants is about as intelligible to her as the chattering of birds. She may have half a dozen associates of her own language and manner of life. Perhaps she is alone, except the members of her own family. Often she finds herself the only white female in the house of worship. At first there is a peculiar charm about all the exercises of the sanctuary. The preaching through an interpreter—the songs of praise which well up out of warm Christian hearts, in an unknown tongue—the devout prayer, though unintelligible, except by the magnetic power of the Spirit's influence, which, when it moves one heart, by a well-known sympathetic influence, touches a spring which causes every other devout heart to vibrate in unison, whatever be the language—the story of the cross, as related by these children of nature—the subdued meekness of expression, and the scalding tears, which often chase each other down over brawny faces—all these, and many other things, operate like a charm, and move the tender sympathies of the female heart.

But the spell is at length broken. With all the holy influences connected with such scenes, they begin to wear an aspect of monotony. Thought is busy within, as she casts around her and feels like a speckled bird, in the midst of a strange people. With the speed of lightning, thought wings its flight across lakes, forests, and plains. Her body is on mission ground, but her mind is with loved ones "far, far away." The influences of the sanctuary, in her native land, where every thing had free course, in her own tongue, rush into her mind unbidden, and unconsciously she falls into the pious moanings of the royal Psalmist: "How can we sing the Lord's song in a strange land? If I forget thee, O Jerusalem, let my right hand forget her cunning. If I do not remember thee, let my tongue cleave to the roof of my mouth; if I prefer not Jerusalem above my chief joy."

Her domestic cares are onerous and trying. In the nature of things she must often be left to serve alone. But, if every thing else differs about her, she must have her household regulations as much after the old sort as possible. She has, it may be, just performed her kitchen duties. With the complaisance wont to characterize woman, after her floor is well scoured and every thing in trim, she catches up her knitting or sewing, and is just about to have a little respite from more active toil. But just now half a dozen, perhaps a dozen, Indians come to the door, and, without knocking, open the door and walk in as though they were lords of the concern. The men usually become seated in a chair. Often the women, with their papooses, squat upon the floor, where it is most convenient. The men fill their long pipes with tobacco, and *kin-i-kin-ick*, a leaf which they use for smoking, or, as a substitute, they often use the bark of red alder. Now, for some time, it is puff and spit. The lady of the house must screw up her olfactories to the utmost, and then if she do not cast some meaning side glances at her insulted floor, as though she sympathized with it, it is because she do n't know how.

But now comes the important part of the scene before us. One of these consequential personages volunteers to become the speaker for the rest. He begins: "*Ka-gate, nee-je, ah-pi-che ne-buk-a-da-min.*

Kah-ga-go ko-koosh, kauh-ga-go pah-qua-zhe-gun, kah-ga-go mon-dah-min, kah-ga-go kee-go, me suh ah-noge ka-go mej-e-um, kah-we-ah. Ka-gate ah-pi-che sun-ah-gut! Ah-pa-gish, nee-je, pun-ge pah-qua-zhe-gun, ki-ya ko-koosh," *etc.* In plain English: "Indeed, my friend, we are very hungry. We have no pork, no bread, no potatoes, no corn, no fish, and so of every thing else. We have no provision of any kind. Indeed this is very hard! I desire, friend, that you would give us some bread and pork." If this can not be afforded, something else is desired as a substitute. What is to be done now? In sympathy to the hungry, the missionary's wife brings forth what is left of the last baking, something else is added, to stop this clamor for a morsel of food, and the hungry are sent away with a glad heart. As they take their leave their benefactress bethinks herself that her domestic cares were not lessened by the short stay of these visitors. The picture here drawn does not apply to those Indians who have availed themselves of the benefits of missionary teaching to any considerable degree. These are mostly honorable exceptions. But this sketch is neither overdrawn nor of rare occurrence.

The Christian matron finds it a difficult thing to train up her children aright surrounded by such influences. Her little ones are at the very age when impressions are indelibly made. In the school there is nothing to excite to emulation. The missionary's children, having the advantage of their mother tongue, are generally in advance of the other scholars, and are rather held in check than aided by their associates. Children must have playmates. If they can have no others, they soon contract an intimacy for the Indian children, rapidly learn their language, and slide imperceptibly into many of their habits. To guard against such an evil, and to secure, as far as possible, a correct training, imposes no small charge on the wife of the missionary.

With her husband she becomes a partner in the great field of evangelical labor, and, to the extent of her ability, becomes a teacher of civilization in the management of her domestic relations. A stranger will soon be struck with the difference between the progress made in housewifery by the Indian women at our stations and those at Catholic stations. The comparison is greatly in favor of the former. This is owing, in a very great degree, to the example set the natives by our female missionaries.

Not the least of her privations are the seasons of her husband's often long absence. Her condition is most lonely, having often scarcely any about her but natives, and, perchance, many of these untamed and ferocious in their appearance—enough to frighten a delicate female, unless possessed of undaunted courage. Added to this, she can not be—she is not—unmindful of exposures and perils of her husband, as he spends wearisome days and nights in the wintery forest, or encounters storms on the raging deep. A missionary's wife thus writes to her husband when many miles had separated them: "*Dear Husband,*— I received yours from Eagle River, and also from La Pointe. We are all well, and feel thankful for the blessing of health. Never did I spend a more anxious Sabbath than the one after you left. I knew you must have a very hard time, which proved to be true. I can assure you *that* night was a very lonely one to me. I went to bed, but not to sleep. My prayer was that the Lord would deliver you. How good the Lord is to those that put their trust in him! Brother J. said I might rest assured you were under White Fish Point. It was not any consolation to me. I never saw the river [Ste. Marie] in such motion as it was that day."*

The feelings of a missionary's wife in her lonely hours may be seen in the following brief extract from a letter to her husband: "I have never missed you as much as I have this time. I felt very uneasy about you after your leaving. Every thing looked gloomy."

What made those hours more lonely was, that at such times disease stealthily found its way occasionally into the family circle, piercing loved ones with painful, if not fatal, darts.

But she whose position we are now viewing becomes the traveler. Her sphere is not local, at least for any length of time. If you would test her reso-

---

*Reference is here made to the stormy Sabbath I spent on the propeller Independence described above.

BIG BEKUENESEC FALLS, MENOMONEE RIVER.

lution, her courage in danger, and her fortitude in the hour of suffering, you must accompany her, perhaps with the infant in her arms, as she coasts, for days and weeks together, in the frail birchen canoe, over noisy waves, beneath the scalding sun, the drenching rain, or falling snow; view her as she sits thoughtfully beside her camp-fire, amid the wild scenes around her. It may be her fortune to meet the fury of the dashing and foaming rapids, or to be hurried down them with wild excitement, amid dangerous rocks or jutting crags. And, anon, she is seen trudging in mud knee-deep across land portages. Old Humphry sets down as an exaggerated expression, wading in mud "knee-deep." His remark is doubtless true where it was designed to apply; but if any person will cross the *Savan Portage*, without getting knee-deep in the slough, he must be remarkable for dexterity as a pedestrian.

We must view our *heroine*—for such she may be justly styled, in the best sense of the term—from one or two other stand-points. We must go to some of the remoter inland stations. Here heathenism is seen yielding its legitimate fruits in abundance. Here are scenes so revolting that the eye of humanity turns away and weeps. Here are sights that move to pity and yearning commiseration; cold, nakedness, and hunger—sickness, pain, and anguish. Death strews his victims around, without pity, and the grave opens to receive them, if perchance their bones are not left bleaching on the ground. Some such scenes have been before given. Here is added an extract from a letter, written to my wife by Mrs. Rev. S. Spates, of Sandy Lake mission, dated January 31, 1850. If the reader can peruse it unmoved, ' e is more of a stoic than the writer:

"Dear Sister Pitezel,—I have long been wanting to write to you, but have never taken my pen in hand to do so till now. We are all well at present; and truly, I think, I feel thankful to the Giver of every good and perfect gift for this great blessing; for never was there a time when it was more important for us to have *good health* for the performance of the duties that devolve on us than at present.

"The Indians, or at least many of them, at this place, lost all their gardens last summer by the great freshet, and, from the same cause, the wild rice crop was entirely destroyed in this region, and, consequently, there is quite a famine among them. There are several large families here who have not a pound of provision, and their only chance to get *any thing* is to cut holes in the ice and try to take fish with a hook, for the water is not clear enough to spear them. If they succeed, they have something to eat; if not, they must wrap up in their blankets, and lie down, amid the cries of their hungry children, to pass the night without food.

"Formerly, when the rice crop was cut off, they could live by hunting. But this winter they all say there are very few tracks of any kind of animals to be seen, so few that they have almost entirely given up hunting. But the Indians at this place are not alone in their suffering. All the Indians north of us, as far as we have been able to learn, are in a still worse condition. They are not only hungry, but are almost naked. The rabbits, previous to this winter, have always been very numerous in that part of the country, and, as their lands have not been purchased by Government, they, of course, have no annuities from that source, and their principal clothing has been made of the skins of rabbits, and their flesh was their main dependence for food. But this winter there were no rabbits to be had, and it is to be feared that a great many of these poor Indians must perish with hunger and cold before spring. You can better imagine than I can describe our feelings, when, a few days since, a *whole band* of these poor, starving, naked creatures made their appearance among us. They were scarcely able to walk. A few of the strongest ones came several days before the others. They said they had eaten nothing for eight days. After recruiting a day or two, they procured a little provision, and started back to meet the others. When they reached them, they were so far gone that they would walk a few steps and fall down. After eating, however, they gathered strength, and all reached here alive. But how all the Indians that are here now are to live till spring I can not tell. To all human appearance, some of them must starve to death. The Lord blessed us with a fine crop of potatoes last fall, amounting to nearly three hundred bushels. By cooking potatoes, we are able to feed a good many of them. We generally give away from ten to thirty portions a day, besides what we let them have to take away with them. Within the past month we have thus fed between three and four hundred Indians.

"But this seems to effect but little toward relieving their sufferings. I frequently think if our good Christian brethren could be with us, and witness with what gratitude they receive a little food, and have them beg for every thing in their sight, even to the potato peelings, and see with what eagerness they gather up the smallest pieces—could they see how stupid, ignorant, filthy, and degraded they are—could they, in a word, behold the image of their blessed Lord in such ruins, such *dreadful ruins*, as we here behold it, their purse-strings would be unloosed, tears of sympathy would flow freely from their eyes, their interest for the cause of missions among the heathen would be greatly increased, and the burden of their prayer would be, O Lord, send forth *speedily* more laborers into thy harvest! There are hundreds, perhaps thousands, of poor Indians in this wilderness who have never heard the name of Jesus. My eyes overflow with tears at this thought; and unless they are soon Christianized and taught to cultivate the soil, they must soon become extinct; for game, which is their principal source of subsistence, is becoming scarcer every year."

This lengthy and touching extract shows with what feelings the missionary's wife looks upon the physical, intellectual, and moral destitution around her; how her noble and generous sympathies bound to meet those crying wants, and how her hands act in concert to deal out bread to the hungry; thus to become eyes to the blind, and feet to the lame. I think of several female missionaries, who have spent years in that remote region, a delineation of whose labors and sufferings for the cause of Christ would be invaluable to the Church. Their own pen could make the record.

THE FAMINE.

"O the long, the dreary winter!
O the cold and cruel winter!
Ever thicker, thicker, thicker,
Froze the ice on lake and river,
Ever deeper, deeper, deeper,
Fell the snow o'er all the landscape,
Fell the covering snow, and drifted
Through the forest—round the village;
Hardly from his buried wigwam
Could the hunter force a passage;
With his mittens and his snow-shoes
Vainly walked he through the forest,
Sought for bird, or beast, and found none,
Saw no track of deer or rabbit,
In the snow beheld no foot-prints;
In the ghastly, gleaming forest
Fell, and could not rise from weakness—
Perished there from cold and hunger."

SONG OF HIAWATHA, pp. 262–3.

CHAPTER XXIX.

INDIAN CHARACTERISTICS.

THE reader may be disappointed if he should not find, in a work of this kind, a chapter, at least, devoted to some of the leading features which indelibly stamp the Indian character. It must be confessed that the subject is a difficult one to treat properly, and this is the more so within the narrow limits assigned to these remarks.

The Indian is wont to look back to palmy days, in his traditional history, when his people could boast of numbers and of prowess; when, comparatively free from diseases, they were rapidly increasing; when they could rally numerous braves, fitted, by training, for the chase, or for war. They think of their once vast forests, rich and luxuriant, and abounding with game—of their lakes and rivers, filled with the finny tribes. They contemplate, with sorrow and dejection, the joyous days, when contact with the "pale faces" had not introduced among them various pestilences and epidemics, by which their thriving settlements were fast depopulated—of those days when they had not come in contact with the worse pestilence of their peculiar vices, to fill up the measure of their already corrupt and sinful moral being.

To form a correct view of Indian character something more is requisite than the passing glance of the traveler. There is danger here of forming a hasty judgment, and drawing "pen and ink sketches," life-like though they may be, as imaginary portraits, yet fail to reflect the original. We look in vain into the dense shades of the wilderness, the home of the red man, for those marks of greatness to be found among many other nations. We see not smiling fields waving with golden harvests. Vainly do we look for thrifty villages and populous cities, with the din and bustle of business, and the ebbing and flowing tide of commerce. The school, the college, the church, and the legislative assembly greet not the eye of the beholder. All is the wildness and ruggedness of nature, untamed and unsubdued. The highest achievement of skill in the mechanic art is to construct the rude wigwam, the snow-shoe, or the birchen canoe. The steamboat has not found its way into the deep and broad river, nor has the flying locomotive, the *ish-ku-ta-o-dau-bon*, the fire-wagon, sped its way over the wide domain. The printing-press, Herschel's telescope, and the electric telegraph would be alike useless to this rude people. Vainly we look for the philosopher, the historian, the discoverer, the inventor, the man of genius.

It would seem to be a natural inference, from such evidences, that the Indians are a very inferior race; that, intellectually, they are far below most other nations. As an existing and general fact, it can not be called in question that, in many respects, they are inferior to their white neighbors. In point of knowledge they confess themselves to be but mere children compared with others. As *men*, they would be slow to admit that they were inferior to the proudest monarch.

But this admission is not sufficient proof of real inferiority in native talent and capability. It has resulted rather from want of opportunity to develop existing talent. Powers of body or mind unused soon become imbecile. It can not be doubted that the tendency of all the scenes and associations surrounding the untutored Indian is to barbarism, to a savage state. It is a tendency downward. Every thing tends to depress and degrade fallen humanity to a deeper degradation, socially, intellectually, and morally. Let these opposing influences operate unrestrained for untold ages, and what must be the necessary result?

The tendency of these influences is demonstrated in the fact that, in numerous instances, where people of other nations have taken up their abode with the Indians, they have gradually adopted their manners and customs. It requires, in such cases, only two or three generations to bring them down to the level of their barbarous neighbors. What then can we expect of the Indian in the midst of his darkness and barbarism?

But with such names to enliven the page of Indian history as Pontiac, Blue Jacket, Osceola, Logan, Tecumseh, and Black-Hawk,* who can question the high intellectual capability of the tribes they represent? Under more favorable auspices, many of them would have been the patrons of the arts and sciences, their eloquence would have resounded in the forum, and the wisdom of their statesmen would have rendered venerable their legislative assemblies. The lines of the poet may apply truthfully to the untutored Indian:

> "Full many a flower is born to blush unseen,
> And waste its fragrance on the desert air."

In many examples in Indian history we have some of the finest specimens of impassioned eloquence on record. For striking and beautiful imagery, terse and forcible illustration, and deep pathos, where shall we look for better examples? Than this fact alone no better evidence could be afforded of a high order of intellect. The book of the Indian orator is always spread out before him. He draws his illustrations from the sun, moon, and stars, and the firmament which environs him like a great wigwam. Forests and mountains, beasts, birds, fishes, and reptiles, rivers, lakes, and oceans, furnish him with appropriate metaphors and striking comparisons. A few brief specimens must suffice.

---

* To this list may be added such names as Mononcue, Between-the-Logs, John Sunday, and Peter Jones, among the Christianized Indians. These were men capable of standing in the presence of governors and kings.

The following brief speech was made by Sastarexy, chief of the Hurons, to La Motte, the French commandant at Detroit. It had reference to the giving up, on the part of the Outawas, of *Le Pesant*, called *The Bear*, to atone for his murderous acts among the Miamis. Sastarexy did not believe that this great bear, so dreaded by the Indians, would be given into their hands. He was for wreaking his vengeance on some of the enemy that were at hand. Le Pesant was at Mackinaw. He addressed La Motte as follows:

"*My Father*,—Let us say to you that we can not believe that the Outawas will do what they have promised; for who is he that can overturn so great a tree; [Le Pesant] whose roots, they themselves say, are so deep in the earth, and whose branches extend over all the lakes? There is meat here; why go farther to seek it? One is certain, the other is uncertain." (Sheldon's Early Hist. Mich., p. 225.)

The following is the closing of a speech made by Logan, a chief of the Cayugas, after all his relatives had been murdered in cold blood, without provocation, by Colonel Cresap, a white man:

"There runs not a drop of my blood in the veins of any living creature. This called on me for revenge. I have sought it. I have killed many. I have fully glutted my vengeance. For my country I rejoice at the beams of peace; but do not harbor a thought that mine is the joy of fear. Logan never felt fear. He will not turn on his heel to save his life. Who is there to mourn for Logan? Not one!" (Frost's Indian Wars, page 153.)

The following is Black-Hawk's speech, after he had failed to effect the deliverance of his people: "Farewell, my nation! Black-Hawk tried to save you, and revenge your wrongs. He drank the blood of some of the whites. He has been taken prisoner, and his flames are stopped. He can do no more. He is near his end. His sun is setting, and he will rise no more. Farewell to Black-Hawk." (Ibid., page 267.)

The Indians are imitative beings. The ingenuity and skill they display in making their nets, snow-shoes, and birch canoes, under proper tuition, will enable them to excel as mechanics. The skill of the women in weaving mats and sacks and making fancy articles of birch bark, which they ornament with colored porcupine quills and painted figures, and their fine specimens of bead-work, show that they can readily learn to manufacture clothes and fancy articles with the needle. Their susceptible progress in the various arts of civilization might be shown by numerous interesting facts, which it would be tedious to relate here.

Some of the most striking features of Indian character, as all their history attests, are love of liberty and independence, intrepidity in the chase or in war, generosity to strangers, patient endurance of fatigue, cold, and hunger, feelings of revenge for wrongs suffered, fortitude in the midst of perils, and contempt of death. See this last remark illustrated in Logan's speech.

But a picture of Indian character can not be drawn without some dark lines. Much of Indian history is a history of wars. These are marked, in many instances, by savage ferocity and by acts of cruelty and inhumanity almost without parallel, unless it is to be found in the treatment they have received from their enemies. Mr. Frost, in speaking of the Indian wars in the time of the American Revolution, says, "The whole course of the contest maintained between the Indians and the Americans, had been marked by an excess of cruelty almost unparalleled in the annals of war. Women and children were put to death as mercilessly as those in arms." (Page 181.) The Indians have often proved treacherous to their best friends. And yet it would be hard to prove from this that treachery characterizes them as a people. They have often, at such times, been influenced by their more knowing *false* friends and ill advisers, to whom they have looked for counsel. In extenuation of the cruelty of the Indians toward others, it may be stated that they have seldom been the aggressors, and have often suffered much before they have sought for revenge. But when once the fires of revenge have been kindled, they have exhibited more of the rage of demons than the reason of men.

Among the Indians, woman is degraded far beneath her appropriate sphere. The term *woman* is one of reproach. To act meanly and cowardly is to act the woman. To be called a woman is an insult scarcely to be endured. To be clad in woman's dress and treated like a woman, as a punishment, is the climax of public disgrace. See an interesting case related in Hall's Life of Rev. John Clark, where Gov. Cass "decided to *make a woman*" of an Indian who had been guilty of a high misdemeanor. The Governor caused him to be divested of his own clothing, instead of which he was invested with "an old, greasy petticoat." "It is said that he never recovered his position with his tribe, but was ever after considered as disfranchised and degraded." (Page 82.)

The women cultivate the patches of corn and potatoes, besides doing the other drudgery about home.

But respecting this Mr. Schoolcraft says: "It is not generally known that this labor is not compulsory, and that it is assumed by the females as a just equivalent, in their view, for the onerous and continuous labor of the other sex, in providing meats and skins for clothing by the chase, and in defending their villages against their enemies, and in keeping intruders off their territories." (Notes to the Song of Hiawatha, page 307.)

For all this, it is an undoubted fact that the men very willingly avoid this labor, when they are far more able to do it than those upon whom the burden falls. The lordly head of the family, in his prime and vigor, and the active youth of sixteen, often lounge about the wigwam for days together, and see aged and decrepit mothers and grandmothers, and superannuated old men, bending under the weight of burdens "grievous to be borne," without lending a helping hand.

There is much of primitive simplicity embodied in their language and hieroglyphics. Like the Hebrew language, their names are highly significant, and are usually given, not arbitrarily, but to express some quality or trait in the person or thing to which they are applied. The *fire-water* for whisky, the *fire-wagon* for the locomotive, the *Great Knife* for the American people, in allusion to the terrible use they made of the *sword* in the Indian wars, may serve as examples. Men and women are named after trees, birds, beasts, and other objects animate or inanimate, to suit their fancy. Tecumseh was appropriately named the "*Crouching Panther.*"

The Indians, like the ancient Israelites, have their *totems*, or family coat of arms. These are preserved in hieroglyphics carved in wood or painted on bark. The totem may be the *bear*, the *eagle*, the *fox*, or any other animal. At the decease of a relative, the totem is placed at the head of the grave. Generations may have passed away, and near relatives may have been scattered far and wide, but wherever they find the same coat of arms, they know that they belong to the same original stock and are descended from the same parents. They thus preserve the identity of their tribes with great care.

The mythology and religion of the Indians is invested with much interest to such as would study

Indian character. I find a paragraph so appropriately written on this subject in Hall's Life of Rev. John Clark, that the reader will be gratified at its insertion here:

"The Indians believed in the Great Spirit, whom they always located in the sky, and to whom they ascribed many of his attributes. They always regard him as omniscient and the hearer of prayer; he is supreme in power and infinite in goodness. But they were at the same time polytheists; they clothed the fields, forests, and waters with divinities, and regarded every part of creation as animated by spirits visible and invisible. Some were malignant and some benign, and they presided over the affairs and destinies of men. These must be propitiated by sacrifice, and their offerings must be followed by fasts to render them acceptable, and by feasts to express gratitude. Such is the ground-work of their religion; but superstition has grafted upon the original stock, till it has become monstrous with demonology, witchcraft, and necromancy. They have no succession in the priesthood, but, like the office of war-captain, it is assumed and exercised by men of more than ordinary acuteness and cunning. It is conferred by the election of *opinion*, but not of votes. While they regard the Great Spirit as having his residence in the sky, they invariably locate their minor divinities in the earth. The idea of a universal deluge is fully entertained by all the Indians, and it is found in their tales and legends, even at the greatest distance from civilization and Christianity. They have also some crude notions of the *incarnation*, as is evident from legends gathered and translated by Mr. Schoolcraft." (Pages 78, 79.)

A few facts may not be amiss here, as illustrative of their idolatrous and polytheistic worship. Some years since, Rev. P. Marksman found at Naomikong, Lake Superior, a singular-shaped stone, evidently worn by the action of water, which he presented me as one of their gods. Many of the islands are designated by the words *manito minis*, which mean *spirit* island. The island of Mackinaw, according to Mr. Schoolcraft, signifies "place of the dancing spirits." A lofty rock islet stands, like a lone monument, in the St. Louis river, near the head of Grand Portage, which the Indians regard with superstitious veneration. Many of them think it daring presumption to attempt to scale its summit. They often coast along it, and lay their grateful offerings of *tobacco* on its ledges, to propitiate the presiding divinity.

All who have ever spent much time among the Ojibwa Indians, have heard something about the wondrous tutelar divinity, "of mysterious birth" and wondrous achievements, designated by several titles, but commonly called *Ma-ne-bu-zho.* When at Kewawenon, John Southwind presented me with a small image of an old man carved in wood, designed to represent this divinity, which, I was told, had descended through four generations. Some of the greatest blessings enjoyed by the Indians are by them attributed to the agency of *Ma-ne-bu-zho*, whose very name is a synonym of wisdom. Several of the legends of this personage, combined with some others of similar character, form the outline of the very singular and attractive poem by Longfellow, entitled "The Song of Hiawatha." Many phases of Indian character are here painted with the hand of the master. The production is a fine addition to the classic literature of American authors, and will be read with great interest by every student of the Indian. Poetic license has been taken with some Indian words and phrases, which might be expected. But whatever the critics may say, his poem will live and be admired as a monument of the author's genius and a beautiful tribute to the fast-fading and disappearing tribes of the wilderness.

From numerous incidents before given in this work, it is but too apparent that the moral traits of heathen Indians give a dark coloring to the picture. Ignorance and stupidity, superstition, idolatry, sorcery, and necromancy, with the long and dark train of heathen vices and abominations, are to be found here. If the apostle Paul had spent years among this people, he could not have traced their moral lineaments into a more complete life-likeness than he has done in the first chapter to the Romans, from which one brief clause is enough: "*Filled with all unrighteousness.*" Here is God's image "*in dreadful ruins.*" Without the Gospel, as a people they are "*without hope.*"

CHAPTER XXX.

PLEA FOR INDIAN MISSIONS

THE Christianization and civilization of the aboriginal tribes of North America have enlisted the warm Christian sympathy and enlarged benevolence of many of the wisest and best men. Such, evidently, do not look upon the efforts of the Church and the nation, in this direction, as visionary and impracticable, but as founded upon reason and the higher demands of revelation. Still it is not to be questioned that skepticism prevails widely among men whose influence is felt, and felt, too, even within the pale of the Church, and the energies of many thus become paralyzed, and the streams of benevolence are dried up or turned out of their course.

When traveling on Lake Superior I fell in company with a gentleman of learning and talent—a statesman—a man of influence as a popular orator, who evinced, in general, great respect for religion, but who considered that "the attempts of missionaries to better the condition of Indians had hitherto proved an utter failure, and that it was to fight against Providence to attempt, under existing circumstances, to better their condition."

In the very able and important reports of Messrs.

Foster and Whitney on the Geology and Topography of the Lake Superior region, after an interesting and highly-appreciatory sketch of the labors and sufferings of Jesuit missionaries, in the vicinity of the lakes, we have the following statement, which, if we understand it, is intended to apply to all missionary efforts bestowed upon the Indians. The idea is, that they have proved a failure. The statement, without qualification, is copied into Sheldon's Early History of Michigan, and is thus embalmed in the history of our country. It is as follows: "The effect of the contact of the two races has been to afford the Indian additional incentives to vice, while his intellectual and moral elevation has been little advanced; and, at this day, it can not be said that he stands higher in the scale of civilization than when first known by the white man." (Part I, page 10.) Here, by a single sweep of the pen, the labors, sacrifices, and, in many instances, eminent successes of missionaries in this field, are scattered to the winds and covered with oblivion. But they may well afford to suffer such a fate when it is remembered that "their record is on high, and their memorial with their God."

These statements may be considered in the light of objections to missionary effort among the Indians. Let us examine them briefly. The first *assumes*, as true, that missionary efforts among the Indians have proved an utter failure. The assumption we deny as unfounded, and rest the matter here for the present. It is said to be "to fight against Providence to attempt, under existing circumstances, to better their condition." If to attempt to carry into effect the authoritative command of Providence, to go into all the world and preach the Gospel to every creature, is to *fight against Providence*, then the Christian Church may plead guilty to the charge. If, on the contrary, the mandate of Heaven is to be obeyed, it is not only to acquiesce in, but to act in harmony with the will of Providence, to labor with a view to the elevation of the red man.

The statement taken from the reports we may admit, in part, what is here affirmed, that "the effect of the contact of the two races has been to afford the Indian additional incentives to vice." But has it not afforded him also limitless incentives to virtue, which were beyond his reach? On the same principle of reasoning, we might say that the means of human progress open up incentives and furnish occasions for the spread of vice among white people; therefore, the means of progress have not bettered the condition of the white people. The progress of vice has evidently kept pace with the march of improvement, if it has not far outstripped it.

Mr. Frost, in the preface to his Indian Wars, makes the following statement as a fact, gathered from Indian history: "Their wars among themselves, in which they persist, thin their numbers from year to year, and their habits of life are by no means favorable to an increase of population, or even to the preservation of their race. Whole tribes have already disappeared, from causes independent of the hostility of the people; and similar causes now in operation threaten their total extermination, even if they should suffer no more from the fatal rifle, or the destroying influence of intoxicating liquors." He adds, "It is hoped that Christian benevolence may yet devise some means by which this interesting and brave people may be preserved, and become instructed in the arts of civilized life." The fact is, the doom of the red man was sealed by causes growing wholly out of his heathen condition. Contact with the white people threw open the gate of knowledge before him, and bid him enter. If the knowledge necessary to point out the path of virtue, opened up new incentives to vice, it is to be viewed as an accident rather than a necessary result. But for the cupidity of those whose efforts have been opposed to the benevolent attempts to elevate the Indian, he would have stood far higher to-day than he does in the scale of civilization.

That the Indian's "intellectual and moral elevation has been little advanced," compared with the desires of the Church, is a painful fact. But we must hesitate before adopting the following: "At this day it can not be said that he stands higher in the scale of civilization than when first known by the white man."

If we should throw aside entirely the reports of missionaries, as not entitled to credit, any one may satisfy himself by consulting the statements of agents and officers of the Government, found in the reports of the Commissioner of Indian Affairs, that great advances have been made among many of these tribes in civilization and Christianity. I will not burden these pages with extracts which might be made from these reports; but against such assertions as the above, generally made without proof, I offer the following statement of a President of the United States, Mr. Tyler, in his message of 1842—Frost's Indian Wars, page 284—"With several of the tribes great progress in civilizing them has already been made. The schoolmaster and the missionary are found side by side, and the remains of what were once numerous and powerful nations, may yet be preserved as the builders up of a new name for themselves and their posterity."

The argument against the elevation of the Indian, from the comparatively few who have been actually Christianized, and partially or wholly civilized, may be as legitimately opposed to the Christian religion in its influence over the nations of the earth. Though eighteen hundred years have elapsed since it was first introduced, it is confined within narrow limits yet, compared with the entire population of the globe. "The whole number of Indians within the states and territories," says Dr. Durbin, "does not exceed four hundred thousand." Admitting that the number of Protestant Church members among these does not exceed eight or ten thousand in the United States and the territories, of which the Methodist Episcopal

Church, and the Methodist Episcopal Church South, embrace between five and six thousand: compare even this number with the whole number of Indians, making allowance for the numbers thus Christianized who have died annually, in holy triumph, and the results tell favorably for the cause; especially when we remember that it has not been half a century since our first Indian missions were commenced, the formidable obstacles to be overcome before those missions could obtain a firm footing, and the adverse influences which have operated since. Hand in hand with this Christianizing process, have been the shop, the farm, the school, and other means of social, civil, and religious elevation. The theorist may conclude that these things have not bettered the condition of the Indian, but the Indian himself knows to the contrary, and testifies to the contrary. Do you say that all this forms only the exception to a general rule? I deny the application of this principle here. The world was bettered by the introduction of Christianity, before a millionth part had actually tested its virtue. The civilizing influences of Christianity can not be introduced into any barbarous or savage nation, without conferring a benefit on the whole. All the North American Indians are bound together by many ties of affinity. Christianity has been introduced among them—it is the leaven hid in the meal, and must affect, more or less, the entire lump. Its work may be slow and gradual, but it must go on and increase.

The Wesleyan missionaries in Canada have been

among the most successful in their missionary efforts among the Indians. The flame which first broke out among them, extended to the distant shore of Lake Superior. The following speeches, published some years ago, in the Christian Advocate and Journal, show the influence of this work on the Canada Indians, and the sympathy they felt for their distant brethren yet without the Gospel. The touching and heart-felt response made by the chief at Kewawenon to the speech of Yellow Head, shows how much those Indians felt their need of the same purifying and elevating Gospel:

SPEECH OF YELLOW HEAD, HEAD CHIEF OF THE CHIPPEWA TRIBE AT LAKE SIMCOE, UPPER CANADA, IN BEHALF OF ALL THE CANADIAN CHIPPEWAS.

"TO ALL THE CHIPPEWAS IN THE UNITED STATES OF AMERICA,—O my nation! My eldest brother! Hear ye what I have to say to you. We have received a great blessing from the Great Spirit. It is the word of the Great Spirit which teaches his holy religion, and which our forefathers never had. This is a good religion for us. I am now old and gray-headed, but I find this to be a very good religion.

"Once I was blind, but the Great Spirit made me see when his light shined upon me through the thick mist that covered me up. When in this evil state of darkness, we had no comfort at all, but were in a most wretched condition. We were lying about taverns and in the streets, or before the doors in the mud, where the white people threw out their dirty slops; while our wives and children, living in huts made of boughs of trees, were naked, cold, and starving. This is the work of the evil spirit, in giving us the fire-water to drink, and this is the way he serves his children and gives them no happiness. We then thought we were living; but we were all dead in sin; and when we think of what we have been it makes us feel miserable. Therefore we speak to you, and tell you to take the religion of the Great Spirit.

"When we embraced this religion it made us happy in our hearts, and we were no longer lying drunk in the streets, but lived in houses like the white men, and our women and children were comfortable and happy. We drank no more fire-water, which makes men act like fools—like the hogs that live in the mud. Hear this, my nation, and take the true religion of the Bible, which will make you happy, and drink no more fire-water, and let me hear from you then, and tell me how you like my words. Now we shake hands with you in all our hearts; also with your women and children. We love you all much in our hearts. This is all I have to say.

"ME SHUKEENCE."

SPEECH OF PENASHE, CHIEF AT KEWAWENON, IN REPLY TO THE FOREGOING.

"I feel truly thankful to hear from our brethren at the east, and that they have found the true religion, and received a blessing from the Great Spirit. I have taken the wampum which they sent us in my hand, and looked at it. It is all white. But the string is red, which tells us that the Son of God came into the world and spilled his blood. Now we must all listen to the words of the Great Spirit. I have now given my answer. We shake hands with you all in our hearts. This is all I have to say.

"PENASHE QUEMEZHAN SHIS SHAANWABETOO."

The facts in the above speeches speak volumes in behalf of the power of the Gospel to elevate the red man. Several similar testimonials from individuals have been before given in our narrative.

But it was not my design to enter into a labored argument on this point. The brief answer made to objections, which have been placed in a strong light, must suffice. If the professing Christian has been skeptical, let him banish his doubts, and come up nobly to his part of this great work. As surely as Christ hath tasted death for every man, is it the will of God that the Indians should share in the inheritance of the purchased possession. But this is a "work of faith," as well as a "labor of love." These missions must, to accomplish their object, live in the heart of the Church. They must share in her warmest sympathies and prayers, and receive her liberal gifts of men and means, not in proportion to the number of converts, but in proportion to the value of a single soul savingly enlightened.

The claims of the Indian upon the Christian sympathies of the nation are great beyond measure. *Christianity* makes us the debtor to this people. But, added to this, we are the inheritors of their once vast forests, broad rivers, and lakes. As a result of the contest between the victors and the conquered, many of their noblest sons have bathed the ground with their blood. Their history is one of aggression of the stronger on the domain of the weaker—a history of wrong, of cruelty, of blood. It is not here intimated that our Government has intended to inflict wrong upon the Indian tribes. It has, doubtless, aimed to adopt a policy which, in the end, would elevate the Indian. That the policy adopted was not always the best, is what might have been expected of erring mortals. Many of the wrongs suffered by the Indians have been despite the well-meant aims of the Department. But, from whatever source they may have arisen, the Indians have been the sufferers, and the only recompense we can make them is to give them the joy, the undying hope, imparted by the Gospel.

One other motive should prompt us to duty here; that is, the present strait of the Indian. His choice is between two alternatives; he must be elevated by means of a Christian civilization, or he must become extinct at no distant day. His fisheries are monopolized by others, and his hunting-grounds have been mostly destroyed. He can live but little longer by the chase. He never can become truly civilized without the entering wedge of Christianity. The pagan religion is interwoven with all the relations of the Indian, and is in direct conflict with civilization. This false prop must be removed before he will lean upon the true one. Unenlightened and uninfluenced by the Gospel, the doom of prophecy hangs, with fearful portent, over the Indian tribes: "*For the nation and kingdom that will not serve thee shall perish; yea, those nations shall be utterly wasted.*" Isaiah lx, 12.

"I beheld, too, in that vision
All the secrets of the future,
Of the distant days that shall be.
I beheld the westward marches
Of the unknown crowded nations.
All the land was full of people,
Restless, struggling, toiling, striving,
Speaking many tongues, yet feeling
But one heart beat in their bosoms.
In the woodland rang their axes,
Smoked their towns in all the valleys;
Over all the lakes and rivers
Rushed their great canoes of thunder.
Then a darker, drearier vision
Passed before me, vague and cloud-like;
I beheld our nations scattered,
All forgetful of my counsels,
Weakened, warring with each other;
Saw the remnants of our people
Sweeping westward, wild and woeful,
Like the cloud-rack of a tempest,
Like the withered leaves of autumn!"

SONG OF HIAWATHA.

Such a song was fitting to be put into the mouth of the wisest man that ever was given to the Indian tribes. But, looking hopefully into the scheme of redemption, we are encouraged by words of wisdom, such as no fabled oracle has ever uttered: "The wilderness and the solitary place shall be glad for them; and the desert shall rejoice and blossom as the rose. It shall blossom abundantly, and rejoice, even with joy and singing: the glory of Lebanon shall be given unto it, the excellency of Carmel and Sharon, they shall see the glory of the Lord, and the excellency of our God."

"Let thrones, and powers, and kingdoms, be
Obedient, mighty God, to thee;
And over land, and stream, and main,
Now wave the scepter of thy reign."

CHAPTER XXXI.

LAKE SUPERIOR REGION—DESTINY—CONCLUSION

THIS region is an interesting portion of our great and growing country. Rich in exhaustless stores of mineral wealth, and scarcely less so in its capabilities of enriching us in science and art, it opens a wide field for industry and enterprise, as well as for scientific research. But till recently it has hardly been known. The pearly waters of the vast lake, for ages on ages, had been shut in by dense woodlands and mountain ranges, hardly disturbed, unless by the gambols of the finny tribe and the birchen canoe, fanned by gentle summer breezes, or lashed to fury by the wild sweep of Boreas. But those days are numbered. The lake now bears on her broad bosom the schooner, with whitened sail, and echoes the puff of the steamer as she plows majestically the crested billows, bearing the fruits of commercial industry and thrift to destined ports. The wilderness, untraversed but by the native and the trader, is now dotted with cabins of miners. The prowling of wild beasts and the savage war-whoop have given way to the woodman's ax and the blast from the miner's shaft, which rends the air. The uncultivated forest is here and there turned into a garden. Villages begin to line the wild shores and the rugged cliffs, and already the vision of crowded cities, with all the moving tides of commerce and fortune, begin to flit across the imagination as though they were reality. As it regards the geological structure of Lake Superior and the various phenomena laid open by scientific exploration and research, we must take little notice of them here, as not falling within the plan or aim of these unpretending pages. Scientific gentlemen, who were every way qualified for such a work, have bestowed vast labor and much patient investigation on these themes, and the results have been given to the world as a rich legacy. These must be consulted by such as would study minutely the developments of the Lake Superior region. They may be found in the able reports of Messrs. Foster and Whitney. In looking into the facts here detailed, no one will overlook our vast indebtedness to the late lamented Dr. Houghton, through whose influence and scientific labors, more than those of any other person, this region was brought into favorable notice. Had he lived to consummate his own comprehensive plans, his country would have been greatly enriched by his contributions to science; but, mysteriously, he was suddenly removed from earth in the midst of his achievements and hard-earned fame, and the result of much of his labor perished with him.

Although the first explorations of white men in this region are comparatively recent, still we are led back nearly two hundred years to the time when

Jesuit missionaries, some of them learned, talented, and refined, and well fitted for any station, traversed the Lake Superior region, and became missionaries among the Indians. The names of Rene Mesnard, Claude Allouez, Claude Dablon, and James Marquette, are embalmed in the history of our country as pioneers into that, then especially, inhospitable clime.

An interesting fact is given us as connected with those early explorations; that is, the evidences of the existence of native copper. In several places large bowlders of this mineral were found, some of them weighing a hundred pounds. This pure virgin copper was regarded by the Indians with superstitious veneration, and some of the specimens preserved by them were worshiped as gods. After New France had been ceded to the British crown, an Englishman by the name of Alexander Henry, who had escaped the horrible massacre of Mackinaw, headed a mining expedition, which was prosecuted for a time near the forks of the Ontonagon river. But the effort was ill-directed and soon abandoned. Up to the year 1844 no successful effort had been made to develop the mineral resources of the country. Since that period the wonderful discoveries and the untold wealth which have been revealed have been published to the world.

In those mining explorations a very interesting fact has been brought to light—the works of a rude people, who had been engaged in mining, certainly not less than four hundred years ago, probably much earlier. Those evidences may be seen on Isle Royal, at Eagle river, at the North-West Mine, and other places. But the most interesting discoveries of this kind were made at the Minnesota Mine, at the Ontonagon. Mr. Samuel O. Knapp, the then intelligent agent of the Minnesota Mining Company, in the spring of 1848, laid open one of these ancient works. The following is an extract from Messrs. Foster and Whitney's Reports: "The depression was twenty-six feet deep, filled with clay and a matted mass of moldering vegetable matter. When he had penetrated to the depth of eighteen feet, he came to a mass of native copper, ten feet long, three feet wide, and nearly two feet thick, and weighing over six tuns. On digging around it the mass was found to rest on billets of oak, supported by sleepers of the same material. This wood, specimens of which have been preserved, by its long exposure to moisture is dark-colored, and has lost all its consistency. A knife-blade may be thrust into it as easily as into a peat-bog. The earth was so packed around the copper as to give it a firm support. The ancient miners had evidently raised it about five feet, and then abandoned the work as too laborious. They had taken off every projecting point which was accessible, so that the exposed surface was smooth." (Part I, page 159.)

Proof of the high antiquity of these works is found in the fact that trees growing over these works are as aged as the forest trees around them. Messrs.

Foster and Whitney speak of a pine stump, thus situated, "broken fifteen feet from the ground, ten feet in circumference, which must have grown, flourished, and died since the earth in which it had taken root was thrown out." Mr. Knapp counted, say they, "three hundred and ninety-five annular rings, on a hemlock, growing under similar circumstances, which he felled near one of his shafts. Thus it would appear, that these explorations were made before Columbus started on his voyage of discovery." (Ibid.)

Ancient stone hammers have been found, in large quantities, in connection with these works. Those taken out of the Minnesota works exceed ten cart-loads, and weighed from five to thirty-nine pounds each. "A copper gad, with the head much battered, and a copper chisel, with a socket for the reception of a wooden handle, were brought to light." These I saw myself, in the possession of Dr. Hickock, of New York, in the summer of 1848. Messrs. Foster and Whitney suppose that this ancient mining was performed chiefly with these stone hammers, with the aid of fire to soften the rock and separate it from the copper.

All is involved in conjecture respecting who were those rude miners. The Indians of the country have no traditionary accounts of this matter. Our authors, quoted above, mention the fact, that copper rings, designed for bracelets, are frequently met with in the western mounds. And they more than intimate that these copper rings are "a strong link in the chain of evidence to connect the ancient mining of this region with the earth works of the Mississippi Valley." (Ibid.)

But with a simple statement of these facts we must leave the reader to his own speculations, respecting the people who, long ago, delved into the mines of Lake Superior, for hidden treasure.

The high latitude of Lake Superior is proof that it can never be a resort for farming purposes. Fort Wilkins is in latitude 47° 27′. Point Kewenaw is less adapted to agriculture than the vicinity of Ontonagon or Grand Island. Yet all along the southern shore of the lake are immense bodies of rich alluvial land, timbered mostly with maple and birch, adapted to the growth of most of the staple commodities of the farmer. The season is short; but vegetation matures with surprising rapidity. The country is good for grazing—oats produce abundantly. Perhaps in no place can field peas be found to do better. Wheat has never been fairly tested. The only doubt is with reference to the deep snows of so long continuance. When at Kewawenon, I planted some eight-rowed Michigan corn one season, which grew thriftily, filled well and matured. But this, perhaps, was an exception to a general rule. No great dependence can be made on corn-growing. The esculent roots grow most thriftily, and produce abundantly; and they usually possess rare culinary properties Farmers may make their avocation lucrative, so far as may be needed to supply the mines. But for general farming purposes, choice must always be made of farms where the growing season is longer, and the winters less severe.

The fisheries and pineries must form an important item in the commerce of Lake Superior. Now that the Ste. Marie's canal, a magnificent national work, so long demanded, has connected the great chain of lakes, a ready market will always be afforded for fish and lumber, as well as other products of the country.

The Lake Superior region has many natural advantages and attractions, to offset against its rugged and forbidding features. Its pure and invigorating atmosphere, pearly waters, savory fishes, and its proverbial healthfulness, must make it a chosen resort for invalids and a fond home for actual residents. The traveler will make it a resort who desires to study nature in her loveliest and wildest aspects. A view of the rising or setting sun on the wide lake, or as his rays kindle the landscape into a picture of loveliness, or are thrown in flecks of light against the perpendicular walls of sand-rock, which here and there form the bold shore, is indescribably beautiful. What can exceed, in grandeur, the coruscations of light, as seen in the Aurora Borealis, or Northern Lights, of a Lake Superior sky? *Mirage* is often seen on the lake in the form of trees, islands, and landscapes. These representations are often beautiful, but by their sudden disappearance show that they are but optical illusions. I have often witnessed this phenomena on the water, and once on land. On my way to Sandy Lake one season, and when within a few miles of the place, there appeared just ahead of us a beautiful little lake. I mistook it at first for Sandy Lake. But as we went on it vanished, and proved to be an illusion. The extreme length of a summer's day is a fact with which all voyagers are familiar. In the longest days, when the sky is clear, morning begins to dawn at two o'clock, and the light of day does not fairly disappear till ten o'clock at night.

In this land, interesting in so many of its features, the hardy pioneer has made his home. The wilderness is no longer to remain a rugged waste, but is to be made tributary to human progress and the wants of man. Thus it is yet to answer the design of a beneficent Creator. The first settlers were a mixed multitude, representing several nations. The miners, chiefly English, German, and Irish. Many of the agents and managers of the mines, and persons in other branches of business, were our own countrymen. Many of those hardy and enterprising backwoodsmen were rough in their appearance as the wild scenes around them. The absence of female society may account for this in part. But there were other reasons which produced carelessness and often recklessness in personal appearance and manners. In many places a company of bachelors, or widowers, for the time being, many of whose families were beyond the Atlantic, were huddled together in mining cabins and shanties, free from the restraints of civilized life—every one at liberty to do that which was right in his own eyes. The razor was seldom used. But it would hardly do to set this down as a relic of barbarism, at a time when many devote more attention to the development of a mustache than to the development of the mind. Red flannel shirts were generally worn, and laboring men, when at work, even in the coldest weather, seldom wore a coat.

The long winters afforded great opportunities for reading and study. These were well improved by some who were quite extensive readers. Many choice books were found in the libraries of intelligent mining agents. But many read little or nothing, and, with the majority of readers, the books that were eagerly devoured were novels and vapid and trashy literature.

It is not wonderful, that with this state of things a generally confessed laxity prevailed in the morals of the great mass, that gambling, drunkenness, Sabbath-breaking, and kindred vices, found here a fruitful soil, on which to grow and thrive.

But with all that has been in conflict with the real progress of the Lake Superior region, recent indications foreshadow a proud destiny as at hand. Bound now to the great east, by a vast chain of lakes and rivers, soon to be connected by railroad to the vast west and the far south, instead of being a barbarous verge, fringing the outskirts of civilization, it is to become the center of eastern and western civilization, drawing from the moral and intellectual resources of both, and enriching both, in turn, by the fruits of industry and enterprise. Her towns and cities must multiply—her population greatly increase, and the vast riches of her mines be rendered more and more available.

Thank God, the institutions of the Church have already a footing among the people, and we trust a firm hold on their generous sympathies. Now is the time of planting. The season for fruit-gathering is at hand. Our schools and churches are destined yet to dot that land—the trees of the forest to "clap their hands." "The inhabitants of the rocks" begin already to "sing and to shout from the top of the mountains."

The writer may be allowed, in conclusion, to express his ardent desire for the continued prosperity of this interesting region; and that the institutions of the Church, as conducing to this result, may keep pace with the progress of the country. His prayer is, that enlarged prosperity may attend the missions among the Indians and the miners, and that the Church may yet have abundant cause of joy, and none of regret, at the expense and pains she has bestowed on the cultivation of this field.

THE END.

A NEW BOOK.

Pitezel's Lights and Shades of Missionary Life

OPINIONS OF THE PRESS.

Lights and Shades of Missionary Life: Containing Travels, Sketches, Incidents, and Missionary Efforts during nine years spent in the region of Lake Superior. By Rev. John H. Pitezel, of the Michigan conference. Illustrated. Price, $1, with the usual discount.

This is a good book, well calculated to animate the Church with a more earnest zeal in the support of missions and the ministry with a bolder heroism in the more difficult and dangerous passages of ministerial duty. God grant his blessing to accompany it, and may it have a wide field!—*Pittsburg Christian Advocate.*

Among the remnant of the old and warlike Indian nations once inhabiting this country, our missionaries have labored to bring, if possible, a perishing race to the knowledge of Christ. To this holy work Mr. Pitezel devoted, at the call of the Church, nine years of active, laborious, and successful effort. He tells his story in a practical, common-sense way. He invents no fictions, varnishes no tales. Nevertheless, the Christian reader will find deep interest in tracing the every-day life of a missionary in such a work.—*Ladies' Repository.*

This is an exceedingly readable book, full of thrilling incidents; containing much valuable information in relation to a region and a people that are now attracting much attention. It will be found a very agreeable companion for old and young during the long winter evenings. We bespeak for it an extended circulation. The mechanical execution is in the best style of the Western Book Concern, which, we confess, is saying a great deal, for in this respect Swormstedt & Poe have few equals, and no superiors.—*Western Christian Advocate.*

It is interesting to the general reader for the observations and facts in regard to the country, and to the members of his Church and all Christians, as portraying the sacrifices, hardships, discouragements, and successes of such a life in such a country and under such circumstances.—*Mich. State Journal.*

The book will be found very interesting as regards the history of the country and the habits of the Indians remaining there. It contains several beautiful engravings.—*Lansing Rep.*

Having enjoyed an acquaintance with brother Pitezel, and many others who are now laboring with the Indians in the Lake Superior region, we were prepared to expect a book full of interest, and giving clear indications of industry and sound judgment. We are not disappointed. The book is valuable for its facts, for its opinions and suggestions. We hope it will have an extensive sale.—*E. O. Haven, D. D., Editor of Zion's Herald, Boston.*

It is an extraordinary narrative of labors, sufferings, and successes, varied by entertaining anecdotes and romantic adventures. Indian life is abundantly illustrated in it.—*Christian Advocate and Journal.*

The descriptions of Lake Superior country and scenery are finely written and are peculiarly attractive.—*Kalamazoo Gazette.*

If you would settle, from calmly and truthfully stated facts, the power of grace to save red men—if you would discern the power of the cross—if you would see "the homes and haunts" of the original proud owners of these woodlands—if you would have your heart affected with convictions of duty toward a neglected people, then order "Lights and Shades of Missionary Life," by John H. Pitezel.—*North-Western Christian Advocate.*

Resolutions of Michigan and Detroit Conferences.

The following resolution was adopted by the Michigan conference:

Resolved, That we recommend to our people Rev. J. H. Pitezel's publication entitled "Lights and Shades of Missionary Life," and will encourage its sale in our charges.

The following is a copy of the resolution passed by the Detroit annual conference:

Resolved, That we heartily commend to our people the book published by Rev. J. H. Pitezel.

www.ingramcontent.com/pod-product-compliance
Lightning Source LLC
LaVergne TN
LVHW021144110826
845150LV00005B/1119

* 9 7 8 1 4 2 5 5 4 8 1 2 4 *